DIASPORA DIPLOMACY

Manchester University Press

Key Studies in Diplomacy

Series Editors: J. Simon Rofe and Giles Scott-Smith

Emeritus Editor: Lorna Lloyd

The volumes in this series seek to advance the study and understanding of diplomacy in its many forms. Diplomacy remains a vital component of global affairs, and it influences and is influenced by its environment and the context in which it is conducted. It is an activity of great relevance for International Studies, International History, and of course Diplomatic Studies. The series covers historical, conceptual, and practical studies of diplomacy.

Previously published by Bloomsbury:

21st Century Diplomacy: A Practitioner's Guide by Kishan S. Rana

A Cornerstone of Modern Diplomacy: Britain and the Negotiation of the 1961 Vienna Convention on Diplomatic Relations by Kai Bruns

David Bruce and Diplomatic Practice: An American Ambassador in London, 1961-9 by John W. Young

Embassies in Armed Conflict by G.R. Berridge

Published by Manchester University Press:

Reasserting America in the 1970s edited by Hallvard Notaker, Giles Scott-Smith and David J. Snyder

Human rights and humanitarian diplomacy: Negotiating for human rights protection and humanitarian access by Kelly-Kate Pease

The diplomacy of decolonisation: America, Britain and the United Nations during the Congo crisis 1960–64 by Alanna O'Malley

Sport and diplomacy: Games within games edited by J. Simon Rofe

The TransAtlantic reconsidered edited by Charlotte A. Lerg, Susanne Lachenicht and Michael Kimmage

Academic ambassadors, Pacific allies: Australia, America and the Fulbright Program by Alice Garner and Diane Kirkby

A precarious equilibrium: Human rights and détente in Jimmy Carter's Soviet policy by Umberto Tulli

US public diplomacy in socialist Yugoslavia, 1950–70: Soft culture, cold partners by Carla Konta

Israelpolitik: German–Israeli relations, 1949–69 by Lorena De Vita

Diplomatic tenses: A social evolutionary perspective on diplomacy by Iver B. Neumann

Diaspora diplomacy

The politics of Turkish emigration to Europe

Ayca Arkilic

MANCHESTER UNIVERSITY PRESS

Published by Manchester University Press
Oxford Road, Manchester M13 9PL

www.manchesteruniversitypress.co.uk

British Library Cataloguing-in-Publication Data
A catalogue record for this book is available from the British Library

ISBN 978 1 5261 4868 1 hardback
ISBN 978 1 5261 9125 0 paperback

First published 2022
Paperback published 2025

EU authorised representative for GPSR:
Easy Access System Europe, Mustamäe tee 50,
10621 Tallinn, Estonia
gpsr.requests@easproject.com

Ayca Arkilic thanks the ERASMUS+ programme of the European Commission, and the support provided by the Jean Monnet Module 'NECOTE - New Challenges and Opportunities in a Transforming Europe' (Project ID 101126961)."

Co-funded by
the European Union

Typeset
by Sunrise Setting Ltd, Brixham

Contents

Figure and tables

Figure

Tables

Acknowledgements

Writing this book was a long but rewarding journey. During the years it took me to convert it from a PhD proposal into a fully fledged research project, I accumulated numerous intellectual and personal debts. No part of this project would have been possible without the guidance I received from many mentors in the Department of Government at the University of Texas at Austin. My thanks first go to my wonderful supervisors, Gary Freeman and Terri Givens. I have been a fortunate beneficiary of their knowledge, friendship and generosity throughout my personal and academic development. My other mentors in Austin, Henry Dietz, Raúl Madrid and Kurt Weyland, played an instrumental role in helping me hone my analytical thinking and writing skills. Special thanks also go to Hilde Coffé (University of Bath), Louise Davidson-Schmich (University of Miami) and Sultan Tepe (University of Illinois Chicago) who have never ceased to support me at every stage of my career.

My colleagues at my new intellectual home, the Political Science and International Relations Programme at Victoria University of Wellington, are simply the best part of my job. Robert Ayson, Fiona Barker, Emily Beausoleil, Alexander Bukh, David Capie, Xiaoming Huang, Stephen Levine, Xavier Márquez, Kate McMillan, Manjeet Pardesi, Kate Schick and Jason Young have been key supporters of my professional advancement. Catherine Abou-Nemeh, Caroline Bennett, Matthew Castle, Patrick Flamm, Mona Krewel, Alexander Maxwell, Julija Sardelić and Claire Timperley offered advice on my work. I also thank Jonette Crysell and Yan Ma for their administrative assistance.

It would be remiss if I did not acknowledge the financial and institutional resources that enabled me to complete this book. In particular, I am indebted to Victoria University of Wellington, the University of Texas at Austin, the French Ministry of Foreign Affairs, the Oxford Centre for Islamic Studies, the European Science Foundation, the Consortium on Qualitative Research Methods and the New Zealand European Union (EU) Centres Network. Aynur İsmayilli-Karakoç, Pia Schneider, Gülce Uygun and Brenda Watson helped me transcribe a significant number of interviews in Turkish, English, French and German. Keleigh Coldron provided excellent copy-editing assistance. Some portions of the book are drawn, in revised form, from my articles published in *Diaspora Studies* and *Mediterranean Politics*. I thank the journal editors for granting copyright permission.

My sincere appreciation goes to the brilliant editorial team at Manchester University Press. Simon Rofe and Giles Scott-Smith believed so much in this project and were very encouraging from its inception until the end. Meticulous suggestions offered by them and the anonymous reviewers significantly improved the book. I also thank Lucy Burns, Robert Byron and Jonathan de Peyer for their endorsement of the project.

Over the course of my fieldwork in France and Germany, I was affiliated with Sciences Po-Paris and the WZB Berlin Social Science Centre. I thank Catherine Wihtol de Wenden of Sciences Po-Paris and Ruud Koopmans of the WZB for welcoming me as a visiting scholar. In France, conversations with Samim Akgönül, Bayram Balcı, Faruk Bilici, Hamit Bozarslan and Stéphane de Tapia challenged me to think in new ways. Thanks to my friends Bilgehan and Gülce, my sojourn in Paris turned into an unforgettable life experience. In Germany, I benefited from stimulating discussions with Dirk Halm, Gerdien Jonker, Werner Schiffauer, Riem Spielhaus, Dietrich Thränhardt and Gökçe Yurdakul. My friends Anna, Armin and Doğa made Berlin a second home for me. I am grateful to Adil Tütüncü and his family for facilitating my fieldwork in Turkey. Most importantly, I owe so much to my interviewees in France, Germany and Turkey, who generously shared their precious time and knowledge with me.

I presented the book's chapters at numerous academic conferences and workshops, such as the annual meetings of the American Political Science Association, the Council for European Studies and the British Association for Islamic Studies; the Humboldt Colloquium; and the Diasporas, (Trans)nationalism and Identities Panel at the University of Otago. A number of scholars also read earlier drafts and provided much needed feedback. In particular, I thank Fatih Abay, Yehonatan Abramson, Selen Artan, Osman Balkan, Jean Beaman, Hanlie Booysen, Benjamin Bruce, Matthew Buehler, Leon Goldsmith, Jonathan Grossman, James Headley, Martin Holland, Eric Jeunot, Ayhan Kaya, Ramazan Kılınç, Alex Kreger, Nikola Mirilovic, Rachel Navarre, Dilan Okçuoğlu, Seçkin Söylemez, James To, Gerasimos Tsourapas and İnci Öykü Yener-Roderburg for their comments. My stay at the Oxford Centre for Islamic Studies and sabbatical at Victoria University of Wellington gave me the opportunity to expedite the writing process. I extend my thanks also to the Centre for European Studies at Harvard University for accepting me as a visiting scholar.

Heartfelt encouragement and solidarity received from close friends across the globe has kept me sane over the years. Beliz, Elif, Emine, Emma, Engin, Eyüphan, Kasia, Mine, Oya and Songül deserve special acclaim for being there in the most challenging moments. I feel the deepest gratitude of all to my wonderful family, to whom this book is dedicated. Being born into such a loving family is the best luck of my life. I thank my parents, Ayşe and Necati, for loving me unconditionally and for always being by my side. I thank my siblings, too, Tunca, Günça and Güven (and their families), for always making me feel strong and supported in life. *İyi ki varsınız ve sizi çok seviyorum*. Finally, I am grateful to my husband, Guy, for his love and kindness. Our heated political discussions, Wellington Film Society nights and trips all around New Zealand have been such a great source of comfort and joy. I look forward to having many more adventures together with the addition of our little boy, Théo Çınar, to the family.

Abbreviations

AABF	Federation of Alevi Unions in Germany *Alevitische Gemeinde Deutschland*
ACORT	Citizens' Assembly of People from Turkey *Assemblée Citoyenne des Originaires de Turquie*
ADD	Alliance of German Democrats *Allianz Deutscher Demokraten*
AfD	Alternative for Germany *Alternative für Deutschland*
AfM	Alternative for Migrants *Alternative für Migranten*
AKP	Justice and Development Party *Adalet ve Kalkınma Partisi*
ANAP	Motherland Party *Anavatan Partisi*
ASTU	Intercultural Citizen Actions *Actions Citoyennes Interculturelles*
ATİB	Turkish-Islamic Union in Europe *Avrupa Türk İslam Birliği*
BIG	Alliance for Innovation and Justice *Bündnis für Innovation und Gerechtigkeit*
CCMTF	Coordination Committee of Turkish Muslims of France *Comité de Coordination des Musulmans Turcs de France*
CDK-F	Democratic Kurdish Council in France *Conseil Démocratique Kurde en France*
CDU	Christian Democratic Union of Germany *Christlich Demokratische Union Deutschlands*
CFAIT	French Council of Turkish Immigrant Associations *Conseil Français des Associations d'Immigrés de Turquie*
CFCM	French Council of the Muslim Faith *Conseil Français du Culte Musulman*

CHP	Republican People's Party
	Cumhuriyet Halk Partisi
COJEP	Council for Justice, Equality and Peace
	Conseil pour la Justice, l'Égalité et la Paix
DEİK	Foreign Economic Relations Board
	Dış Ekonomik İlişkiler Kurulu
DIK	German Islam Conference
	Deutsche Islam Konferenz
DİTİB	Turkish-Islamic Union for Religious Affairs
	Diyanet İşleri Türk İslam Birliği
Diyanet	Directorate of Religious Affairs
	Diyanet İşleri Başkanlığı
DP	Democrat Party
	Demokrat Parti
ELCO	Teaching Language and Culture of Origin
	Enseignement Langue et Culture d'Origine
ELELE	House of Workers from Turkey
	Maison des Travailleurs de Turquie
FEYKA	Federation of Kurdish Associations in France
	Federasyona Komeleyên Kurd li Fransayê
FN	National Front
	Front National
FUAF	Federation of Alevi Unions in France
	Fédération Union des Alévis en France
HDP	People's Democratic Party
	Halkların Demokratik Partisi
IFB	Islamic Federation Berlin
	Islamische Föderation Berlin
IMF	International Monetary Fund
ISI	import-substitution industrialisation
İB	Directorate of Communications
	İletişim Başkanlığı
KOMKAR	Federation of Associations from Kurdistan
	Yekitîya Komalên Kurdistan
KRM	Coordination Council of Muslims in Germany
	Koordinationsrat der Muslime in Deutschland
MENA	Middle East and North Africa
MHP	Nationalist Movement Party
	Milliyetçi Hareket Partisi
NAV-DEM	Democratic Society of Kurdish People in Germany
	Navenda Civaka Demokratîk ya Kurdên li Elmanyayê

NSU   National Socialist Underground
             Nationalsozialistischer Untergrund
PEGIDA   Patriotic Europeans against the Islamisation of the Occident
             Patriotische Europäer gegen die Islamisierung des Abendlandes
PEJ   Equality and Justice Party
             Parti Égalité et Justice
PKK   Kurdistan Workers' Party
             Partiya Karkerên Kurdistanê
RN   National Rally
             Rassemblement National
SPD   Social Democratic Party of Germany
             Sozialdemokratische Partei Deutschlands
TBB   Turkish Union in Berlin-Brandenburg
             Türkischer Bund in Berlin-Brandenburg
TBMM   Grand National Assembly of Turkey
             Türkiye Büyük Millet Meclisi
TGB   Turkish Community of Berlin
             Türkische Gemeinde zu Berlin
TGD   Turkish Community in Germany
             Türkische Gemeinde in Deutschland
TİKA   Turkish Cooperation and Coordination Agency
             Türk İşbirliği ve Koordinasyon Ajansı Başkanlığı
TMV   Turkish Maarif Foundation
             Türkiye Maarif Vakfı
TRT   Turkish Radio and Television Corporation
             Türkiye Radyo Televizyon Kurumu
UETD   Union of European Turkish Democrats
             Avrupalı Türk Demokratlar Birliği
UID   Union of International Democrats
             Uluslararası Demokratlar Birliği
YEE   Yunus Emre Institute
             Yunus Emre Enstitüsü
YEK-KOM   Federation of Kurdish Associations in Germany
             Yekitîya Komalên Kurd li Elmanyayê
YTB   Presidency for Turks Abroad and Related Communities
             Yurtdışı Türkler ve Akraba Topluluklar Başkanlığı
ZMD   Central Council of Muslims in Germany
             Zentralrat der Muslime in Deutschland

Chronology of key events

1923	Mustafa Kemal Atatürk establishes the Republic of Turkey
1924	Turkey establishes the *Diyanet*
1946	Turkey transitions from a single- into a multi-party system
1960	Military coup overthrows the Democrat Party government in Turkey
1961	Turkey and Germany sign the first labour-recruitment agreement
1963–1967	Turkey introduces its First Five-Year Development Plan
1967	Turkey establishes the General Directorate of Foreign Relations and Services for Workers Abroad
1968–1972	Turkey introduces its Second Five-Year Development Plan
1971	Military coup overthrows the Justice Party government in Turkey
	The *Diyanet* starts dispatching religious personnel abroad
	Turkey establishes the Directorate of External Services
1973	Oil crisis brings the demand for guest workers from Turkey to a halt in Europe
1975	Turkey establishes the State Industrial and Workers' Investment Bank
1976	Turkish Parliament passes legislation prohibiting the establishment of party branches outside Turkey
	Turkey establishes the Directorate General for Education of Workers' Children Abroad
1978	Abdullah Öcalan establishes the Kurdistan Workers' Party
	Turkey establishes the Turkish Councillorship for Religious Services and the Religious Services Attachés
	Massacre in Kahramanmaraş kills scores of Alevi citizens
1980	State-run Turkish Radio and Television Corporation begins daily broadcasts in Europe
	Military coup overthrows the Justice Party government in Turkey
1981	Turkey permits dual citizenship
1982	All Turkish political parties are banned from receiving financial support from and collaborating with immigrant organisations

2007–11   Justice and Development Party introduces the Alevi Opening and the Kurdish Opening

2008   New law allows expatriates who have renounced their Turkish citizenship to receive invalidity, old age and survivor's pensions

2009   Eurozone crisis erupts
           Blue Card replaces Pink Card
           Turkey's e-consulate system opens

2009–11   Ahmet Davutoğlu, Turkey's Minister of Foreign Affairs, promotes a neo-Ottoman foreign policy agenda

2010   Turkey establishes the Presidency for Turks Abroad and Related Communities
           Turkey launches the Office of Public Diplomacy
           Alliance for Innovation and Justice Party becomes the first political party established by Turkey-originated German citizens

2011   Turkey's economic and democratic backsliding gains momentum

2012   Turkey establishes the Turks Abroad Advisory Board

2013   Gezi Park protests begin

2014   Turkish presidential election becomes the first election for which Turkish citizens abroad are able to vote in their host countries

2016   Turkey signs a refugee deal with the EU
           Military coup attempt fails and marks the official collapse of the alliance between the Justice and Development Party and the Gülen Movement in Turkey
           Turkey establishes the Turkish Maarif Foundation

2017   Turkey–EU relations begin to worsen due to diplomatic row over pro-Turkish diaspora rallies
           Turkish constitutional referendum results in a shift from a parliamentary into a presidential system

2018   Turkey establishes the Directorate of Communications and the Union of International Democrats

2020   COVID-19 pandemic breaks out
           France vows to restrict the number of foreign religious personnel serving in the country
           Several European countries ban Turkish ultranationalist Grey Wolves

1

Introduction

On 11 February 2008, 20,000 individuals gathered in Cologne's colossal Lanxess Arena to hear the leader of the incumbent Justice and Development Party (AKP) and Turkish prime minister,[1] Recep Tayyip Erdoğan, speak. Erdoğan's visit took place a week after an apartment-block fire in the southern German city of Ludwigshafen in which nine Turks, including five children, died.[2] The 'Big Reunion', as the organisers of the rally called it, resembled a pop concert, with light shows, giant screens and cheerful music. After several long hours of waiting, the audience was asked to stand to sing the Turkish national anthem, followed by the German national anthem, before Erdoğan arrived. Finally, a loudspeaker announced that 'the architect of Turkey, the man [you] all have been waiting for, is here!' Erdoğan let the audience applaud and scream for quite a while and invited Turkish parliamentarians, ministers and Turkey's ambassador to Germany to the stage before he began his address to the diaspora: 'The Turkish people are a people of friendship and tolerance ... Wherever they go, they bring only love and joy.'[3] He continued:

> Today there are 3 million Turks in Germany ... Assimilation is a crime against humanity. No one should expect you to see yourselves as 'the other' in today's Germany ... You must learn German to gain an advantageous position in this country, but our children must also learn Turkish. Turkish is your native language ... With its large population, Turks in Germany should play an essential role in German politics. Why don't we have mayors, political party leaders and lobby groups in Germany, the Netherlands and Belgium? Why don't we have more representatives in the European Parliament? ... Despite their smaller population, some groups are able to pressure their host states through their lobby power. Why can't we do the same to protect our interests? ... I expect Turks in Europe to act as Turkey's ambassadors and help us join the EU.[4]

Erdoğan also criticised the German government's failure to respond to xenophobic attacks targeting Turkish-origin Germans and condemned Germany's reluctance to accept Turkey into the EU.[5] Despite the generally peaceful atmosphere, the 'Big Reunion' generated controversy in Germany for several reasons. First, no other Turkish head of state or party leader had come to Europe before this event to address the diaspora.[6] Second, the rally became the largest political event post-war Germany had ever witnessed; even the historical speech Chancellor Helmut Kohl delivered after the fall of the Berlin Wall in 1989 attracted only 10,000 people.[7] During her election campaigns, no more than a few thousand people came to listen to Chancellor Angela Merkel.[8] Third, according to some German newspapers and policymakers, the spectacle disseminated provocative messages: *Die Welt* wrote that Erdoğan's words were harming German Turks' integration, and Günther Beckstein, the governor of Bavaria at the time, called Erdoğan's messages 'nationalistic' and 'highly displeasing'.[9] Chancellor Merkel also criticised Erdoğan's remarks. She underscored that Turks' allegiance to the German state should not be questioned and suggested that her government would raise the issue of Turkish integration within Germany in further discussions with Turkey's prime minister.[10]

Erdoğan addressed emigrants from Turkey in other European countries as well. At a rally held in Paris in 2010, the first of its kind in France, he once again reminded the diaspora how important they were and encouraged them to actively and assertively participate in French and European politics without forgetting their national identity and roots: 'Becoming a French citizen wouldn't make you less Turkish. Pursue your legal rights in France ... You must take this step. If you don't, others will take advantage of this. Unite, act together, fight together, be strong, be assertive ... If you take these steps, you will contribute immensely to your country [Turkey].'[11]

This book takes a closer look at Turkey's burgeoning diaspora diplomacy. Diaspora diplomacy is a relatively new phenomenon. *The Palgrave Macmillan Dictionary of Diplomacy* defines it as collaborating with expatriate communities, which can provide political, financial and even moral support for the home state.[12] Other scholars refer to the concept as 'engaging a country's overseas community to contribute to building relationships with foreign countries'[13] or 'a collective action that is driven, directed and sustained by the energy and charisma of a broad range of migrants who influence another country's culture, politics and economics in a manner that is mutually beneficial for the homeland and the new home base'.[14]

In this book, I define 'diaspora diplomacy' as the desire to advance foreign policy interests, relations and negotiations via diasporic communities at multiple levels (local, national and supranational). Since the goal is to advance foreign policy interests (not necessarily to improve diplomatic relations), the outcome of these efforts may or may not be mutually beneficial for the home state, the host state(s) and the diasporas. This conceptualisation posits that diaspora diplomacy can be counterproductive. It also disaggregates the diaspora and looks at differences within it rather than treating the group as a unitary actor. In doing so, it takes into consideration the fact that not all segments of a diaspora community might be willing to promote the foreign policy goals of their home state. As such, sending states may engage in diaspora diplomacy by empowering 'loyal' émigré groups, controlling 'disloyal' groups and even protecting their diaspora allies against the threat of 'harmful' diasporas. The book's goal is to identify some general mechanisms – in terms of actors, issues, processes, the nature and content of diaspora diplomacy activities and the degree of cooperation between home and host states – that help explain when the outcome of diaspora diplomacy efforts is positive or negative, and to generate a definition that emphasises the agency of the diaspora group itself in explaining such outcomes.

This definition reveals that diaspora diplomacy efforts are different from 'diaspora engagement policies'. The latter promote a state-oriented perspective that centres around home states' activities and discourse aimed at engaging with their nationals abroad at the individual and collective level through symbolic nation-building, institution-building and the provision of a set of rights and obligations.[15] The term 'diaspora engagement policy', therefore, does not capture the new forms of diplomacy carried out by the diaspora that are complementary to official government efforts. Diaspora diplomacy does not view the diaspora's links with the origin state merely as a top-down relationship and maintains that diaspora communities have their own agency, goals and political clout. In fact, as I show in this study, certain diaspora groups refuse to take part in diaspora diplomacy.

This book examines Turkey's diaspora outreach efforts as an example of diaspora diplomacy, rather than seeing them merely as diaspora engagement, because Turkey's changing relations with its diaspora have turned certain segments of Turkey's overseas population into active political players with significant implications for the country's diplomatic relations. The core contention of this book is that while Turkey's diaspora diplomacy has not replaced traditional diplomatic channels between Turkey and European countries, it has emerged as a new force complementing and enhancing Turkey's official endeavours. A form of unprecedented political activism is being carried out by Turkey's diaspora with encouragement from the Turkish state, which seeks to defend and advance Turkey's interests internationally. Since the beginning of the 2000s, Ankara has increasingly conceived of its diaspora in Europe as a political leverage tool. Turkey's desire to put pressure on and influence relations with European countries has resulted in the empowerment of select, ideologically proximate diaspora organisations, mainly conservative-nationalist and Sunni Islamic groups, across Europe.[16] These groups have organised political demonstrations, press speeches and signature campaigns, and have run for office at the local, national and EU level. They have even formed their own political parties in Europe.

Turkish bureaucrats state that foreign policy is not carried out solely with traditional diplomacy but also with cultural, economic and commercial diaspora networks.[17] The Turkish diaspora's diplomacy has focused on advancing Ankara's five foremost official foreign policy goals, which are listed by Turkey's Ministry of Foreign Affairs as: (1) the denial of the Armenian genocide; (2) the establishment of closer relations with the EU; (3) the promotion of Turkey as an independent and strong regional power, and the preservation of a distinct Turkish identity in Europe; (4) the disempowerment of terrorist (Kurdish separatist and Gülenist[18]) groups abroad; and (5) combating Islamophobia and racism in Europe.[19] These goals shape the ways in which Turkey interacts with its diasporas and other states. While EU membership remains a distant dream for Turkey currently, and conservative-nationalist diaspora groups have done more harm than good in this regard (as explained in the book), joining the EU remains an official foreign policy goal and Turkey wishes to do this by instrumentalising the large Turkish diaspora in Europe. In fact, many analysts acknowledge that 'Turkish-European citizens play an important role in the economic, political, cultural, and social ties between the EU and Turkey' and that they are 'an asset to Turkey's efforts to join the EU'.[20]

One of the most concrete examples of Turkish expatriates' recent active citizenship in Europe took place in 2012, when French Turks organised their largest collective demonstration in response to a French Senate bill that criminalised the denial of the 1915 mass killings of Armenians by Ottoman Turks as genocide.[21] Eventually the bill was ruled unconstitutional by the French Constitutional Council.[22] In Germany, a political campaign led by resident Turks before the 2013 German federal elections was, in a similar vein, the largest collective action coordinated by the Turkish diaspora in the country. Turks were urged to participate in German elections, challenge Islamophobia and lobby the EU to accelerate accession negotiations with Turkey.[23]

As noted earlier, while diaspora diplomacy may increase global engagements, it does not always lead to positive outcomes: it may complicate an origin country's bilateral and multilateral relations, as evidenced by Turkey's contested diaspora diplomacy and the resulting pushback from European countries. This book argues that diaspora diplomacy is not the only element harming Turkey's relations with Europe. Yet it has been a significant and overlooked contribution to the worsening of relations. Ankara has placed heavy emphasis on religion and ethno-nationalism in its kin-based patriarchal diaspora policy and promoted a new diaspora identity that demands absolute loyalty from and evokes a sense of obligation among overseas Turks regardless of their citizenship status. These developments have been regarded not only as an infringement upon national sovereignty and an intervention in domestic affairs, but also as a security threat by most European states, including Austria, Belgium, France, Germany and the Netherlands. Given that these countries are influential EU member states, the broader ramifications of Turkey's diaspora diplomacy have also undermined relations with Brussels.

The objectives of the book

The first goal of this book is to understand the reasons behind the Turkish government's growing interest in its diaspora. Erdoğan's declaration that expatriates constitute an intrinsic part of the Turkish nation marks a drastic change from the rhetoric of the past. In the early days of large-scale emigration from Turkey to Europe in the 1960s and 1970s, Turkish bureaucrats tended to view emigrants as uncivilised, low-skilled 'villagers' (*köylü*) or 'remittance machines' (*döviz makinesi*). In the 1980s and 1990s, official meetings and parliamentary proceedings identified emigrants as 'immigrant workers', 'Turkish citizens abroad' (*yurtdışı Türkler*) or 'expatriates' (*gurbetçiler*). These expressions had a derogatory undertone. Since the early 2000s, Turkey has deliberately reframed the position of its emigrants in its state discourse and has opted for the term 'diaspora'.[24] This is surprising given that the term had previously been used by the Turkish government to address former non-Muslim ethnic groups of the Ottoman Empire, such as Armenians, Greeks and Jews, who emigrated to Europe and the Americas in the nineteenth century. Today, Turkish officials emphasise that members of the diaspora are considered to be equal citizens to their compatriots in Turkey and that anyone who has emigrated from Anatolia regardless of religious or ethnic background belongs to the Turkish diaspora.[25] Another startling rhetorical change is Ankara's extolling of diasporans as qualified, hard-working and influential people. The messages conveyed at mass Turkish rallies in Europe reflect this transformation.

Ankara's relationship with its diaspora community has entered a new stage not only with the promotion of a more inclusive discourse addressing Turkey's emigrants but also with the institutionalisation of its diaspora engagement policy. Since the AKP's rise to power in 2002, Turkey has increased the size and budget of the state institutions that play a paramount role in diaspora affairs, especially the Directorate of Religious Affairs (*Diyanet*), Turkey's formal religious institution. Turkey's diaspora policy-making has gained momentum since the formation of the Presidency for Turks Abroad and Related Communities (YTB) in 2010. The YTB is an overarching diaspora institution designed to coordinate the government's official activities targeting emigrants from Turkey. Other diaspora institutions established by Ankara include the Yunus Emre Institute (YEE), founded in 2007, which promotes Turkish language, identity, culture and history abroad. The Directorate of Communications (İB)[26] is responsible for improving Turkey's global image and extending its soft power beyond Turkey's borders; the Union of International Democrats (UID)[27] organises pro-Turkish rallies and streamlines the diaspora's political lobbying activities in Europe; and the Turkish Maarif Foundation (TMV) provides educational services abroad.

Turkey also introduced external voting in 2014, marking a key moment in its new diaspora agenda.[28] With the outbreak of the COVID-19 pandemic in 2020, Turkey has reshaped the contours of diaspora engagement, characterised by new financial aid programmes and the further digitalisation of diaspora engagement tools to cater to the needs of the diaspora. What accounts for the relative neglect, even contempt, with which the Turkish government treated its expatriates in the immediate aftermath of World War II and how can we explain the turnaround in the last two decades? Despite the fact that a large number of Turkish citizens have lived in Europe since the 1960s, why has Turkey shown unprecedented interest in its émigré population only recently?

This book also examines the impact of Turkey's policy change in diaspora affairs on emigrant groups from Turkey. Have Turkey's new engagement policies and rhetoric resonated with members of its overseas population? Has Turkey been able to mobilise its diaspora effectively? The majority of diasporans attending pro-Turkish rallies in Europe see Erdoğan as a hero, yet these rallies have also aggravated polarisation within the diaspora community. While a significant number of conservative Turks follow Erdoğan with admiration, at almost every rally several hundred Alevi, Kurdish, Gülenist and left-leaning secular individuals protest against him. The AKP's authoritarian turn and extraterritorial suppression of dissident diasporans, particularly after the 2013 Gezi Park protests[29] and the 2016 failed coup, have led to fear and resentment in the diasporic space. Turkey's surveillance initiatives and repressive transnational state apparatuses have mainly targeted Gülenists abroad.[30] This book maps the variation within Turkey's diasporas concerning the response to Turkey's new diaspora strategy in order to assess the impact, capacity and cohesion of Turkey's diaspora diplomacy.

Finally, the book explores European states' reaction to Turkey's expanding sphere of influence over its diaspora. Although Turkey had expressed an interest in joining the EU in the 1960s, Turkey's EU hopes showed no momentous progress over the years due to the country's political and economic instability (with the exception of Turkey's recognition as a candidate for full EU membership at the 1999 Helsinki Summit). The 2016

EU–Turkey refugee deal became a bargaining chip[31] for Turkey vis-à-vis European countries as it led to a significant drop in irregular migration flows from Turkey into the EU.[32] The deal quickly became a central aspect of dialogue between Turkey and the EU and temporarily accelerated Turkey's EU-accession process.[33]

Yet Turkish diaspora engagement policy and diaspora diplomacy have become an increasing source of suspicion and frustration in Europe. In 2017, the Netherlands prohibited Mevlüt Çavuşoğlu, Turkey's Minister of Foreign Affairs, from visiting the country to address Turkish voters, citing the planned rally's risks to public order and security.[34] German and Austrian authorities also prevented several pro-Turkish meetings and rallies as they saw them as an intervention in their domestic affairs.[35] In contrast, French officials declared that such gatherings posed no threat to them.[36] However, following the beheading of a French school teacher by a radical Islamist in 2020, French President Emmanuel Macron announced a draft bill that asserted that France's secular values should be protected against foreign influence.[37] Macron's declaration built on a consultative process, which started in 2018 and underscored the need to establish a system that would oversee places of worship, donations and religious personnel working in France.[38] According to this plan, through a new national council and a ten-point charter, religious personnel (imams) would have to be certified by the state and pass courses on secularism, civil liberties and theology, and a chief imam would serve as the highest religious authority in France. Macron's suggested measures also included offering Arabic instruction in public (state) schools, supervising private religious education, restricting home schooling and combating speech or activities that contradict republican values.[39] The investigation of several *Diyanet* imams on suspicion of spying on Gülen followers in Europe, the ban on some ultranationalist Turkish diaspora organisations and the closure of mosques by European authorities have also reinforced rifts between Turkey and Europe.

The argument

The first part of the book shows that Turkey's current diaspora policies are motivated by political goals and that the new active Turkish diaspora engagement policy started with the AKP's rise to power in 2002. Since 2003, Turkey has increasingly sought to build leverage and legitimise its presence in Europe through its diaspora population. 2003 was a turning point for the AKP's new diaspora policy because a parliamentary commission was set up that year by Turkey's Parliament, the Grand National Assembly of Turkey (TBMM), to address diasporans' socio-economic, political, cultural and religious problems. Turkish policymakers have actively mobilised select sub-groups of the Turkish diaspora to participate in host-state politics and to affect host-government policies towards international issues that concern Ankara. Turkey's new diaspora outreach policies have also sought to consolidate the political power of the AKP and its leader Erdoğan by drumming up expatriate votes. Moreover, they have been geared towards extending the reach of the regime's authority into transnational space. This is a striking change: Turkey's pre-2000 diaspora engagement policy was driven mainly by economic or security-related concerns, such as securing remittance flows from Europe into Turkey and controlling subversive Islamist and Kurdish political dissidence.[40]

Turkey's new diaspora strategy arose through a confluence of domestic, transnational and international factors.[41] Domestically, the conservative AKP's economic and political reforms, the Europeanisation process, the promotion of a new identity based on Sunni-Muslim nationalism and neo-Ottoman foreign policy orientations have transformed Turkey's state–diaspora relations. Transnationally, heightened economic, social and political visibility of Turkey's expatriates in their host countries, against the backdrop of their transition from temporary to permanent settlement in the 1990s, has led the Turkish state to reconsider the efficacy of its diaspora as a source of influence in advancing the national interest abroad. Internationally, the nature of the relationship between the homeland and host countries varies over time, as does the homeland's perception of the possibilities and limits of action within this power structure.[42] Turkey's diaspora policies between the 1960s and 1990s were characterised by the asymmetry of power between Turkey and Europe.[43] Turkey submitted its application for full EU membership in 1987, though Turkey's poor economic and political standing, as well as problems with Cyprus and Greece, resulted in the rejection of Turkey's membership bid by the EU in 1997. However, two years later the EU granted Turkey candidacy status.[44]

Following the beginning of full EU-accession negotiations in 2005, and the augmenting of Turkish leverage with the unfolding of the 2015 European refugee crisis, Turkey's perception of its capabilities in the context of its relations with the Turkish diaspora and host states has changed significantly. Turkey's pattern of changing relations with the diaspora reflects its self-perception as an emerging regional power. The rise of Islamophobia and anti-immigrant attitudes in host countries following 9/11 has also compelled Turkey to reach out to its community in Europe.

The second part of the book concentrates on the impact of Turkey's new diaspora engagement policy on its expatriates in the two European states that host the largest emigrant populations from Turkey: France and Germany. Turkey has forged a multi-tiered diaspora policy that has favoured ideologically proximate diaspora groups over non-conformist ones because the former are seen as better able to serve the political interests of the homeland. This differentiation is reflected in the recent empowerment of Turkish conservative-nationalist and Sunni Islamic diaspora organisations vis-à-vis other groups. The attention and favouritism of the Turkish state has enhanced the identity and rationale of the former, bolstered by extensive organisational capacity-building assistance. Turkish policymakers have undertaken 'identity work' through government-sponsored rallies in French and German cities and expanded outreach and official correspondence with conservative Turkish organisations. The result has been a fundamental shift in collective self-perception among the leaders of these organisations. Having experienced a shared sense of marginalised self-identity in their host countries for decades, the Turkish state's active diaspora engagement has dramatically boosted Turkish Muslim leaders' collective self-worth and sense of efficacy. Moreover, by providing technical and financial support, the Turkish state has contributed to a surge in mobilising capacity and activity among these groups. Leadership and capacity-building seminars, special funding programmes and training in navigating the law and regulatory environment have been central to the heightened visibility and political usefulness of Turkish conservative-nationalist and Sunni Islamic organisations in France and Germany. These organisations' political activities constitute significant examples of diaspora diplomacy because most of these conservative diaspora leaders hold German or French citizenship and have the potential to affect European politics as voters and politicians. The book also details the divisions within Turkey's diasporas and suggests that the Turkish government's strategy of selective preferment has caused resentment among diaspora groups that are not buttressed by the Turkish government. In doing so, it examines the fragmentation within the diaspora community as a factor impeding the effectiveness of Turkey's diaspora diplomacy.

The final section of this book demonstrates that Turkey's assertive diaspora engagement policy and the empowerment of conservative diaspora groups have complicated Turkey's – and diasporans' – relations with Europe. Members of the diaspora community have found themselves increasingly torn between Turkey and their countries of settlement. Moreover, most European policymakers have interpreted Turkey's recent outreach activity and Turkish Muslim groups mobilising at Ankara's behest as an intervention in their domestic affairs. Turkish diaspora engagement policy and diaspora diplomacy have traditionally generated backlash and complicated the Turkish diaspora's relations with policymakers more so in Germany than in France, where the issue of Islam, immigration and radicalisation has historically been understood as a North African problem. The large community of

North African Muslims in France and their colonial past have kept this group under the spotlight and, simultaneously, freed the comparatively smaller Turkish population to exist in the shade. Thus, Turks in France, unlike those in Germany, have enjoyed a privileged 'invisibility' in the eyes of policymakers, at least until recently. This status has also stemmed from the popular French imaginary of Turkey as a like-minded country, with its strong and centrist state tradition and secular regime, and of Turks as a liminal group between Europe and the Middle East. As a *laïc* state, France has also typically relied on foreign countries' assistance in the governance of its Muslims much more than Germany has, a position that has started to change under Macron.

Bridging diaspora and diplomacy studies

Diasporas predate the emergence of nation-states yet they were not seen as political and financial assets until the 1990s.[45] Despite diasporas' key role as agents of change and shapers of policies in both home and host states, relations between origin states and their diasporas have mostly been investigated as an issue of 'domestic politics'.[46] Diaspora scholars have described and categorised the strategies and policies directed by home states to diasporas[47] and addressed how and why states cultivate closer ties with diaspora groups.[48] Others have explored domestic, transnational and international factors that lead states to harness their émigré populations and to build diaspora organisations[49] or looked at ethical dimensions of extraterritorial citizenship, de-ethnicisation or de-territorialisation.[50]

As Fiona B. Adamson has succinctly summarised,[51] other branches within diaspora studies have examined the role of diasporas in democratisation, economic development, foreign policymaking, civil wars and terrorism, as well as war termination, post-conflict reconstruction and peacebuilding. Some studies have examined how diasporas strive to establish new nation-states.[52] However, these works have been primarily concerned with the impact of the diaspora on the politics of the homeland or on the politics of the host country rather than with international relations. Moreover, current scholarship on diasporas has focused mainly on state–diaspora relations and disregarded how diasporas engage with other audiences and stakeholders for diplomatic purposes. It is thus crucial to disentangle diasporas from the state and bounded territory to scrutinise the link fully and systematically between diaspora and diplomacy.[53]

Similarly, the specialised literature on migration in the Middle East and North Africa (MENA) has foregrounded the significance of emigration flows for domestic concerns, including citizenship; state authority, capacity and strength; identity; and democracy;[54] as well as for economic development and remittances.[55] Apart from a few studies, such as Gerasimos Tsourapas's book tracking the impact of labour emigration from Egypt on the country's relations with Saudi Arabia and other Arab countries, the MENA migration literature has not sufficiently explored how population flows from sending countries go beyond 'low politics' to shape relations at the state-to-state level.[56]

Recent diplomacy scholarship has gone beyond the traditional focus on state-led diplomacy to draw our attention to polylateralism in the field: namely, the pluralisation of actors engaging in various forms of diplomatic activity.[57] 'New diplomacy' has assigned a proactive role to non-state actors, such as citizens and associations, in this context.[58] While some have referred to diasporas in passing – mostly as a vehicle for public diplomacy[59] or a mode of soft power[60] – this literature has not approached diaspora groups as diplomatic actors in their own right that at times advocate for home-state interests and at other times act independently. Given that diasporas may communicate to and spatially bind multiple audiences, including non-state actors, and thus affect governance and society in both sending and receiving countries, it is surprising that the diaspora and diplomacy literatures have paid scant attention to the question of how diasporas, as in-between political subjectivities, blur the strict division between the domestic and the foreign.[61]

This book aims to contribute to the recent emerging scholarship on diaspora diplomacy[62] in various ways. First, the limited research that has connected diasporas and diplomacy has rarely gone beyond single case studies,[63] nor have such works analysed the broader implications of diaspora diplomacy for foreign affairs, state power, sovereignty, territorialisation and de-territorialisation,[64] mostly viewing diaspora diplomacy in relation to economic and public diplomacy.[65] Moreover, the existing scholarship on diaspora diplomacy has provided insufficient empirical evidence of how diaspora diplomacy operates in reality.[66] This book will fill this gap by examining the new role the Turkish diaspora has in Europe as an agent of diplomatic goals, and the plethora of transnational and international diplomatic tensions that arise from this process, based on cross-country analysis. In addition, a detailed discussion of how Turkey's diaspora outreach efforts have sought to extend the Turkish state's legitimacy beyond its borders and how Turkish expatriates have become part of a larger de-territorialised nation enables this work to contextualise diaspora studies within international relations[67] and diplomacy studies.

Second, and perhaps more importantly, existing scholarship on this topic has mostly investigated 'good diaspora diplomacy'. Kishan S. Rana's research on India's diaspora diplomacy[68] and Joaquin Jay Gonzalez's book on the Filipino community's numerous acts of diplomacy in host states[69] probe the positive effects of diaspora diplomacy for the home or host countries. In a similar vein, in examining the Nordic and Baltic countries' diaspora diplomacy, Ieva Birka and Didzis Klavins look at how the foreign affairs ministries in these countries 'promote the systematic relationship, for mutual benefit, between the country of origin government, diaspora group-ings in countries of residence, and the various interest associations in both the country of origin and country of residence'.[70] In contrast, this book focuses on an understudied aspect of the literature: contentious diaspora diplomacy. I suggest that the current definition of diaspora diplomacy should be expanded in a way to account for the negative effects of such engagement for bilateral and multilateral relations. Thus, this book contrib-utes to the developing literature in this field by prompting a debate on 'unsuccessful' diaspora diplomacy to enhance our understanding of the conditions under which diaspora diplomacy may fail or generate negative and unintended consequences.

A third contribution is that while there is scholarly emphasis on the linkages between diasporas and diplomacy, we still have limited knowledge of the value and impact of such engagement.[71] With few exceptions,[72] most scholarly works typically assume that states develop homogeneous policies towards the diaspora or conclude that all diaspora groups are inclined to promote home-state interests collectively. This literature views diasporas mainly as actors of diplomacy that are at the service of sending states.[73] This book illustrates that the impact of Turkey's diaspora diplomacy has been limited due to the increasing heterogeneity of Turkey's diasporas and some diaspora members' reluctance to abide by Turkey's claim to their identity and role. In fact, certain Turkey-originated diaspora groups (Alevis, secular-ists, Kurds and Gülenists) have lobbied other state and non-state actors to advocate for their own interests at the expense of official Turkish policy. By contending that the lack of cohesion within the diaspora weakens the effec-tiveness of diaspora diplomacy, the book contributes to our understanding of the conditions under which diaspora diplomacy operates.

This study's fourth contribution is to examine the causal mechanism by which an origin state's engagement with a certain diaspora group directly influences the political-mobilisation patterns of that diaspora in host coun-tries. While some have suggested that states may implement differentiated policies that target diaspora groups according to specific criteria,[74] studies have not sufficiently theorised why this might be the case. Other researchers have argued that the divergent policies of origin states depend upon emi-grant communities' perceived utility in staying abroad versus the utility of being back at home[75] or asked why ethno-culturally defined states develop favourable policies to integrate some returnees from their historical diasporas while overlooking others.[76] Some have demonstrated that sending states favour elite diaspora groups to boost the homeland's global competitiveness.[77] In contrast, this book reveals that states may implement multi-tiered diaspora policies even when nationals abroad do not send remittances and are not expected to return to the homeland. It argues that origin states empower those diaspora members that are more likely to promote their foreign policy interests, and that they do so by instilling a sense of self-esteem, collective identity and group consciousness in select members of the diaspora through the provision of technical, financial and legal support.

Finally, despite its position as a key emigrant-sending country, the diaspora diplomacy scholarship has largely omitted Turkey. Existing research on Turkey's emigrants has mostly concentrated on the economic, political and social impact of this emigration on the homeland or host states. While the post-2000 discourse, policies and institutions directed by the Turkish state towards its nationals abroad have attracted scholarly attention,[78] these studies have not examined the implications of Turkey's diaspora diplomacy for various actors and at multiple levels. This book aims to fill this empirical lacuna in the literature.

Conceptual framework and methodology

Alan Gamlen defines 'diaspora' as temporary or permanent extraterritorial groups that interact with their origin states.[79] Rogers Brubaker also emphasises an orientation towards the origin state, real or imagined, as a defining feature of the term.[80] Emigrants from Turkey in Europe form a 'diaspora' because they share a common history and identity that distinguishes them from their host societies. Moreover, Turkey's overseas nationals have established close economic, emotional, socio-political and cultural ties to their homeland, albeit contested at times, and have formed institutions, organisations and parties since the first wave of emigration to Europe.[81]

In this book I define the Turkish diaspora as immigrants and their descendants who originate from Turkey and are involved in the politics of the homeland regardless of their cultural, ethnic, linguistic, political or religious background. While the diaspora is divided across multiple lines, and the book also discusses Kurds who are widely present in the diaspora, the term 'Turkish' will be used throughout the book for three reasons. First, its usage is common within the immigration literature since it is an overarching term. Second, as noted above, Turkey's parliamentary proceedings have opted for the term 'Turkish diaspora' to refer to emigrants from Turkey since the early 2000s. Third, the book's focus is on diaspora diplomacy conducted by Turkish conservative-nationalist and Sunni Islamic organisations. However,

'Turkey's diasporas', 'emigrants from Turkey' and 'Turkish citizens abroad' will also be utilised to highlight diversity within the diaspora. The other terms employed to address members of the émigré population are 'immigrants', 'expatriates', 'overseas Turks', 'Euro-Turks', 'diasporans', 'German Turks' and 'French Turks'. I use the word 'emigrant' in reference to the point of departure and 'immigrant' in reference to the new country of arrival.

In analysing Turkish diaspora diplomacy, one needs to clarify in what ways it is different from diaspora engagement policies and emigration policies. As discussed previously, diaspora engagement policies refer to origin states' activities and discourse aimed at engaging with their expatriates at the individual and collective level and may also take place at the subnational and transnational level. I confine my policy analysis to national-level actors, such as ministries, embassies, consulates and political parties. Emigration policies, on the other hand, are all state policies that spur or hinder the extraterritorial movement of populations, such as agreements on seasonal work, return policies, retention schemes and exit restrictions.[82] Turkey's migration policies started with a focus on emigration policy and transformed into diaspora engagement policy over time. While this book touches upon Turkey's emigration and diaspora engagement policies, the main focus is on diaspora diplomacy, which emphasises the agency of the diaspora community. The book's discussion of diaspora mobilisation focuses on the civic or informal dimension – that is, repertoires of political action outside traditional political channels, such as demonstrations, press releases and signature campaigns.[83] The term is used interchangeably with others, including collective political action, political participation and politicisation.

The book is based on fourteen months of fieldwork in three countries: Turkey, France and Germany. The first round of research, in Ankara, Paris, Strasbourg, Berlin and Cologne, was conducted in 2013–14, with a second round of follow-up data collection in Ankara, Paris and Berlin in 2019. The findings draw from over 110 semi-structured, in-depth interviews conducted with policymakers, journalists and leaders of Turkey's diaspora organisations. I recruited participants by contacting them via phone or email and by visiting them in their offices. I also benefited from my existing networks and used the snowballing technique, whereby an initial contact referred me to new informants.[84] A careful examination of Turkish, English, French and German news sources (including *Anadolu Ajansı*, *Hürriyet*, *Hürriyet Daily News*, *Sabah*, *Euractiv*, *Reuters*, *Le Monde*, *Le Point*, *Deutsche Welle* and *Der Spiegel*), governmental and organisational documents, national censuses, electoral data and existing surveys also formed the empirical basis of this book.

To track the evolution of Turkey's policies of engagement with its diaspora from the 1960s, and the Turkish state's changing relations with European host countries and the EU, interviews were carried out in Turkey's capital with officials from: the AKP; the YTB; the *Diyanet*; the Ministry for EU Affairs; the Ministry of Foreign Affairs; the Ministry of Labour and Social Security; the YEE; and the İB. Conversations with diplomats from the EU Delegation to Turkey, the German Embassy in Ankara and the French Embassy in Ankara improved my analyses. I also conducted interviews with Turkish diplomats from Turkey's embassies and consulates in France and Germany.

To gain a deeper understanding of the Turkish diaspora's mobilisation, perceptions, practices, goals and discourses as well as their links to their origin and settlement countries, interviews were conducted in France and Germany with the officials of the largest and most active Turkey-originated diaspora organisations in both countries. These included, but were not limited to: the Turkish-Islamic Union for Religious Affairs (DİTİB); the UID; the National Vision (*Millî Görüş*); the Council for Justice, Equality and Peace (COJEP); Citizens' Assembly of People from Turkey (ACORT); the House of Workers from Turkey (ELELE); and the Federation of Alevi Unions in France (FUAF). I also spoke with the representatives of: the Union of Islamic Cultural Centres (*Süleymancılar*); the Turkish Community in Germany (TGD); the Turkish Union in Berlin-Brandenburg (TBB); the Turkish-Islamic Union in Europe (ATİB); the Islamic Federation Berlin (IFB); the Turkish Community of Berlin (TGB); the Federation of Alevi Unions in Germany (AABF); the Ahlal Bayt Alevi Federation of Europe; the Kurdish Institute of Paris; the secular Republican People's Party (CHP); and the pro-Kurdish People's Democratic Party (HDP). Selecting a combination of diaspora organisations has enabled me to delve into why the homeland engages with such organisations differently across host countries.

As a Turkish migrant studying the politics of Turkish emigration to Europe, I benefited from the literature on 'insider research' and 'positionality'.[85] As Magdalena Nowicka and Anna Cieslik note, researchers who are migrants themselves need constantly to co-construct and renegotiate their status vis-à-vis their research participants, become a 'temporary' insider only during the conduct of the research and 'must not only display who they are but also who they are not'.[86] During my fieldwork, all of my interviewees greeted me positively: regardless of their ideological position, they were happy to see a rare scholarly interest in their views and willingly provided a detailed account of their experiences. They invited me to their offices and homes, shared Turkish tea and food and introduced me to new respondents. However, Gülenist respondents have been keeping a low public profile, particularly since the 2016 aborted coup. Therefore, I relied on secondary literature and journalists' interviews to examine how Gülenist organisations interpreted Turkey's increasing sway over its diaspora in Europe.

Additionally, I carried out interviews with French and German journalists, policymakers and diplomats. In France, I spoke with individuals from: the Ministry of Europe and Foreign Affairs; the Ministry of the Interior; the Ministry of Justice; the French Council of the Muslim Faith (CFCM); the High Council for Integration; and *Le Monde*. In Germany, I interviewed experts from: the Federal Foreign Office; the Federal Ministry of the Interior; the Federal Ministry of Labour, Integration and Social Affairs; the Federal Agency for Civic Education; the Federal Ministry for Economic Affairs and Energy; the German Islam Conference (DIK); the Berlin Senate for Integration and Migration; and the Christian Democratic Union (CDU)-associated Konrad Adenauer Foundation. I also spoke with parliamentarians from various political parties, such as the Green Party, the Left Party and the Social Democratic Party of Germany (SPD).

I employed thematic analysis to interpret my interview data. Thematic analysis is the process of identifying patterns or themes within qualitative data.[87] After familiarising myself with the material, I generated codes, sorted them into themes, searched for common themes within broader patterns of meaning and reviewed, defined and named themes to consolidate explanation.[88] In the write-up stage, I compared and contrasted varying narratives and created a coherent account that includes quotes and excerpts from the interviewees.

Finally, this research draws on careful analysis of secondary literature, governmental and organisational reports and national censuses to trace the wider process of diaspora policy transformation in Turkey, the diaspora community's links to home and host states and Ankara's changing diplomatic relations with European countries. The archival research conducted for this book involved studying official government documents, such as Turkish law and legal decrees and constitutional reforms relevant to Turkish citizens abroad, parliamentary minutes, statements by public officials and the annual reports of the *Diyanet* and the YTB. The Euro-Turks Barometer[89] and the Trajectories and Origins Survey[90] were also utilised to gauge the degree of integration of Turkey-originated immigrants and their descendants in France and Germany.

This study's analytical focus is on diaspora organisations for several reasons. As the de facto representatives of immigrant-origin citizens in Europe, these organisations constitute the main claims-making actors and co-constructors of political debates pertinent to immigration and integration, and serve as a bridge between their home states and local communities.[91] Moreover, since 9/11, Turkey-originated diaspora organisations have become increasingly salient actors in Europe.[92] This book pays particular attention to diaspora organisations because the majority of scholarly analysis on origin states' diaspora engagement policies adopt a top-down perspective, which has discouraged them from collecting much needed empirical data from individuals in the diaspora. These studies fail to detail how diaspora organisations perceive or respond to sending states' outreach activities. The extensive, multi-site fieldwork underpinning this research is a particular strength of the book.

Why study Turkey's diaspora population in France and Germany?

There are an estimated 6.5 million Turkish citizens living abroad (8 per cent of Turkey's population), with approximately 5.5 million in western Europe, meaning emigrants from Turkey are the largest Muslim immigrant group in Europe.[93] Kurds are the most populous ethnic minority in Turkey and reside mainly in eastern and south eastern Turkey.[94] While the proportion of ethnic Kurds in Turkey stands at 17.7 per cent, they constitute around 25–30 per cent of the emigrant population.[95] The Kurdish population in Europe, which includes Kurdish Alevis, is between 1.5–1.7 million.[96] There are 850,000–950,000 Kurds in Germany and 230,000–250,000 in France.[97] Kurds from Turkey constitute 75 per cent of the Kurdish diaspora in the West.[98] Alevis, an ethno-religious community, comprise approximately 20 per cent of the Turkish population and form the second largest religious group in the country.[99] They do not follow orthodox Sunni Islamic practices, such as veiling of women, fasting during Ramadan and gender-segregated worshipping in mosques. Alevi mystical poetry and music rituals performed in houses of worship (*cemevis*) form key elements of the Alevi collective identity.[100] The Alevi population in Europe is more than 1 million, with 150,000 in France and 600,000 in Germany.[101] Not all Turks and Kurds in Europe hold Turkish citizenship. Table 1.1 details the presence of emigrants from Turkey in major western European countries.

Turkish and Kurdish workers began to arrive in western Europe in small numbers through private initiatives in the mid-1950s. However, from the 1960s, large waves arrived as a result of short-term labour-recruitment agreements signed between Ankara and several European governments.[102] Labour shortages and the demographic challenges of the post-war era were the rationale for importing labour.[103] The first agreement was struck with West Germany in 1961, followed by similar agreements with Austria (1964), Belgium (1964), the Netherlands (1964), France (1965), Sweden (1967), Switzerland (1971), Denmark (1973) and Norway (1981).[104] Even though the economic downturn caused by the 1973 oil crisis brought the demand

Table 1.1 Turkey's diaspora population in Europe

Country	Turkish population numbers (percentage relative to host country population)
Germany	3,000,000 (3.6)
France	800,000 (1.1)
Netherlands	410,000 (2.4)
Austria	300,000 (3.4)
United Kingdom	250,000 (0.3)
Belgium	220,000 (1.9)
Switzerland	120,000 (1.4)
Denmark	70,000 (1.2)
Sweden	60,000 (0.6)
Norway	16,000 (0.3)
Finland	13,000 (0.2)

Source: Turkish Ministry of Foreign Affairs: www.mfa.gov.tr/sub.tr.mfa?199113bb-f534-408f-a373-64fe1946f1b7.

for guest workers to a halt in Europe, most workers had obtained residency permits by then.[105] The introduction of lenient family-reunification and asylum policies in the mid-1970s once again increased the inflow of Turkish citizens to European countries, this time spearheaded by spouses and dependents.[106] Emigration to Europe continued in the 1980s and 1990s and became mostly political, with a surge of asylum applications from Alevis, Kurds and other political dissidents fleeing Turkey's oppressive military regime. By the mid-1980s, policymakers in Turkey and Europe accepted that Turkish citizens abroad were no longer temporary residents.[107] Turkey's socio-economic and democratic deterioration, the rise of political Islam and a faltering EU-accession process, triggered another wave of emigration to Europe in the 2000s, led by secular individuals, highly skilled emigrants, students and sacked public employees.

Unlike other Muslim emigrant groups from North Africa, Sub-Saharan Africa and South Asia, Turks do not share colonial ties with any European state. This has had significant repercussions for Turkish emigration to Europe. While colonial linkages mean Maghrebis are concentrated in France and South Asians in the UK, Turks have spread across Europe. The absence of a colonial relationship between Turkey and European countries also means that second- and third-generation Turkish emigrants have much more readily retained their Turkish national identity and language and have been less inclined to fully integrate into their host states. As an official from the French Ministry of the Interior explained, the lack of a colonial relationship has led to a very strong influence of the homeland culture over Turks in

Europe.[108] Turks abroad also tend to be more conservative than Turks in the homeland. According to a 2012 survey, 16 per cent of Turks living in Turkey reported strong religious beliefs compared to 37 per cent of the Turkish diaspora.[109]

Since France and Germany are the most populous and influential EU countries, and home to the highest number of Turks in Europe, this book focuses on the Turkish diaspora in these two countries. France and Germany host around 800,000 and 3 million Turks respectively.[110] France is a particularly important case. Home to the headquarters of both the European Parliament and the Council of Europe, France constitutes a critical lobbying centre not only for loyal diaspora groups but also for non-conformist groups. In addition, Turks in France remain an under-studied community in the literature: existing books and studies have mostly examined Turks in Germany, the Netherlands, Belgium, the United Kingdom and the United States, with France significantly over-looked.

This book delves into Turkey's diaspora population in France and Germany also because these countries share many similarities yet have crucial institutional differences. For example, France and Germany are both representative democracies with highly developed capitalist economies. They also have similar immigration profiles: they host the largest Muslim populations in Europe and are the most popular emigration destinations for Turks in the region, as noted above. However, as discussed in Chapters 6 and 7, these countries have different immigration, citizenship and integration policies and relations with their Turkish community.[111] This wide institutional variation enables an analysis that can control for the explanatory power of host-state-related factors and thus more clearly illustrate the sending country's effects on the simultaneous empowerment of the select subgroups of the Turkish diaspora in two distinct contexts.

Chapter outline

Following this introduction, the book is organised into seven chapters. Chapter 2 focuses on the transformation of Turkey's diaspora policies from the 1960s to the present day. It explains why Turkey has adopted a proactive diaspora outlook from the 2000s onwards compared to earlier passive policies. While the Turkish state's diaspora policies in the past were driven mainly by economic incentives, they are presently shaped by political goals. The chapter examines Turkey's motives, discourses and concessions towards its diaspora across three time periods: (1) the 1960s–1970s, (2) the 1980s–1990s and (3) 2000–21.

Chapter 3 considers Turkey's engagement with Turkey-originated diaspora organisations in France, focusing on the diaspora outreach activities of various state institutions. It argues that Ankara's engagement with the Turkish community in France follows deliberate policy goals, such as increasing the lobbying capacity of Turkish diaspora organisations, canvassing expatriate votes and strengthening national legitimacy by evoking a sense of home-state loyalty among French Turks. This chapter unpacks how Turkey has empowered conservative-nationalist and Sunni Islamic organisations in France.

Chapter 4 unravels Turkey's involvement in the diasporic field in Germany by examining the outreach activities of various state institutions. The chapter shows that, as in France, engagement with the Turkish community in Germany follows specific political goals and that Ankara's diaspora engagement policies have prioritised certain pro-government Turkish diaspora groups at the expense of others. This asymmetrical treatment explains the curious transition of conservative-nationalist and Sunni Islamic organisations in Germany from passive to active citizenship.

Chapter 5 delves into the intricacies of the diasporic space in Europe by looking at the intra-diasporic politics as well as at the ongoing clashes the AKP government has been experiencing with Alevi, secular, Kurdish and Gülenist diaspora groups. The chapter examines Turkey's authoritarian turn since 2011 and shows that the deepening tension between pro- and anti-AKP diaspora groups and the internal schisms within Turkey's émigré community have weakened Turkey's diaspora diplomacy, generated unrest within European host states and negatively affected Turkey–EU relations.

Chapters 6 and 7 explore how the French and German governments have responded to Turkey's changing relations with its expatriates. They demonstrate that Turkish diaspora engagement policy and diaspora diplomacy have generated backlash and engendered entangled relations with policy-makers in both countries, but more so in Germany than in France. To explain this disparity, these chapters focus on these countries' different immigration, citizenship and integration policies, as well as state policies towards Islam, with a focus on the Turkish community. The chapters conclude that emigrants from Turkey in France have traditionally enjoyed a privileged status vis-à-vis Turks in Germany due, in large part, to the historical relations with, and size of, the Turkish community in each country and the different ways the countries have engaged with Islam.

Finally, Chapter 8 draws together the key analytical implications of the book's main findings. Against the backdrop of literature on the international politics of state–diaspora relations, it critically discusses whether Turkey presents an extreme case, thus breaking new ground, or whether Turkey's diaspora diplomacy is in keeping with other examples, such as the Caribbean and MENA countries, India, the People's Republic of China and the Philippines. The chapter concludes by discussing how this research speaks to a broader range of timely issues, including the continuing supremacy of the nation-state in an age of globalisation, populist nationalism, authoritarianism and immigrant integration. It also offers avenues for future research.

Notes

1 Erdoğan served as Turkey's prime minister between 2003 and 2014.
2 D. Crossland, 'Erdogan's Visit Leaves German Conservatives Fuming', *Der Spiegel*, 12 February 2008, www.spiegel.de/international/germany/the-world-from-berlin-erdogan-s-visit-leaves-german-conservatives-fuming-a-534724.html
3 F. Ataman, 'Erdogan's One-Man Show', *Der Spiegel*, 11 February 2008, www.spiegel.de/international/germany/cologne-s-turkish-spectacle-erdogan-s-one-man-show-a-534519.html
4 'Başbakan Erdoğan, Köln Arena Stadyumu'nda Türkler'le Bir Araya Geldi', *Haberler*, 10 February 2008, www.haberler.com/basbakan-erdogan-koln-arena-stadyumu-nda-turkler-haberi/
5 *Ibid.*
6 F. Ataman, 'Erdogan's One-man Show'.
7 *Ibid.*
8 *Ibid.*
9 D. Crossland, 'Erdogan's Visit Leaves German Conservatives Fuming'.
10 *Ibid.*
11 'Fransa'daki Türklere Anayasa Değişikliğini Anlattı', *CNN Türk*, 7 April 2010, www.cnnturk.com/2010/dunya/04/07/fransadaki.turklere.anayasa.degisikligini.anlatti/571245.0/
12 G. R. Berridge and L. Lloyd, *The Palgrave Macmillan Dictionary of Diplomacy* (Basingstoke: Palgrave Macmillan, 2012).
13 K. S. Rana, 'Diaspora diplomacy and public diplomacy', in *Relational, Networked and Collaborative Approaches to Public Diplomacy: The Connective Mindshift*, eds R. S. Zaharna, A. Arsenault and A. Fisher (London: Routledge, 2012), p. 70.
14 J. J. Gonzalez, *Diaspora Diplomacy: Philippine Migration and Its Soft Power Influences* (Maitland: Mill City Press, 2012), p. 239.
15 A. Gamlen, 'Diaspora engagement policies: What are they, and what kind of states use them?', *Oxford Centre on Migration, Policy and Society Working Paper* 32 (2006), p. 9.
16 Z. Sahin-Mencutek and B. Baser, 'Mobilizing diasporas: Insights from Turkey's attempts to reach Turkish citizens abroad', *Journal of Balkan and Near Eastern Studies* 20:1 (2018), 86–105; A. Arkilic, 'Empowering a fragmented diaspora: Turkish immigrant organizations' perceptions of and responses to Turkey's diaspora engagement policy', *Mediterranean Politics* (2020), doi: 10.1080/13629395.2020.1822058

17 'Yunus Emre Bülteni', *YEE* (September 2009), p. 7, www.yee.org.tr/sites/default/files/yayin/eylul_2009.pdf

18 Fethullah Gülen is a Muslim cleric and the leader of the Gülen Movement (also known as *Hizmet*). Founded in Turkey in the 1970s, the Gülen Movement is a transnational Islamic social network that runs schools, thinktanks and educational and entrepreneurial centres across the world. Gülen has been living in the United States since the 1990s. Gülen supporters are accused of plotting the 2016 failed coup attempt and are regarded by Turkish authorities as a terrorist group called the FETÖ (Pro-Fethullah Terror Organisation).

19 'Main Issues', *Turkish Ministry of Foreign Affairs* (2021), www.mfa.gov.tr/sub.en.mfa?395d59f6-c33c-4364–9744-cff90ec18a3e

20 Y. Aljamal, 'Can Diasporas Ease Tensions in International Politics?', *Politics Today*, 6 December 2020, https://politicstoday.org/can-diasporas-ease-tensions-in-international-politics/

21 'Turks Stage Mega March in Paris', *Daily Sabah*, 21 January 2012, www.dailysabah.com/world/2012/01/21/turks-stage-mega-march-in-paris

22 'French Genocide Law "Unconstitutional" Rules Court', *France24*, 28 February 2012, www.france24.com/en/20120228-france-turkey-genocide-armenia-sarkozy-freedom-expression

23 E. Yalaz, 'Immigrant Political Incorporation: Institutions, Groups and Inter-Ethnic Context' (PhD dissertation, Rutgers University, 2014).

24 D. Aksel, *Home States and Homeland Politics: Interactions between the Turkish State and Its Emigrants in France and the United States* (London: Routledge, 2019).

25 K. Öktem, *Turkey's New Diaspora Policy: The Challenge of Inclusivity, Outreach and Capacity* (Istanbul: Istanbul Policy Centre, 2014).

26 The İB was originally founded in 2010 as the Office of Public Diplomacy under the Prime Ministry. It changed its name in 2018.

27 The UID's previous name was the Union of European Turkish Democrats (UETD), an institution established in Cologne in 2004. The organisation changed its name after Germany's Federal Office for the Protection of the Constitution announced in 2018 that the UETD was incompatible with Germany's constitutional order and that through the UETD the Turkish government collected large amounts of information on Turkish opposition groups based in Germany.

28 For more information, see: A. Arkilic, 'The 2017 Turkish constitutional referendum: Domestic and transnational implications', *New Zealand Journal of Research on Europe* 12:1 (2018), 55–72; A. Arkilic, 'Turkish populist nationalism in transnational space: Explaining diaspora voting behaviour in homeland elections', *Journal of Balkan and Near Eastern Studies* 23:4 (2021), 586–605.

29 The Gezi Park demonstrations started as an environmental movement in Istanbul's Gezi Park in May 2013 and quickly evolved into large-scale protests against the AKP's democratic backsliding, increasing authoritarianism and encroachment on secularism at home and abroad.

30 G. Tsourapas, 'Global autocracies: Strategies of transnational repression, legitimation and co-optation in world politics', *International Studies Review* (2020), doi: 10.1093/isr/viaa061

31 For a detailed discussion on how migration is used for foreign policy purposes, see: K. Greenhill, *Weapons of Mass Migration: Forced Displacement, Coercion and Foreign Policy* (Ithaca: Cornell University Press, 2010).

32 A. Kaya, 'Migration as a leverage tool in international relations: Turkey as a case study', *Uluslararası İlişkiler* (January 2021), 1–19.

33 A. Kaya, *Turkish-origin Migrants and Their Descendants: Hyphenated Identities in Transnational Space* (Basingstoke: Palgrave Macmillan, 2019); F. B. Adamson and G. Tsourapas, 'Migration diplomacy in world politics', *International Studies Perspectives* 20:2 (2019), 113–28.

34 K. Faheem, 'Netherlands Cancels Turkish Foreign Minister's Visit in Spiralling Feud between Europe and Turkey', *Washington Post*, 11 March 2017, www.washingtonpost.com/world/netherlands-cancels-visit-by-turkish-foreign-minister-in-spiraling-feud-between-europe-and-turkey/2017/03/11/acc2c8ba-0655–11e7-a391–651727e77fc0_story.html

35 A. Arkilic, 'How Turkey's Outreach to Its Diaspora Is Inflaming Tensions with Europe', *Washington Post*, 26 March 2018, www.washingtonpost.com/news/monkey-cage/wp/2018/03/26/how-turkeys-outreach-to-its-diaspora-is-inflaming-tensions-with-europe/

36 'Reality Check: Is Banning Turkish Rallies EU Policy?', *BBC*, 13 March 2017, www.bbc.com/news/world-europe-39221689

37 'Turkey Accuses Macron of Supporting Hate Crimes with His New Plan against "Islamist Separatism"', *Duvar English*, 5 October 2020, www.duvarenglish.com/diplomacy/2020/10/05/turkey-accuses-macron-of-supporting-hate-crimes-with-his-new-plan-against-islamist-separatism/

38 R. S. Alouane, 'Islam, made in France? Debating the reform of Muslim organizations and foreign funding for religion', *Brookings Institution* (2019), www.brookings.edu/blog/order-from-chaos/2019/05/01/islam-made-in-france-debating-the-reform-of-muslim-organizations-and-foreign-funding-for-religion/

39 K. Piser, 'Macron Wants to Start an Islamic Revolution', *Foreign Policy*, 7 October 2020, https://foreignpolicy.com/2020/10/07/macron-wants-to-start-an-islamic-revolution/; 'Macron Hails French Muslim Charter to Combat Extremism', *France24*, 18 January 2021, www.france24.com/en/france/20210118-french-muslim-council-draws-up-charter-to-combat-extremism

40 E. Østergaard-Nielsen, *Transnational Politics: Turks and Kurds in Germany* (London: Routledge, 2003).

41 A. Arkilic, 'Explaining the evolution of Turkey's diaspora engagement policy: A holistic approach', *Diaspora Studies* 14:1 (2021), 1–21.

42 A. Délano, *Mexico and Its Diaspora in the United States: Policies of Emigration since 1848* (Cambridge: Cambridge University Press, 2011).

43 E. Østergaard-Nielsen, 'Turkey and the "Euro-Turks": Overseas nationals as an ambiguous asset', in *International Migration and Sending Countries:*

Perceptions, Policies and Transnational Relations, ed. E. Østergaard-Nielsen (Basingstoke: Palgrave Macmillan, 2003), pp. 77–99.

44 P. Kubicek, 'The Europeanisation and grassroots democratisation in Turkey', *Turkish Studies* 6:3 (2005), 361–77.

45 I. Manor, 'The contradictory trends of digital diaspora diplomacy', *Exploring Digital Diplomacy Working Paper 2* (2016), https://digdipblog.files.wordpress. com/2017/08/the-contradictory-trends-of-digital-diaspora-diplomacy.pdf

46 J. F. Hollifield, 'The politics of international migration', in *Migration Theory: Talking across Disciplines*, eds C. Brettell and J. F. Hollifield (London: Routledge, 2000), pp. 137–85.

47 L. Brand, *Citizens Abroad: State and Emigration in the Middle East and North Africa* (New York: Cambridge University Press, 2006); A. Gamlen, 'Diaspora engagement policies'; F. Ragazzi, 'A comparative analysis of diaspora policies', *Political Geography* 41 (2014), 74–89.

48 E. Østergaard-Nielsen, *Transnational Politics*; L. Varadarajan, *The Domestic Abroad: Diasporas in International Relations* (Oxford: Oxford University Press, 2010); D. Naujoks, *Migration, Citizenship, and Development: Diasporic Membership Policies and Overseas Indians in the United States* (Oxford: Oxford University Press, 2013); A. Gamlen, 'Diaspora institutions and diaspora governance', *International Migration Review* 48:1 (2014), 180–217; M. Koinova and G. Tsourapas, 'How do countries of origin engage migrants and diasporas? Multiple actors and comparative perspectives', *International Political Science Review* 39:3 (2018), 311–21; A. Gamlen, M. Cummings and P. Vaaler, 'Explaining the rise of diaspora institutions', *Journal of Ethnic and Migration Studies* 45:4 (2019), 492–516.

49 R. C. Smith, 'Migrant membership as an instituted process: Transnationalisation, the State and the extra-territorial conduct of Mexican politics', *International Migration Review* 37:3 (2003), 297–343; A. Délano, *Mexico and Its Diaspora in the United States*; A. Délano and A. Gamlen, 'Comparing and theorizing state–diaspora relations', *Political Geography* 41 (2014), 43–53; A. Gamlen, *Human Geopolitics: States, Emigrants and the Rise of Diaspora Institutions* (Oxford: Oxford University Press, 2019).

50 J. M. Lafleur, 'Why do states enfranchise citizens abroad? Comparative insights from Mexico, Italy and Belgium', *Global Networks* 11:4 (2011), 481–501; M. Collyer, 'A geography of extra-territorial citizenship: Explanations of external voting', *Migration Studies* 2:1 (2014), 55–72.

51 F. B. Adamson, 'Sending states and the making of intra-diasporic politics: Turkey and its diaspora(s)', *International Migration Review* 53:1 (2019), 210–36.

52 E. Mavroudi, 'Palestinians in diaspora, empowerment and informal political space', *Political Geography* 27:1 (2018), 57–73; L. Berkowitz and L. Mügge, 'Transnational diaspora lobbying: Europeanization and the Kurdish question', *Journal of Intercultural Studies* 35:1 (2014), 74–90.

53 E. L. Ho and F. McConnell, 'Conceptualizing "diaspora diplomacy": Territory and populations betwixt the domestic and foreign', *Progress in Human Geography*, 43:2 (2019), 235–55.

54 H. De Haas, 'Between courting and controlling: The Moroccan state and "its" emigrants', *Oxford Centre on Migration, Policy and Society Working Paper 54*

(2007); G. Parolin, *Citizenship in the Arab World: Kin, Religion, and Nation State* (Amsterdam: Amsterdam University Press, 2009); W. Pearlman, 'Competing for Lebanon's diaspora: Transnationalism and domestic struggles in a weak state', *International Migration Review* 48:1 (2014), 34–75.

55 N. Iskander, *Creative State: Forty Years of Migration and Development Policy in Morocco and Mexico* (Ithaca: Cornell University Press, 2010); P. Fargues, 'International migration and the nation state in Arab countries', *Middle East Law and Governance* 5 (2013), 5–35.

56 G. Tsourapas, *The Politics of Migration in Modern Egypt: Strategies for Regime Survival in Autocracies* (Cambridge: Cambridge University Press, 2018).

57 G. Wiseman, '"Polylateralism" and new modes of global dialogue', in *Diplomacy: Problems and Issues in Contemporary Diplomacy*, eds C. Jönsson and R. Langhorne (Thousand Oaks: Sage, 2004); A. F. Cooper, J. English and R. C. Thakur, *Enhancing Global Governance: Towards a New Diplomacy* (New York: United Nations University Press, 2002); S. Riordan, *The New Diplomacy* (Cambridge: Polity Press, 2003); P. Kerr and G. Wiseman, *Diplomacy in a Globalising World* (Oxford: Oxford University Press, 2013); C. Bjola and M. Holmes (eds), *Digital Diplomacy: Theory and Practice* (London: Routledge, 2015); E. L. Ho and F. McConnell, 'Conceptualizing "diaspora diplomacy"'.

58 D. Stone and E. Douglas, 'Advance diaspora diplomacy in a networked world', *International Journal of Cultural Policy* 24:6 (2018), 710–23.

59 Public diplomacy differs from traditional diplomacy. While the latter is concerned with the relationship between the representatives of states or other international actors, the former refers to official communication aimed at societies, organisations and individuals abroad (J. Melissen, *The New Public Diplomacy: Soft Power in International Relations* (Basingstoke: Palgrave Macmillan, 2005), p. 5).

60 Public diplomacy is a key dimension of soft power. See: *ibid.*, p. 4. Joseph Nye defines soft power as 'the ability to get what you want through attraction rather than coercion or payments [which] … arises from the attractiveness of a country's culture, political ideals and policies' (J. S. Nye, *Soft Power: The Means to Success in World Politics* (New York: Public Affair, 2004), p. x).

61 E. L. Ho and F. McConnell, 'Conceptualizing "diaspora diplomacy"'.

62 M. Mwagiru, 'Diplomacy of the diaspora: Harnessing diasporas in Kenya's foreign policy', *Diaspora Studies* 4:1 (2011), 39–58; M. Tomiczek, 'Diaspora diplomacy: About a new dimension of diplomacy – the example of a new emigration non-governmental organisation', *Journal of Education Culture and Society* 2 (2011), 105–23; D. L. Trent, 'American diaspora diplomacy: US foreign policy and Lebanese Americans', *The Clingendael Institute Discussion Papers in Diplomacy No. 125* (2012); A. A. Torrealba, 'Three main approaches of diaspora diplomacy in foreign policy', *Actual Problems of Economics and Law* 11:2 (2017), 154–69; J. Dickinson, 'Visualising the foreign and the domestic in diaspora diplomacy: images and the online politics of recognition: #givingtoindia', *Cambridge Review of International Affairs* 33:5 (2020), 752–77.

63 There are exceptions: N. Mirilovic, 'Regime type and diaspora politics: A dyadic approach', *Foreign Policy Analysis* 14 (2018), 346–66.

64 E. L. Ho and F. McConnell, 'Conceptualizing "diaspora diplomacy"'.

65 I. Birka and D. Klavins, 'Diaspora diplomacy: Nordic and Baltic perspective', *Diaspora Studies* 13:2 (2020), 117.

66 *Ibid.*, 118.

67 Y. Shain and A. Barth, 'Diasporas and international relations theory', *International Organisation* 57:3 (2003), 449–79; F. B. Adamson and M. Demetriou, 'Remapping the boundaries of "state" and "national identity": Incorporating diasporas into IR theorising', *European Journal of International Relations* 13:4 (2007), 489–526.

68 K. S. Rana, 'Diaspora diplomacy and public diplomacy'.

69 J. J. Gonzalez, *Diaspora Diplomacy*.

70 I. Birka and D. Klavins, 'Diaspora diplomacy', 118.

71 L. Kennedy, 'Diaspora and Diplomacy', Diaspora and Diplomacy Conference, University College Dublin, 24–26 May 2018, Dublin Ireland, https://networks.h-net.org/node/20292/discussions/1246497/diaspora-and-diplomacy

72 M. Koinova, 'Diaspora mobilisation for conflict and post-conflict reconstruction: contextual and comparative dimensions', *Journal of Ethnic and Migration Studies* 44:8 (2017), 1–19; A. Délano Alonso and H. Mylonas, 'The microfoundations of diaspora politics: Unpacking the state and disaggregating the diaspora', *Journal of Ethnic and Migration Studies* 45:4 (2019), 473–91.

73 E. L. Ho and F. McConnell, 'Conceptualizing "diaspora diplomacy"'.

74 B. S. Heisler, 'Sending countries and the politics of emigration and destination', *International Migration Review* 19:3 (1985), 469–84; P. Levitt and R. De la Dehesa, 'Transnational migration and the redefinition of the state: Variations and explanations', *Ethnic and Racial Studies* 26:4 (2005), 587–611; N. L. Green and F. Weil (eds), *Citizenship and Those Who Leave: The Politics of Emigration and Expatriation* (Champaign: University of Illinois Press, 2010).

75 G. Tsourapas, 'Why do states develop multi-tier emigrant policies? Evidence from Egypt', *Journal of Ethnic and Migration Studies* 41:13 (2015), 2192–214.

76 H. Mylonas and M. Žilović, 'Foreign policy priorities and ethnic return migration policies: Group-level variation in Greece and Serbia', *Journal of Ethnic and Migration Studies* 45:4 (2019), 613–35.

77 E. L. Ho, '"Claiming" the diaspora: Elite mobility, sending state strategies and the spatialities of citizenship', *Progress in Human Geography* 35:6 (2011), 757–72.

78 C. Ünver, 'Changing diaspora politics of Turkey and public diplomacy', *Turkish Policy Quarterly* 12:1 (2013), 181–9; Y. Aydın, 'The New Turkish Diaspora Policy', *Stiftung Wissenschaft und Politik* (2014), www.swp-berlin.org/fileadmin/contents/products/research_papers/2014_RP10_adn.pdf; Z. Yanaşmayan and Z. Kaşlı, 'Reading diasporic engagements through the lens of citizenship: Turkey as a test case', *Political Geography* 70 (2019), 24–33; Y. E. Ok, '"Diaspora diplomacy" as a foreign policy strategy', *IFAIR* (2018), https://ifair.eu/2018/11/01/diaspora-diplomacy-as-a-foreign-policy-strategy/; B. Baser, 'Governing Turkey's diaspora(s) and the limits of diaspora diplomacy', in *The Routledge Handbook of Turkish Politics*, eds A. Özerdem and M. Whiting (London: Routledge, 2019), pp. 202–13; K. Burgess, *Courting Migrants: How States Make Diasporas and Diasporas Make States* (Oxford: Oxford University Press, 2020).

79 A. Gamlen, 'The emigration state and the modern geopolitical imagination', *Political Geography* 27:8 (2008), 841.

80 R. Brubaker, 'The diaspora "diaspora"', *Ethnic and Racial Studies* 28:1 (2005), 1–19.

81 Y. Aydın, 'Turkish diaspora policy: Transnationalism or long-distance nationalism?', in *Turkish Migration Policy*, eds İ. Sirkeci and B. Pusch (London: Transnational Press, 2016), pp. 169–81.

82 A. Weinar, 'Emigration policies in contemporary Europe', *European University Institute CARIM-East Research Report* (2014), p. 5.

83 R. Zapata-Barrero, L. Gabrielli, E. Sánchez-Montijano and T. Jaulin, 'The political participation of immigrants in host states: An interpretative framework from the perspective of origin countries and societies', *European University Institute INTERACT Report* (2013), http://hdl.handle.net/1814/29565

84 R. Atkinson and J. Flint, 'Accessing hidden and hard-to-reach populations: Snowball research strategies', *Social Research Update* 33 (2001), 1–4.

85 R. Merton, 'Insiders and outsiders: A chapter in the sociology of knowledge', *American Journal of Sociology* 78:1 (1972): 9–47; K. Narayan, 'How native is a "native" anthropologist?', *American Anthropologist* 95:3 (1993): 671–86; G. Rose, 'Situating knowledges: Positionality, reflexivities and other tactics', *Progress in Human Geography* 21:3 (1997), 305–20; L. Voloder and L. Kirpitchenko (eds), *Insider Research on Migration and Mobility: International Perspectives on Researcher Positioning* (London: Routledge, 2013).

86 M. Nowicka and A. Cieslik, 'Beyond methodological nationalism in insider research with migrants', *Migration Studies* 2:1 (2014), 7.

87 V. Braun and V. Clarke, 'Using thematic analysis in psychology', *Qualitative Research in Psychology* 3:2 (2006), 77–101.

88 V. Braun and V. Clarke, 'Thematic analysis', in *APA Handbook of Research Methods in Psychology, Vol. 2: Research Designs*, ed. H. Cooper (Washington DC: APA), 57–74.

89 M. Erdoğan, 'Euro-Turks Barometer', *Hacettepe University Migration and Politics Research Centre Report* (2013), http://fs.hacettepe.edu.tr/hugo/dosyalar/ETB_rapor.pdf

90 C. Beauchemin, C. Hamel and P. Simon (eds), *Trajectories and Origins: Survey on the Diversity of French Population* (Berlin: Springer, 2018).

91 M. Schrover and F. Vermeulen, 'Immigrant organisations', *Journal of Ethnic and Migration Studies* 31:5 (2005), 823–32; S. Carol and R. Koopmans, 'Dynamics of contestation over Islamic religious rights in western Europe', *Ethnicities* 13:2 (2013), 165–90.

92 R. Kastoryano, *Negotiating Identities: States and Immigrants in France and Germany* (Princeton: Princeton University Press, 2002); K. Rosenow-Williams, *Organising Muslims and Integrating Islam: New Developments in the 21st Century* (Leiden: Brill, 2012); A. Arkilic, 'The limits of European Islam: Turkish Islamic umbrella organisations and their relations with host countries – France and Germany', *Journal of Muslim Minority Affairs* 35:1 (2015), 17–43.

93 'Turkish citizens living abroad', *Turkish Ministry of Foreign Affairs* (2021), www.mfa.gov.tr/the-expatriate-turkish-citizens.en.mfa

94 'Minorities and indigenous peoples in Turkey', *Minority Rights Group* (2021), https://minorityrights.org/country/turkey/

95 S. Cagaptay and E. C. Sacikara, 'Turks in Europe and Kurds in Turkey Could Get Erdogan Elected', *Washington Institute*, 23 July 2014, www.washingtoninstitute.org/policy-analysis/view/turks-in-europe-and-kurds-in-turkey-could-elect-erdogan

96 'Kurdish diaspora', *Kurdish Institute of Paris* (December 2016), www.institut-kurde.org/en/info/kurdish-diaspora-1232550988

97 *Ibid.*

98 *Ibid.*

99 C. Jenkins, S. Aydin and U. Cetin (eds), *Alevism as an Ethno-religious Identity: Contested Boundaries* (London: Routledge, 2018).

100 A. Arkilic and A. E. Gurcan, 'The political participation of Alevis: A comparative analysis of the Turkish Alevi Opening and the German Islam Conference', *Nationalities Papers: The Journal of Nationalism and Ethnicity* 49:5 (2021), 949–66.

101 A. Gorzewski, 'Alevis in France: Striking a Balance between Old and New', *Qantara*, 7 November 2008, https://en.qantara.de/content/alevis-in-france-striking-a-balance-between-old-and-new

102 İ. Sirkeci, 'Revisiting the Turkish migration to Germany after forty years', *Siirtolaisuus-Migration* 29:2 (2002), 9–20; G. Yurdakul, *From Guest Workers into Muslims: The Transformation of Turkish Immigrant Associations in Germany* (Newcastle upon Tyne: Cambridge Scholars, 2009).

103 N. Abadan-Unat, *Bitmeyen Göç: Konuk İşçilikten Ulus-Ötesi Yurttaşlığa* (Istanbul: Bilgi University, 2002).

104 Turkey also signed a bilateral agreement with Australia in 1967. See: A. İçduygu, 'International migration and human development in Turkey', *United Nations Development Programme Human Development Research Paper No. 2009/52* (2009).

105 A. Akgündüz, *Labour Migration from Turkey to Western Europe, 1960–1974: A Multidisciplinary Analysis* (Aldershot: Ashgate, 2008).

106 P. L. Martin, *The Unfinished Story: Turkish Labour Migration to Western Europe* (Geneva: International Labour Office, 1991).

107 E. Østergaard-Nielsen, *Transnational Politics*.

108 B. Ercan-Argun, *Turkey in Germany: The Transnational Sphere of Deutschkei* (London: Routledge, 2003); Interview, French Ministry of the Interior official, Paris, 14 January 2019.

109 S. Cagaptay and E. C. Sacikara, 'Turks in Europe and Kurds in Turkey'.

110 'Avrupa', *Turkish Ministry of Foreign Affairs* (2021), www.mfa.gov.tr/sub.tr.mfa?199113bb-f534–408f-a373–64fe1946f1b7

111 R. Brubaker, *Citizenship and Nationhood in France and Germany* (Cambridge, MA: Harvard University Press, 1992); P. Ireland, *The Policy Challenge of Ethnic Diversity* (Cambridge, MA: Harvard University Press, 1994); R. Koopmans and P. Statham (eds), *Challenging Immigration and Ethnic Relations Politics* (Oxford: Oxford University Press, 2001); J. S. Fetzer and C. J. Soper, *Muslims and the State in Britain, France and Germany* (Cambridge: Cambridge University Press, 2005).

2

'From guest workers to brothers and sisters': The transformation of Turkey's diaspora engagement policies

Turks have now spread to 150 countries across the world. We naturally see our diaspora as a diplomacy tool. However, we do not ask them to serve as a diplomatic agent for us. We do not have a political agenda. They do this voluntarily. Our diaspora belongs not only to us but also to Europe. That's why our citizens are an important source of soft power for both Turkey and Europe.[1]

Turkey is a latecomer to diaspora engagement affairs. Since the 1960s, Ankara has strived to connect with members of the Turkish community abroad through various state agencies. Turkey's earlier policies in the 1960s and 1970s were largely ad hoc, uncoordinated and restricted to attracting money back home, providing temporary support and controlling subversive Islamist and Kurdish political dissidence. During the 1980s and 1990s, Turkish officials acknowledged emigrants' permanent status in Europe but prioritised a security-oriented approach towards them. Turkey began to craft an institutionalised diaspora engagement policy driven by new political incentives with the AKP's rise to power in 2002.

Since 2003, Turkish bureaucrats have realised that an integrated and enfranchised diaspora, armed with the rights and prerogatives of citizenship, would be politically beneficial for both Turkish emigrants and their homeland. To this end, they have developed a keen interest in changing the image of Turks from low- to high-skilled immigrants. Official capacity-development programmes have urged the Turkish expatriate community to participate in European elections, obtain dual citizenship and learn the language of their host country. Through its nationals abroad, Turkey now presents itself as a rising great power, extends the state's legitimacy and 'soft power' beyond borders and lobbies against host-state policies and developments that are deemed inimical to Turkey's interests. This chapter will provide an historical and multidimensional overview of Turkey's changing diaspora engagement policy with a focus on the often intertwined domestic, transnational and international factors that have shaped this area of policy. It will first look at policies introduced before 2003. It will then analyse the ambitious diaspora policy framework adopted in the post-2003 era.

Turkey's pre-2003 diaspora engagement policies

The 1960s and 1970s: From undesired peasants to workers abroad

Turkey's emigration policies until the 1960s were motivated by the country's modernisation and nation-building process.[2] Following the collapse of the Ottoman Empire, Mustafa Kemal Atatürk, a secular and nationalist military officer with a Western-oriented elite tradition, established the Republic of Turkey in 1923. The new regime's ruling cadre was very different from the Ottoman sultans, for whom Islam had played a significant role in politics and society.[3] Atatürk and his administration emphasised 'Turkishness' over the predominantly Islamic character of the Ottoman Empire to neutralise the resilient cultural elements of the Ottoman era, which were seen as backward.[4] Kemalist reformers' efforts went far beyond modernising the state apparatus, as the country changed from a multi-ethnic empire to a secular, republican nation-state that penetrated the daily lives of the people.[5] The abolition of the Caliphate, the Arabic alphabet and call to prayer, Islamic education organisations and movements and the wearing of Islamic clothing in public space struck conservatives as the monopolisation of governmental and societal power by the new Western-oriented modernist elite.[6] In the early days of the Republic, Turkish officials sent students to Europe and North America to create an intellectual community who would ideally return to Turkey upon completion of their Western education and contribute to the country's modernisation process.[7] The republican elite also sought to restructure the national and cultural identity of the state and its citizens on the basis of homogeneous national culture, which induced forced migration waves and population exchanges.[8] These policies replaced the non-Muslim population of Turkey, which was regarded as a 'threat' to the newly founded Republic, with Turkish Muslims from former Ottoman lands.[9]

Emigration policies from the 1960s were significant, as they not only transformed the nature of emigration, from student outflows and forced migration to labour emigration, but also increased exponentially the number of Turks and Kurds moving abroad. After two devastating world wars, European countries' labour shortages and demographic challenges necessitated them to request temporary workers from Turkey, North Africa, Yugoslavia and southern Europe.[10] At the same time, Turkey was grappling with grave political and economic problems that served as push factors. Following Turkey's transition from a one-party system under the CHP into a multi-party system in 1946, the Democrat Party (DP) rose to power in 1950 as the first party in Turkey with a religious undertone.[11] In 1960, the military junta toppled the DP, the prime minister (Adnan Menderes) and the president

(Celal Bayar) on the basis that they posed a threat to the core principles of the secular Kemalist regime. In the aftermath of the execution of three DP leaders, including Menderes, a new election took place in 1961 and İsmet İnönü and Cemal Gürsel became the new prime minister and president respectively.[12]

Political turmoil hit the Turkish economy hard, which was already struggling due to its state-driven import-substitution industrialisation (ISI) economic model. ISI prioritised technology over labour, produced goods only for an internal market and, therefore, did not create sources of foreign revenue. Turkey's agrarianism, low level of urbanisation, underdevelopment of the industrial working class and rapidly growing population exacerbated economic distress.[13] Turkey's First Five-Year Development Plan (1963–67) identified the 'export of surplus labour power' as a key component of economic progress.[14] The provision of low-skilled Turkish and Kurdish guest workers from rural Anatolia was expected to be a short-term win–win situation for Turkey and Europe: it would aid the recovering but labour-short economies of post-war Europe and serve as a transitory solution to Turkey's unemployment and slow-development problem. In addition, Turkey hoped to benefit from guest workers' skills and experiences upon their return.[15] Earthquakes in eastern Turkey during this period also led to Kurdish outflows from Turkey.[16]

Turkey's emigration policies during the 1960s and 1970s reflected 'a state of ambivalence'[17] and were mainly restricted to attracting remittances, providing information to guest workers regarding their migratory status and encouraging them to return to Turkey to contribute to the homeland's economic development.[18] Turkey's Second Five-Year Development Plan (1968–72) concluded that remittances constituted a significant income source for the Turkish economy and listed measures to multiply them.[19]

The country's economic and political strife deepened with a recession and a violent conflict between left-wing workers and students and right-wing Islamists and militant nationalist groups. These developments culminated in the 1971 military coup that eclipsed politics once again. The army ousted the incumbent centre-right Justice Party's (AP) leader and prime minister, Süleyman Demirel, arguing that he had lost his grip on power and was unable to quell escalating violence. Once martial law was declared, an alternative government of technocrats rose to prominence under the new prime minister, Nihat Erim (who was then replaced by Ferit Melen in 1972, himself replaced by Naim Talu in 1973, who was then replaced by Bülent Ecevit in 1974).[20] The new government banned Necmettin Erbakan's *Millî Görüş*-inspired[21] National Order Party due to its anti-secular agenda. Other influential Islamist figures, such as Fethullah Gülen, who was a preacher at that time, and leaders of the Union of Islamic Cultural Centres, also faced political pressure following the 1971 coup.[22] With the closure of political parties at home, radical leftist groups in exile mobilised abroad to promote their parties' agendas and to oppose the military junta.[23] In 1976, the TBMM passed legislation that prohibited the establishment of party branches beyond Turkish soil.[24] After its formation in 1978 by Abdullah Öcalan to establish an independent Kurdish state, the Kurdistan Workers' Party (PKK) began mobilising migrant workers.[25] In the same year, a massacre killing hundreds of Alevi citizens in the south eastern city of Kahramanmaraş by ultranationalists and conservative Sunnis fuelled sectarian tensions within and beyond Turkey's borders.[26]

The Ministry of Foreign Affairs, the Ministry of Labour and Social Security,[27] the *Diyanet*, the Ministry of Finance and the Ministry of Education were the main official bodies administering Turkey's emigration policies during this era. The Directorate for Consular Affairs, under the Ministry of Foreign Affairs, was particularly important as it oversaw relations with expatriates. The Ministry of Labour and Social Security signed bilateral labour agreements with the Ministry of Foreign Affairs and regulated the recruitment and movement of guest workers.[28] The General Directorate of Foreign Relations and Services for Workers Abroad in the Ministry of Labour and Social Security, established in 1967, coordinated health and social security matters related to guest workers and provided assistance to Turks in their new destinations.[29] The State Planning Organisation and the Turkish Employment Service also regulated the flow of labour migrants.[30]

The *Diyanet* was founded in 1924 following the abolition of the Ottoman Caliphate to bring all religious activity under secular state control.[31] In the 1970s, the *Diyanet*'s main tasks were to provide temporary religious and cultural aid and to constrain the activities of Islamist and Kurdish groups outlawed in Turkey.[32] In 1971, it dispatched its first group of imams to Europe.[33] With the foundation of the Directorate of External Services in the same year, which became the Directorate of External Affairs in 1976, the *Diyanet* began to play a more influential role in the Turkish diaspora's religious and cultural life.[34] In 1978, Ankara established the Turkish Councillorship for Religious Services as part of Turkish embassies, and the Religious Services Attachés as part of Turkish consulates.[35]

The Ministry of Finance and the Ministry of Education were the other prominent state institutions active in emigration policymaking. The former administered the inflow of remittances and investments along with the now defunct Ministry of Village Affairs, the Real Estate Credit Bank and the State Industrial and Workers' Investment Bank.[36] While remittances sent by Turkish workers in 1964 amounted to $45 million and rose to $1.4 billion in ten years, the oil crisis of 1974 led to a sharp decline in remittances.[37] Turkey also offered tax, job and investment benefits to returning workers and created village development cooperatives and workers' joint-stock companies. The ultimate goal was to facilitate the integration of returning immigrants and to support investment in rural areas. However, these efforts did not result in balanced economic improvement across the country.[38] The Ministry of Education in the meantime sought to teach Turkish language, culture and Islam to descendants of Turkish emigrants through the Directorate General for Services for Education Abroad and the Directorate General for Education of Workers' Children Abroad founded in 1976.[39] Turkey also initiated the Teaching Language and Culture of Origin (ELCO) programmes that operate under bilateral agreements signed between Turkey and some countries (like France) that send Turkish language teachers abroad to teach young members of the diaspora their native language outside regular school hours.[40]

However, official documents addressed Turkey's diasporas negatively in these two decades: Turks abroad were seen as uncivilised, low-skilled 'peasants' (*köylü*) or 'remittance machines' (*döviz makinesi*).[41] An examination of TBMM proceedings from these decades attests to this attitude: overseas Turks were cited as 'workers abroad' (*yurtdışı işçileri*). Parliamentarians believed that Turkish workers would be short-term residents in Europe only and revealed a conscious reluctance to use the word 'immigrant' (*göçmen*) *at all* in official documents.[42]

The 1980s and 1990s: From workers abroad to immigrants

By the 1980s, Turkish officials realised that most Turkish guest workers were not returning to the homeland. Accordingly, bureaucrats prioritised the steady inpouring of remittances. This realisation, coupled with Turkey's economic liberalisation and transition into the export-led growth strategy in the 1980s, revitalised the flow of remittances. Remittances reached $2 billion in 1980 and climbed to $3.4 billion by 1995 (before starting to decrease in the late 1990s).[43]

Turkey continued to send religious personnel and language teachers to European countries through the *Diyanet* and the Ministry of Education. The state-run Turkish Radio and Television Corporation (TRT) also began daily broadcasts in Europe in 1980. The TRT's overseas-oriented programmes targeted both adults and young people, promoted Turkish nationalism and Atatürk's reforms and solicited moral and economic support for the Turkish army fighting oppositional forces.[44]

As the political situation became increasingly chaotic in Turkey throughout the 1980s, security became the dominant theme in Turkey's emigration policy. Previously, the main cleavage shaping the Turkish diaspora was a political one between the right and left. By the 1980s, there was a plethora of other dividing lines, between secularists and conservatives, Turkish and Kurdish nationalists, and Sunnis and Alevis,[45] and the 1980 military coup – orchestrated by General Kenan Evren, who later became president – terminated the conflict between the right- and left-wing camps. In 1984, an armed conflict between the Turkish army and the PKK broke out and aggravated political unrest.[46]

In the wake of the military coup, the Turkish government put pressure on the PKK, various left-wing organisations and Islamist movements. Over 20,000 leftists were detained across the country, 8,000 of them Kurdish rebels accused of separatism. Leftist and Kurdish intellectuals, activists and politicians soon fled Turkey and mobilised in various European countries, mainly Germany.[47] Oppositional Islamists also felt threatened following the closure of the *Millî Görüş*-linked National Salvation Party in 1980 and an arrest warrant against Fethullah Gülen. Additionally, targeted bombs and arson attacks by extremist Turkish nationalists rekindled fear and trauma within the Alevi community, increased the number of asylum appeals from Turkey to European countries and exported homeland tensions to the transnational space.[48]

These changes affected state–diaspora relations tremendously, leading Turkish bureaucrats to become more concerned with containing and co-opting dissident group activities and exerting influence on immigrant organisations. Kenan Evren's regime (1980–83) regarded secular immigrant organisations as 'allies' because they imported the Turkish state's nationalist and secular discourse to Europe. On the other hand, Alevi, Kurdish, leftist and 'alternative' Islamic organisations were labelled 'enemies' and placed under state surveillance.[49] To combat dissident groups, Turkey encouraged the establishment of coordinating committees composed of quasi-umbrella organisations affiliated with the nationalist state ideology and required all immigrant organisations to provide information regarding their leadership, members and activities to the Ministry of the Interior.[50] This era thus showed a 'reactive' rather than 'proactive' approach to the diaspora.[51] By 1982, it was illegal for any political party to receive financial support from, and to collaborate with, immigrant organisations.[52]

Turks abroad were addressed as 'immigrants' for the first time in official documents in the 1980s, alongside the terms 'expatriates' (*gurbetçiler*)[53] and 'overseas Turks' (*yurtdışı Türkler*).[54] Remittances remained a significant topic of formal discussion in the TBMM throughout the 1980s. Concerns over dissident groups, the threat of radical Islam and the protection of the cultural identity of younger generations were other key themes in the parliamentary sessions.[55]

A landmark amendment in Turkish citizenship law in 1981 signalled an important shift in the Turkish government's perception of their community abroad. This amendment recognised dual citizenship for the first time on the condition of a permission document issued by the Ministry of the Interior. However, a clause of the law (which was removed in 1992) revoked the citizenship of political dissidents living abroad.[56] According to Yaşar Aydın, the introduction of this law represented a transfiguration of Turkey's policy towards its émigré population into a 'diaspora policy'.[57] The Turkish government took additional steps to establish firmer relations with its diaspora in the 1980s, such as the introduction of paid military service.[58] Moreover, the 1982 Constitution became the first Turkish constitution to stress the need to maintain relations with Turkish immigrants.[59]

In the period succeeding the 1980 military coup, Turkey re-established its parliamentary multi-party democracy under the centre-right Motherland Party (ANAP) and its leader Turgut Özal (Turkey's prime minister from 1983 to 1989 and president from 1989 to 1993). Neoliberal reforms undertaken by Özal presented a clear break from the ISI policies of the previous decades.[60] The restoration of democracy and economic liberalisation brought about a more flexible policy towards Turkish diaspora organisations. Several diaspora leaders noted that Özal was the first state official to recognise Turkish immigrant organisations' lobbying potential.[61] However, as a French bureaucrat from the Ministry of the Interior emphasised, his agenda was mainly economic.[62] In 1984, the *Diyanet* founded the Presidency of External Affairs in Ankara and the first overseas *Diyanet* branch (the DİTİB), in Germany. Together with the Turkish Councillorship for Religious Services and the Religious Services Attachés, the DİTİBs continue to actively monitor Turkish citizens in Europe.[63]

In 1985, new legislation (Law No. 3201) allowed Turkish citizens abroad to benefit from retirement at home through pensions accumulated overseas. The threat of waning ties between Turkey and its overseas population, strict citizenship policies in some countries and the assimilation of Turks in Europe became another source of worry for Turkish officials. In 1986, the Ministry of Foreign Affairs, in cooperation with the Ministry of Culture, took initiatives to promote Turkish culture, language and art abroad through its Turkish Cultural Centres.[64] Turkey also introduced expatriate voting in 1987 through an amendment (Law No. 3377) to the 1961 Law on Elections and Electoral Registers (Law No. 298). Overseas Turks living abroad for more than six months were now allowed to vote in general elections and referenda, using polling stations set up at Turkey's external borders[65] (although take-up was limited due to technical and administrative challenges).[66]

In 1995, the Citizenship Law was amended to create the Pink Card programme. Holders of a Pink Card – replaced by a Blue Card in 2009 – who renounced Turkish citizenship to take the citizenship of their country of settlement became eligible for all Turkish citizenship rights except for voting and running for seats in local and national elections. These rights included: residence, acquisition of property, eligibility for inheritance and employment.[67] This was a strategic move to retain ties with the Turkish diaspora and utilise their economic and political potential.[68] In 1995, Turkish policymakers revised the Turkish Party Law to allow political parties to establish party branches abroad. The effects of this reform were mostly symbolic as no political party opened an overseas office until the 2000s.[69] That said, Turkish and Kurdish diaspora organisations did provide informal support to Turkish political parties from the 1970s (until the establishment of party missions abroad).[70]

Yet the Turkish government's relations with 'undesired' diaspora groups, such as Kurds and Alevis, remained turbulent in this decade: the conflict between Turkey and the PKK deepened, the 1993 Sivas arson attack and the 1995 Gazi neighbourhood shootings in Istanbul resulted in the death of many Alevi individuals,[71] and Turkish intelligence captured Abdullah Öcalan in Kenya in 1999.[72] In 1997, too, *Millî Görüş* supporters sought refuge in Europe once Erbakan's Welfare Party (RP) was shut down by the military.[73]

In terms of the institutionalisation of policies, a handful of Turkish parliamentarians set up special commissions and published reports on the conditions of Turkish citizens abroad, and some ministries even opened sub-units to assist immigrants.[74] The fight against discrimination, xenophobia and the education of Turkish children in Europe became more serious concerns for Turkish bureaucrats.[75] In 1998, the Advisory Board for Turkish Citizens Living Abroad and the High Committee for Turkish Citizens Living Abroad were established by the Prime Ministry to facilitate dialogue between Ankara and Turks living abroad, to tackle legal problems encountered by overseas Turks and to aid their integration.[76] However, these attempts did not prove effective: they were typically put forward as ephemeral proposals by individual politicians and lacked clear-set strategies. Most excluded conservative immigrants in the process.[77] The consular services, likewise, fell short in reaching out to the Turkish community abroad. Their top-down attitude, cumbersome and costly services and inability to contest the rise of racist attacks targeting Turks in Europe alienated the diaspora.[78]

During Turkey's EU harmonisation process in the mid-1990s, and particularly after its recognition as a candidate for full EU membership at the 1999 Helsinki Summit, official documents began to cite members of the Turkish diaspora as 'Euro-Turks' (*Avrupa Türkleri*), and their economic and political lobbying potential as 'goodwill ambassadors' was emphasised by Turkish parliamentarians.[79] However, as expressed by a *Millî Görüş* representative in Germany in 2000, Turkey's efforts were unsuccessful at that time:

[Ankara wants us to be] like the Armenians in the United States, but Turkey is very poor at this. They say, 'go, settle and ... lobby for us' ... But ... you have to take care of your people if you want their support and Turkey never did. People here were faced with a lot of ... state discrimination ... Even here when they go to the [Turkish] consular departments ... And this creates an atmosphere where Turkey cannot say: 'So I did this for you and now you do something for me'.[80]

Turkey's post-2003 diaspora engagement policies

From Euro-Turks to brothers and sisters: The evolution of Turkey's new diaspora framework

Since 2003, Turkey has embarked on a new diaspora engagement strategy based on a nuanced understanding of, and increasing rapprochement with, the diaspora. This scheme has built on previous Turkish governments' outreach endeavours yet moved beyond them, too. A significant change is how the state approaches emigrant Turks rhetorically. Since 2003, Turkey has deliberately reframed the position of Turkish citizens abroad in its state discourse and called for a change in the definition of the diaspora. Contemporary parliamentary proceedings now explicitly use the term 'diaspora' to refer to the émigré population alongside 'citizens living abroad' (*yurtdışı vatandaşlar*) as 'the state began to stress the continuation of the citizenship status of emigrants despite their permanency as residents or even citizens of another country'.[81] The messages conveyed during rallies organised by Turkish officials in Europe reflect this. These mass gatherings extol overseas nationals as 'equal citizens' and representatives of Turkey in Europe. As explored in Chapters 3 and 4, they also praise their lobbying power overseas.

Turkey's current diaspora policy is driven mainly by political ambitions as remittances no longer contribute to Turkey's economic development. While remittances made up 4 per cent of Turkey's GDP in 1974, this figure had dropped to 1.6 per cent by 1993. In 2003, remittances as a share of the Turkish economy declined further to 0.2 per cent. As Figure 2.1 shows, presently they make up only 0.1 per cent.

Forging a formal diaspora engagement policy from 2003 onwards coincided with the configuration of a new political elite that splintered from the reformist wing of the *Millî Görüş*. In the 2002 parliamentarian elections, the AKP won nearly 35 per cent of the total vote and became the first party in eleven years to win an outright parliamentary majority.[82] During the first two terms of his reign (2002–07 and 2007–11), the party's leader, Erdoğan, promoted a new party identity premised on democratic, liberal and pluralistic values, and an open-market economy. An official from the YTB argued that

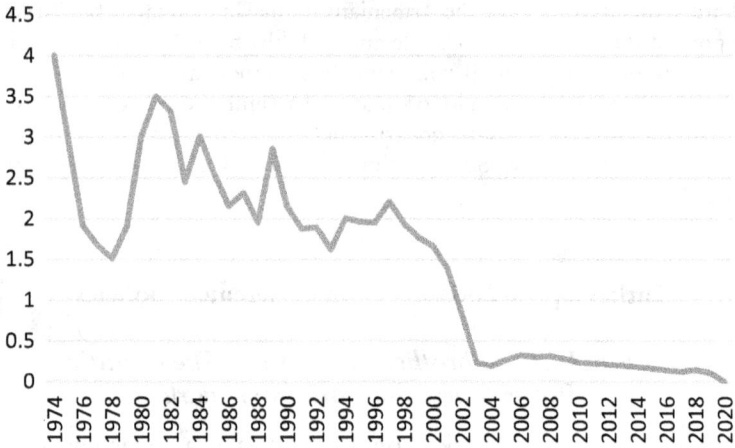

Figure 2.1 Personal remittances received, 1974–2019 (percentage of Turkey's GDP)

Source: World Bank: https://data.worldbank.org/indicator/BX.TRF.PWKR.DT.GD. ZS?locations=TR.

the development of a proactive diaspora agenda is closely linked to 'the AKP government's strong political will' and 'Turkey's growing economic and political power and visibility in the region'.[83] An AKP deputy agreed that Turkey's diaspora policy began to consolidate at a time when Turkey gained political and economic confidence and stability.[84]

While in recent years Turkey's economic growth has slowed down, with rising unemployment rates, dependence on foreign capital and external debt,[85] the Turkish economy thrived in the earlier years of the AKP rule. With an average annual growth rate of 7.5 per cent, it became one of the fastest-growing economies in the world.[86] A strict World Bank and International Monetary Fund (IMF) privatisation and recovery programme – initiated by the preceding, short-lived (1999–2002) coalition government of the left-wing Democratic Left Party (DSP), the centre-right ANAP and the ultra-nationalist Nationalist Movement Party (MHP) in the aftermath of the 2001 financial crisis – enabled the AKP to lower the country's inflation, attract unprecedented foreign direct investment and increase exports and imports.[87] Turkey's GDP per capita income rose from $2,800 in 2001 to $10,000 by 2011, and the unemployment rate, inflation rate and budget deficit had all reached record lows by 2012.[88] As the Turkish economy improved, the AKP government began to form stronger relations with emigrants from Turkey.

In addition to serving as a promoter of economic liberalisation and an expansion-oriented development model, the AKP's commitment in its first term to bringing the country closer to the EU led the government to pass an array of constitutional and judicial reforms.[89] The party's inclusion of cultural pluralism into the state discourse in its second term[90] had one of the most salient impacts on Turkey's diaspora agenda. The Alevi Opening (*Alevi Açılımı*) and the Kurdish Opening (*Kürt Açılımı*) were the first comprehensive official initiatives aimed at responding to Alevis' and Kurds' identity-based demands, which sent a positive message to Alevi and Kurdish diaspora groups in Europe. The Alevi Opening paved the way for the election of Alevi-origin MPs to the TBMM, increased broadcasting of Alevi-focused programming on the TRT, fast-breaking dinners (*iftar*) organised during the Alevi holy month of Muharram and seven official workshops that sought to create a bridge between the Turkish state and Alevi leaders.[91] The AKP also entered peace talks with the PKK and announced the Kurdish Opening, which pledged to launch a new state-owned television channel that would broadcast in Kurdish, disarm the PKK and grant amnesty to its militants, restore the original Kurdish names of certain cities in south eastern Turkey, offer elective Kurdish courses at public schools and amend the constitution in order to redefine the meaning of Turkish citizenship.[92] However, as will be demonstrated in Chapter 5, these initiatives failed through Turkey's economic and democratic backsliding from 2011 onwards.

Another significant domestic change that transformed state–diaspora relations was the shifting of emphasis from secularism in the Kemalist conception of nationhood to a Sunni-Islamic narrative and the introduction of a new foreign policy agenda inspired by neo-Ottomanism.[93] Ahmet Davutoğlu, the Minister of Foreign Affairs between 2009–14 and the architect of this understanding, posited that Turkey is not a 'regional' or 'peripheral' power that merely follows the order of superpower allies, but a 'central superpower' with multiple regional identities.[94] This neo-Ottoman ideal was conspicuous in a 2011 speech Erdoğan gave, which depicted the electoral triumph of the AKP as an accomplishment for all Muslims around the world.[95] The AKP elite's conception of a new Turkey based on the Ottoman imperial dream of becoming 'bigger' and 'better'[96] has required reinforcing ties with Turks abroad as well as with kin and related communities.

Transnationally, through their move from temporary to permanent settlement, Euro-Turks have become more active in their host countries' economic and political life, particularly since the 1990s. Permanent settlement has affected emigrants from Turkey in various ways. Turkish businesses in Europe have thrived over the last two decades and enhanced bilateral economic relations between Turkey and Europe:[97] it is estimated that 200,000 Turkish entrepreneurs in Europe will have provided jobs for more than 1 million people by 2023.[98] In addition, Euro-Turks' educational attainment has improved over the last two decades.[99]

The Turkish diaspora has also attained a stronger political position in Europe through increased naturalisation rates. Today almost half of the people of Turkish-origin living in Europe have citizenship of their country of settlement.[100] Of the 4.6 million holders of Turkish citizenship recorded by Turkish consular services in Europe, 461,407 became citizens of their host countries between 2005 and 2014.[101] In 2016 alone, 32,800 Turks in Europe became citizens of an EU country (half were granted German citizenship; the second biggest group were granted French citizenship), making the community the largest group to acquire EU citizenship after Moroccans, Albanians, Indians and Pakistanis.[102]

In Germany, as will be explained in Chapter 4, a change in citizenship law in 2000 doubled the number of ethnic Turks with the right to vote, increasing their importance as a voter bloc.[103] Today 1.6 million Turks hold German nationality and half a million have dual Turkish–German citizenship.[104] A recent report by the German Statistics Institute noted that among all immigrant groups, Turks have become German citizens in the greatest numbers.[105] German Turks have also become important players in both local and national politics: since 1994, many of them have been elected to the Bundestag, the German Federal Parliament. While some of these politicians, such as Green Party deputy Cem Özdemir, have openly criticised AKP policies, the overall growing political role that Turkey-originated expatriates play in European politics has encouraged the Turkish state to harness them as a political asset. In Germany, as of 2021, there are three Turkey-originated members of the European Parliament, sixteen members of the Bundestag, forty-eight members of state parliaments and 423 members of municipality councils.[106] Since the 2000s, an increasing number of French Turks have also begun to play an increased role in local and national politics across the political spectrum. While there are no Turkish-origin parliamentarians in France, 200 French Turks have been elected to provincial councils, sixteen of them serving as deputy mayor and 184 as council members.[107] France grants dual citizenship to Turks; approximately 360,000 Turks are French citizens.[108]

Turks in Europe have even formed their own political parties. These include the Alliance for Innovation and Justice Party (BIG), a local party established by German Turks in Cologne in 2010, and the Equality and Justice Party (PEJ), the first political party established by French Turks in 2015. Other newly formed pro-Turkish political parties in Europe include the DENK, which secured three parliamentary seats in the Netherlands in 2017; the Alliance of German Democrats (ADD) and the Alternative for Migrants (AfM), established by German Turks in 2016 and 2019 respectively; and the New Movement for the Future Party (NBZ), formed in Austria in 2016.[109]

Bureaucrats from the Turkish Consulate in Paris[110] and the YTB[111] reported that Ankara now views Euro-Turks as both a socio-economic *and* political power in Europe. Euro-Turks' voting potential in Turkish elections is another reason why Turkey has shown a considerable interest in its diaspora in recent years. For example, Germany has become the fourth largest constituency after Istanbul, Ankara and Izmir: 1.5 million German Turks are eligible to cast their ballot in Turkish elections.[112] In France, 326,375 Turks can vote in homeland elections.[113]

Internationally, Turkey's growing visibility in the global arena has brought about a new Turkish diaspora policy, according to Turkish officials.[114] Although Turkey had applied for EU membership in 1987, Turkey–EU relations remained sluggish due to Turkey's economic and political weakness until the late 1990s, when the EU began to serve as a key external actor fomenting political change in Turkey.[115] Once Turkey was officially recognised as a candidate for full membership to the EU in 1999, Ankara enjoyed a more balanced set of conditions and incentives.[116] Following the beginning of full accession negotiations at the 2005 Luxembourg Summit, Turkey's negotiation position vis-à-vis the EU grew progressively stronger.[117]

The 2007–08 global economic recession and the 2009 Eurozone crisis further altered Turkey's perceptions of its power in relation to the EU. While Europe was coping with financial stress, Turkey paid off its remaining debt to the IMF and witnessed a dramatic increase in foreign investment.[118] Amid spiralling economic turmoil, Turkish officials began to depict Europe as a conflict-ridden region with stagnant economies and Turkey as a powerful country.[119] The words of a Turkish bureaucrat mirror this perception change: 'In the past, Turkish officials' meetings with European bureaucrats would start by responding to criticisms directed at Turkey. Today, *we* raise questions and *we* criticise the EU.'[120] In a similar vein, at a 2014 diaspora rally in Germany, President Erdoğan warned that 'For decades, our [Turkish] identity, values, and beliefs have been insulted … Today's Turkey is different.'[121]

As diplomats from the Turkish Embassy in Paris emphasised, the outbreak of the European refugee crisis and the 2016 EU–Turkey refugee deal amplified Turkey's leverage vis-à-vis the EU. According to the deal, Turkey would limit the influx of irregular migrants crossing into the EU from Turkey.[122] In return, the EU vowed to resettle, on a 1:1 basis, Syrians residing in Turkey who had qualified for asylum in the EU. The EU would also provide visa liberalisation and €6 billion to Turkey.[123] Turkey has become the country hosting the largest refugee population in the world,[124] and while the deal is still in place, Turkey has repeatedly threatened to terminate it on the basis that the EU seems reluctant to grant visa freedom to Turks.[125]

Another watershed that has brought Turkish expatriates closer to their homeland is the rise of Islamophobia in Europe, particularly after 9/11. The political environment and debates in European host countries have changed immensely and negatively for Turkish expatriates since the early 2000s, as evidenced by the popularity of far-right and anti-immigrant parties.[126] Growing hostility against Muslims has driven Turkey to reach out to the now vulnerable Turkish community in Europe. An official from the Turkish Consulate in Berlin explained that, as Islamophobic acts targeting Turks in Germany had become more widespread and severe since the 2000s, Ankara had to be more zealous in the diasporic space.[127] On the basis of these developments, the YTB announced that 'in the 2000s, new needs have emerged ... Our diaspora in Europe face educational and employment hardships, institutionalised racism, discrimination, Islamophobia and citizenship rights issues.'[128] Bureaucrats from the Turkish Embassy in Paris[129] and the YTB[130] also confirmed that Turkey's urge to protect its citizens abroad from the perils of rising Islamophobia and far-right parties is natural and should be praised rather than criticised.

The institutionalisation of Turkey's diaspora policies

AKP officials have significantly expanded the organisational capacity, quality and budget of the existing diaspora institutions and created new ones, too. For example, in 2002 Turkey had 163 diplomatic missions and by 2018 that number had increased to 239 (ninety-two based in Europe), making Turkey the fifth largest diplomatic network in the world.[131]

Since the AKP's rise to power, Turkey has diversified its consular services as well. Of particular note here is the issuing of two directives (No. 3846 and No. 3847) in 2003 by the then Minister of Foreign Affairs, Abdullah Gül, to Turkish embassies and consulates in Europe. These directives mandated Turkish diplomats to establish closer relations with formerly stigmatised Islamic organisations, such as the *Millî Görüş* and the Gülen Movement.[132] As an official from the Turkish Consulate in Berlin explained, in the past, bureaucrats from the Ministry of Foreign Affairs had been reluctant to form close relations with conservative immigrant organisations. However, 'this negative stance has finally disappeared and the gap between the state and the public has diminished'.[133] Another diplomat confirmed that Turkish officials' relations with Turkish expatriates have changed tremendously since 2002: 'When I first assumed this position, I requested that my personnel treat Turkish citizens better ... A "good governance" revolution has begun in Turkey.'[134]

As will be discussed in subsequent chapters, the effects of the AKP on the formerly liminal *Millî Görüş* and the Gülen Movement were visible from the early days of the AKP's rise to power.[135] The AKP formed a particularly a special relationship with the Gülen Movement, which provided a strong economic, political and media boost to the AKP and in return acquired key positions within the state bureaucracy, the judiciary, the police and the military. This partnership enjoyed its golden days during the second term of the AKP, started to deteriorate in 2010 and officially collapsed when the AKP accused Gülenists of plotting the 2016 coup attempt.[136]

The *Diyanet* has also undergone major changes since 2002. Its branches abroad, the DİTİBs, have ceased to serve as the tool of the secular state and evolved into a promoter of AKP ideology abroad.[137] As a *Diyanet* official noted, since the 2000s there has been a process of rapprochement between the Turkish government and conservative organisations in Europe, as evidenced by the *Diyanet*'s willingness to send imams to them.[138] In addition to providing religious services to emigrants from Turkey, *Diyanet* personnel abroad are now responsible for shaping European attitudes about Turks and for promoting Turkey's accession to the EU.[139]

Another striking change is the amplification of the *Diyanet*'s budget.[140] In 2002, it constituted 0.6 per cent of Turkey's overall government spending and rose to 1.1 per cent in 2018.[141] In 2020, the *Diyanet*'s total budget stood at 10.5 billion Turkish lira ($1.7 billion) and was larger than eight core ministries in Turkey, including the Ministry of Foreign Affairs, the Ministry of the Interior, the Ministry of Finance and the Ministry of Culture and Tourism. By 2022, its budget is expected to rise to 13 billion Turkish lira ($2.1 billion).[142]

The number of short- and long-term religious personnel assigned to Europe has also increased considerably since 2002. After an initial decade of rapid growth (from twenty in 1980 to 797 in 1990), the number of personnel sent by the *Diyanet* increased more slowly during the 1990s (from approximately 900 in 1990 to 1,100 in 2000).[143] It accelerated again between 2002 and 2015, when their number nearly doubled, from approximately 1,100 to 1,900.[144] Today there are 2,000 *Diyanet* personnel in over 100 countries, with the majority of them working in Europe.[145]

Turkey's post-2000 diaspora engagement policy is also administered by new diaspora institutions. Tied to the Ministry of Culture and Tourism, the YTB's 305 employees provide assistance to the following groups: overseas Turkish citizens; kin and related communities in the Balkans, Caucasus and Central Asia; and international students in Turkey.[146] In addition to its diaspora, Turkey has actively sought to use its kin and related communities to advance Turkish foreign policy interests.[147] Since its establishment, the YTB has worked closely with other government agencies, including the Ministry of Foreign Affairs, the Ministry of Labour and Social Security, the Ministry for EU Affairs and the Turkish Cooperation and Coordination Agency (TİKA).[148]

A commission established by the TBMM in 2003 paved the way for the creation of the YTB. After visiting Turkish communities in Europe to address their problems in various areas, the commission published a report highlighting overseas Turks' permanent status abroad.[149] It recommended that Turkey should tap into diaspora Turks' growing socio-economic and political power in Europe and that Turks abroad should acquire the citizenship of their countries and become more active in Europe's political life. The report also decreed that Turkey's diaspora policy should be guided by a holistic, long-term and multilateral strategy. Consequently, in 2012, the YTB set up the Turks Abroad Advisory Board with seventy representatives from different countries.[150]

In addition to working towards capacity development of diaspora youth and strengthening their ties to Turkey through scholarship programmes, homeland tours, internship opportunities and diaspora youth academies,[151] the YTB also focuses on the empowerment of Turkish diaspora organisations. For example, the Diaspora Organisations Summit, held in Ankara in June 2012, attracted 500 members of the Turkish diaspora from seventeen countries. These participants had been recommended by Turkish embassies and consulates, the UID and the DİTİB. The two-day summit declared that Turks abroad should form a strong diaspora and act as 'Turkey's ambassadors'.[152] According to YTB officials, the institution's main objectives were to work with Turkish citizens abroad to help them overcome their problems; to assist their integration into European societies by strengthening their social status; to preserve the native language, culture and identity of Turkish citizens living abroad; and to remind them of their social and cultural ties to the homeland.[153]

The YTB has provided generous financial assistance to like-minded Turkish organisations operating abroad. Between 2011 and 2020, it provided $17 million to support over 1,000 civil society projects in seventy countries.[154] Between August and October 2017, YTB officials visited 589 civil society organisations and met with 2,320 civil society representatives in countries with sizeable Turkish populations.[155] In 2019, they held thirty-six empowerment meetings with leaders of Turkish civil society organisations in thirty-two different cities abroad.[156] Financial assistance has increased as the institution has stabilised over time.[157] Funding has been provided to organisations in a variety of areas, including anti-discrimination, active citizenship and equal participation, justice, bilingual education, academic and professional development, family and the preservation of native culture.[158] However, as will be explored in the following three chapters, the YTB's support has mainly targeted conservative-nationalist and Sunni Islamic organisations and has excluded diaspora groups viewed as dissident, terrorist or marauders (*çapulcu*).

With the outbreak of the COVID-19 pandemic in 2020, Turkey introduced new programmes and services to cater to the needs of the Turkish diaspora. These include the creation of hotlines for emergency situations, the deepening of communication between the YTB and Turkish immigrant organisations, regular COVID-19 updates from Turkish consulates, the improvement of social media channels, the digitalisation of the diaspora engagement tools and the establishment of new funding and donation programmes.[159] One such programme, the Diaspora COVID-19 Programme for Support and Cooperation, has assisted seventy projects and 200,000 people through collaboration between the YTB and Turkish diaspora organisations.[160]

The promotion of Turkish identity, culture, history and language is another key objective of Turkey's new diaspora framework. The YEE was inaugurated in May 2007 (Law No. 5653) with this purpose in mind. Today it operates as the cultural pillar of Turkey's diaspora engagement policy and coordinates cultural and public relations activities previously performed by the Ministry of Foreign Affairs and the Ministry of Culture and Tourism.[161] According to Ahmet Davutoğlu, foreign policy is not carried out solely via traditional diplomacy but also via cultural, economic and commercial diaspora networks.[162] The YEE seeks 'to enhance Turkey's recognition, credibility and prestige in the international arena' and 'to increase the number of people who forge bonds with, and are friendly to, Turkey all around the world'.[163] Over time, the institution has inaugurated fifty-eight Turkish Cultural Centres in forty-eight countries, many in Europe.[164] The YEE's director pointed out that:

> The Institute, carrying out operations as Turkey's face in 'cultural diplomacy' (*kültürel diplomasi*) will open 100 Cultural Centres by 2023, which marks the 100th foundation anniversary of the Turkish Republic. Our goal is to further promote Turkey around the world with [the] right sources, Turkish instruction, and culture-arts activities, and to contribute to the world's cultural heritage with events based on intercultural interaction.[165]

Since 2011, the institution has administered the Turkology Project, which teaches Turkish culture and language at 101 universities in fifty countries.[166] In addition, it organises summer schools and a Cultural Diplomacy Academy that provides a twelve-week training programme for scholars, university students, young professionals, journalists and civil society workers.[167] My interviews also revealed that the YEE provides financial assistance to Turkish immigrant organisations for projects on the advancement of Turkish language and culture. YEE bureaucrats believe that there is a heightened demand for Turkish language and culture due to Turkey's rise as an economic and political power[168] and its intellectual opening to the world.[169]

Turkish officials concluded that the YEE seeks to strengthen Turkey's linkage to its ancestral lands and perpetuate the neo-Ottoman 'common history and heritage' rhetoric[170] and that the Cultural Centres are the most important instrument for the promotion of Turkish culture and interests during Turkey's EU-accession process.[171]

The İB is another new diaspora institution. Founded in July 2018 (Law No. 30488), it works towards improving Turkey's global image by 'empowering the Turkey brand' and by 'enhancing the power of representation at individual and corporate level, which will provide a momentum for "New Turkey"'.[172] Turkish officials stated that together with the other diaspora institutions, the İB's main task is to corroborate Turkey's image as a powerful country and to refresh ties with the diaspora.[173]

The İB's first director, İbrahim Kalın, linked the establishment of the institution to Turkey's rise as a 'soft power'. According to Kalın, since the early 2000s Turkey's increasing international legitimacy and economic development qualify it as a soft power in international politics and this creates opportunities for new spheres of influence of which the Turkish diaspora constitutes an important tool. In his view, Turkish citizens no longer see themselves as 'a small footnote in the Euro-centric historical narrative' and they desire to see Turkey as a dynamic actor creating its own history.[174]

To improve, coordinate and administer Turkish civil society organisations' lobbying activities in Europe, the AKP also established the UID. An UID official echoed the statements of other diaspora organisations, arguing that the institution's establishment reflects Turkey's rise in the global arena. He listed the UID's main objective as to contribute to Euro-Turks' deeper political integration into European societies through their increased participation in local, national and European elections, to promote dual citizenship rights for Turks, to lobby for Turkey's EU membership and to fight Islamophobia.[175] The UID defines the Turkish diaspora as a community that resides outside Turkey's borders, is organised, lacks full belonging to its host country, has a vision centred around Turkey's past and future and retains emotional, financial and political ties to Turkey. UID officials expect the Turkish diaspora not only to support Turkey's EU bid and to engage in lobbying activities, but to act in unison (*yeknesaklık*).[176]

The UID has thirty-six offices across Europe, with fourteen located in Germany.[177] While each branch abides by local legislation, they are steered by the UID's headquarters in Cologne. These offices organise diaspora rallies prior to Turkish elections and referenda, and demonstrations on issues of importance to the Turkish government. They also periodically host AKP officials, as well as affiliated experts and academics, and gather information about Gülen supporters in Europe.[178] The UID's former chairperson,

Süleyman Çelik, argued that the institution 'has no "organic" ties to the AKP, but merely maintains good relations to government circles and thus fulfils an important function'.[179] A bureaucrat from the French Ministry of the Interior suggested that, as the 'long arm of the AKP in Europe', the UID is also active at the supranational level as it lobbies the European Commission.[180]

The TMV was established in June 2016 (Law No. 6721), shortly after the aborted coup. Together with the Ministry of Education, the TMV is the sole legal entity to provide educational services outside Turkey's borders.[181] The TMV's president, Professor Birol Akgün, explained that the institution strives to represent Turkey's values and invigorates its presence in the world: 'Turkey is now an emerging actor and a rising star in the international arena. It cannot only rely on improving its economic relations with other countries; people-to-people relations are as important as intergovernmental relations to render the interactions between the countries sustainable. Education is an important component of this integration process.'[182] Yet Akgün acknowledged that the institution simultaneously seeks to eliminate terrorist threats by taking over the Gülen-linked schools and educational centres abroad: the TMV has assumed administration of nearly 200 schools in seventeen countries linked to Gülenists and 'opened 71 new schools … to provide alternative schools in [strategic] priority areas and satisfy the education need of the Turkish diaspora'.[183] Today the institution provides education to around 30,000 students in 270 schools across thirty-five countries.[184]

Even though Turkey's new diaspora agenda is mainly political, the AKP also seeks to maximise Turkey's economic capacity in Europe through Turkish-origin business people. To this end, the World Turkish Business Council was founded in 2007 under the auspices of the Foreign Economic Relations Board (DEİK). Calling its activities an example of 'commercial diplomacy' (*ticari diplomasi*), the DEİK brings together overseas Turkish business associations to 'awaken and enhance their lobbying activities' and 'to establish a stronger image for Turkey in the world'.[185] The institution also seeks to curb the influence of the Armenian diaspora.[186] DEİK chairperson, Rifat Hisarcıklıoğlu, explained:

> We want to be one of the most active and powerful diasporas in the world. In the past, the words 'lobbying' and 'diaspora' had a negative connotation for us. We no longer need to fear. We have the necessary experience, knowledge, energy and motivation to succeed … Perhaps we have reached out to our diaspora much later than other countries. However, we have a very strong human potential abroad … Sharing the motto 'Global Power Turkey', our entrepreneurs and businesspeople finally came together … As citizens of a country which no longer is a regional but a global power, we must work together.[187]

New political and socio-economic concessions for diaspora Turks

Since 2003, Turkey has introduced significant political and socio-economic rights for Turkey's diasporas. For the first time in 2012, Law No. 5749 granted Turkish citizens abroad the right to cast their votes by regular ballot at polling booths in their countries of residence. However, due to legal and procedural complications, it was not until the August 2014 Turkish presidential elections that overseas voters over the age of eighteen who were registered on the electoral roll could vote on the soil of their host countries.[188] Initially, overseas Turkish citizens' turnout rate in the 2014 presidential elections was very low. This outcome was caused by serious logistical problems: ballot boxes were placed only in big cities, mail ballots were not accepted and voting procedures were poorly explained. With the June 2015 parliamentary elections, members of the diaspora gained the opportunity to cast their votes at more polling stations over an extended period. These elections also introduced two major changes: immigrant-origin citizens were included in Turkish political parties' election platforms for the first time and diaspora candidates were placed in electable positions on party lists, ensuring they had a real prospect of being elected as deputies in the TBMM.[189] The June parliamentary elections were repeated in November 2015 because the four parties in Parliament failed to secure a parliamentary vote of confidence. In the November 2015 elections, the 2017 constitutional referendum – which equipped Erdoğan with unparalleled power as the country transitioned from a parliamentary into a presidential system – and the 2018 elections, the overseas-voter turnout increased further (see Table 2.1).

Table 2.1 Expatriate turnout in Turkish elections and referenda

Election	Total number of registered voters	Total number of cast votes	Voter turnout (percentage)
2014 presidential	2,798,726	530,116	18.9
2015 parliamentary (June)	2,899,072	1,056,078	36.4
2015 parliamentary (November)	2,899,069	1,298,325	44.7
2017 referendum	2,972,676	1,424,279	47.9
2018 parliamentary and presidential	3,047,323	1,525,279	50

Sources: Turkish Supreme Electoral Council, *Sabah* and *Habertürk* election archives: www.ysk.gov.tr/tr/secim-arsivi/2612, www.sabah.com.tr/secim-sonuclari, https://www.haberturk.com/secim.

In the above-mentioned elections and referendum, the AKP became the most popular party among diaspora voters and received a higher percentage of votes overseas than at home. The other prominent parties that attracted a significant vote share from expatriates in these elections were the CHP (the main opposition party), the HDP and the MHP. In the 2014 presidential elections, AKP leader Erdoğan defeated the joint MHP–CHP candidate, Ekmeleddin İhsanoğlu, as well as the HDP's candidate, Selahattin Demirtaş, receiving 62.5 per cent of the total diaspora votes. From 2015 onwards, the AKP and the MHP have been political allies. In the 2017 constitutional referendum, 59.1 per cent of overseas voters supported the AKP government's proposal to replace the existing parliamentary system with a presidential system. In the 2018 presidential elections, Erdoğan once again secured victory against his opponents by garnering 59.4 per cent of the external votes (see Table 2.2).

In addition to political concessions, Turkey has granted socio-economic rights to its expatriates. Some European countries, including Germany, Austria and Denmark, require foreigners to renounce their original nationalities if they wish to gain citizenship. This policy used to create legal problems for Euro-Turks upon their return to Turkey. In order to remedy this situation and legalise their status, Turkey introduced the Blue Card programme in 2009, which grants expatriates who abandoned their Turkish nationality to obtain the citizenship of their country of residence the right to

Table 2.2 Expatriate voting behaviour in Turkish elections and referenda (percentage of votes cast)

Election	AKP	CHP	MHP	HDP
2014 presidential	62.5 (Erdoğan)	29.1 (İhsanoğlu, joint candidate)		8.3 (Demirtaş)
2015 parliamentary (June)	49.9	17.2	9.2	20.2
2015 parliamentary (November)	56.2	16.4	7.1	18.2
2017 constitutional referendum	59 (voted yes to AKP proposal)	-	-	-
2018 parliamentary	51	17.6	7.9	17.3
2018 presidential	59.3 (Erdoğan)	25.7 (İnce)	-	11 (Demirtaş)

Sources: Turkish Supreme Electoral Council, *Sabah* and *Habertürk* election archives (presidential candidate in parenthesis): www.ysk.gov.tr/tr/secim-arsivi/2612, www.sabah.com.tr/secim-sonuclari, www.haberturk.com/secim.

Table 2.3 The evolution of Turkey's state–diaspora relations

Time period	Main policy motive	Discourse towards Turkey's diasporas	Concessions granted to Turkey's diasporas
1960s–1970s	Economic Religious and cultural	Negative: 'remittance machines', 'workers abroad'	Facilitation of remittance inflows Tax, job and investment benefits upon return to Turkey Health and social security assistance Transfer of religious personnel and Turkish language teachers to Europe Radio and television broadcasting in Europe
1980s–1990s	Economic Religious and cultural Political	Negative/neutral: 'expatriates', 'overseas Turks', 'Euro-Turks' Selective: 'traitors'	Facilitation of remittance inflows Transfer of religious personnel and Turkish language teachers to Europe Creation of Turkish Cultural Centres Dual citizenship Military service and retirement benefits Pink Card Establishment of party branches abroad
2000–21	Political	Positive: 'diasporas', 'equal citizens', 'ambassadors of Turkey' Selective: 'terrorists', 'marauders'	New diaspora institutions Diaspora youth empowerment Civil society empowerment External voting Blue Card Welfare and tax benefits Discounted military service E-government COVID-19-related funding schemes

possess land, live, work and inherit in Turkey. As stated previously, the Blue Card replaced the Pink Card and provides a more comprehensive and systematic framework.[190] An official from the Ministry of Labour and Social Security explained that the AKP passed another law (No. 3201), in 2008, to entitle overseas citizens who have renounced their citizenship to receive invalidity, old-age and survivor's pensions.[191]

Additionally, the AKP has facilitated the émigré community's mobility by reducing passport fees and extending the registration period for foreign-registered cars and mobile phones owned by overseas Turks and their descendants. The establishment of an online portal and e-consulate system in 2009 for Turks abroad has ensured the rapid and efficient processing of visa applications, birth and ID registrations, passport renewals and extensions.[192] In 2012, the TBMM introduced new amnesty legislation, offering tax incentives for inward remittances.[193] Moreover, in 2016, the AKP ratified a law to allow Turkish citizens living abroad for more than three years to pay only €1,000 (as opposed to €6,000) to become exempt from mandatory military service. Citizens, however, need to be at least thirty-eight years old to benefit from the exemption.[194] Table 2.3 charts the transformation of Turkey's state–diaspora relations from the 1960s onwards.

Conclusion

Over the last two decades, Turkey has woven a new diaspora engagement strategy based on a more positive narrative towards Turkish citizens abroad, the establishment of new diaspora institutions and a series of political and socio-economic privileges extended to the diaspora. Until the 2000s the Turkish state's diaspora policies were driven mainly by economic incentives, but its current agenda is shaped by political goals. Turkish officials have strived to improve the Turkish diaspora's quality of life and change the negative image of Turks and Turkey abroad. Diaspora outreach policies have sought to consolidate the political power of the AKP and extend the state's legitimacy beyond its borders.

This chapter has shown that Turkey's diaspora policies are a result of an amalgamation of domestic, transnational and international factors. Domestically, the AKP's rise to power in 2002 resulted in drastic economic and political reforms, and the promotion of a new identity based on neo-Ottomanism and Sunni-Muslim nationalism, which have transformed Turkey's state–diaspora relations. Significant developments such as the 2016 aborted coup also played a role. Transnationally, Turkish expatriates' growing socio-economic and political clout in their host countries has prompted

Turkey to reconsider the efficacy of its diaspora as a source of influence abroad as well as a noteworthy electorate in national elections. Various international developments have also shaped Turkey's new diaspora agenda, including Turkey's heightened bargaining power vis-à-vis the EU since the early 2000s, particularly after the 1999 Helsinki Summit and the European refugee crisis, and the rise of Islamophobia in the post-9/11 era. The chapter has shown that domestic factors have played the most significant role in shaping Turkey's diaspora agenda. It has examined the domestic dimension both as an independent factor and also in relation to transnational and international factors. The configuration of a new political elite has changed the ways in which Turkey interacts with its transnational diaspora and perceives its international position vis-à-vis European countries.

Notes

1 Interview, YTB official, Ankara, 25 June 2019.
2 K. Kirişçi, 'Turkey: A transformation from emigration to immigration', *Migration Information Source*, 1 November 2003, www.migrationpolicy.org/article/turkey-transformation-emigration-immigration
3 M. Heper, 'Turkey: Yesterday, today and tomorrow', *Southeast European and Black Sea Studies* 1:3 (2001), 1–19.
4 D. Shankland, *The Alevis in Turkey: The Emergence of a Secular Islamic Tradition* (London: Routledge, 2003).
5 N. Göle, 'The quest for the Islamic self within the context of modernity', in *Rethinking Modernity and National Identity in Turkey*, eds S. Bozdoğan and R. Kasaba (Seattle: University of Washington Press, 1997), pp. 69–81.
6 K. Karpat, *Social Change and Politics in Turkey* (Leiden: Brill, 1973).
7 A. İçduygu and D. Aksel, 'Migration realities and state responses: Rethinking international migration policies in Turkey', in *Social Transformation and Migration*, eds S. Castles, D. Özkul and M. A. Cubas (Basingstoke: Palgrave Macmillan, 2015), pp. 115–31.
8 A. İçduygu, Y. Çolak and N. Soyarık, 'What is the matter with citizenship? A Turkish debate', *Middle Eastern Studies* 35:4 (1999), 187–208.
9 K. Kirişçi, 'Disaggregating Turkish citizenship and immigration practices', *Middle Eastern Studies* 36:3 (2000), 1–22.
10 N. Abadan-Unat, *Bitmeyen Göç*.
11 I. Yücel, 'Turkish experiments in democracy: The Democratic Party and religion in politics through the eyes of French diplomats', *Journal for the Study of Religions and Ideologies* 15:43 (2016), 144–76.
12 'Inonu Named to Form a Turkish Government', *New York Times*, 11 November 1961, www.nytimes.com/1961/11/11/archives/inonu-named-to-form-a-turkish-government.html
13 F. B. Adamson, 'Sending states'.

14 A. İçduygu, 'International migration and human development in Turkey'.

15 S. Sayarı, 'Migration policies of sending countries: Perspectives on the Turkish experience', *Annals of the American Academy of Political and Social Science* 485 (1986), 87–97.

16 B. Baser, 'The Kurdish diaspora in Europe: Identity formation and political activism', *Bogazici University-TUSIAD Research Report DPF 2013-RR01* (2013), https://cadmus.eui.eu/bitstream/handle/1814/28337/Bahar_Baser_RR_ 01_2013.pdf?sequence

17 C. Ünver, 'Changing diaspora politics of Turkey and public diplomacy'.

18 D. Aksel, 'Kins, distant workers, diasporas: Constructing Turkey's transnational members abroad', *Turkish Studies* 15:2 (2014), 195–219.

19 F. B. Adamson, 'Sending states'.

20 H. Kösebalaban, *Turkish Foreign Policy: Islam, Nationalisation and Globalisation* (Basingstoke: Palgrave Macmillan, 2011); E. B. Ekinci, '1971 Military Memorandum: A Political Downturn', *Daily Sabah*, 19 August 2016, www. dailysabah.com/feature/2016/08/19/1971-military-memorandum-a- political-downturn

21 The *Millî Görüş* is a political Islamist ideology founded by Necmettin Erbakan in 1969. It espouses the brotherhood of global Islamic community (*ummah*), the formation of an Islamic government and an anti-Western position in domestic and foreign policy. After the dissolution of the *Millî Görüş*-oriented Islamist parties in the 1970s and 1980s, Erbakan lived in Switzerland before returning to Turkey to establish another Islamic party (the Welfare Party) in 1983.

22 R. Çakır, *Ayet ve Slogan* (Istanbul: Metis, 2001).

23 L. Nell, 'The shadow of homeland politics: Understanding the evolution of the Turkish radical Left in the Netherlands', *Revue Européenne des Migrations Internationales* 24:2 (2008), 121–45.

24 L. Mügge, 'Managing transnationalism: Continuity and change in Turkish state policy', *International Migration* 50:1 (2012), 20–38.

25 K. Burgess, *Courting Migrants*, p. 94.

26 E. Sinclair-Webb, 'Sectarian violence, the Alevi minority and the Left: Kahramanmaraş 1978', in *Turkey's Alevi Enigma: A Comprehensive Overview*, eds P. White and J. Jongerden (Leiden: Brill, 2003), pp. 215–35.

27 The Ministry of Labour and Social Security was merged with the Ministry of Family and Social Policies in 2018 to form the Ministry of Family, Labour and Social Services. In 2021 it was divided into two ministries to form the Ministry of Labour and Social Security and the Ministry of Family and Social Services.

28 A. Akgündüz, *Labour Migration from Turkey to Western Europe, 1960–1974*.

29 K. Burgess, *Courting Migrants*.

30 D. Aksel, 'Kins, distant workers, diasporas'.

31 *Ibid.*

32 L. Mügge, 'Managing transnationalism'.

33 İ. Gözaydın, *Diyanet: Türkiye Cumhuriyeti'nde Dinin Tanzimi* (Istanbul: İletişim, 2009).

34 'Tanıtım', *Diyanet* (16 April 2018), https://disiliskiler.diyanet.gov.tr/sayfa/53/ tanitim

35 Z. Çıtak, 'Between "Turkish Islam" and "French Islam": The role of the Diyanet in the Conseil Français du Culte Musulman', *Journal of Ethnic and Migration Studies* 36:4 (2010), 619–34.

36 D. Aksel, *Home States*.

37 G. Bettin, S. Paçacı Elitok and T. Straubhaar, 'Causes and consequences of the downturn in financial remittances to Turkey: A descriptive approach', in *Turkey, Migration and the EU: Potentials, Challenges and Opportunities*, eds S. Paçacı Elitok and T. Straubhaar (Hamburg: Hamburg University Press, 2012), pp. 133–66.

38 A. İçduygu, 'International migrant remittances in Turkey', European University Institute *CARIM Research Report No. 7* (2016), http://cadmus.eui.eu/bitstream/ handle/1814/11687/CARIM_ASN_2006_07.pdf

39 D. Aksel, *Home States*.

40 M. A. Akıncı, 'Fransa'daki Türk toplumun Türkçe ile ilişkisi', *HAL Archives-Ouvertes* (2018), https://hal.archives-ouvertes.fr/hal-02367261/

41 Z. S. Artan, 'From Village Turks to Euro Turks: The Turkish State's Perceptions of Turkish Migrants in Europe' (MA Thesis, Bosphorus University, 2009).

42 *Ibid.*

43 For the reasons behind the decline of remittances in the post-1998 era, see: G. Bettin, S. Paçacı Elitok and T. Straubhaar, 'Causes and consequences'; A. İçduygu, 'International migration and human development in Turkey'; A. İçduygu, 'International migrant remittances in Turkey'.

44 E. Østergaard-Nielsen, 'Turkey and the "Euro-Turks"', pp. 77–99.

45 E. Østergaard-Nielsen, *Transnational Politics*.

46 O. Tekdemir, *Constituting the Political Economy of the Kurds: Social Embeddedness, Hegemony, and Identity* (London: Routledge, 2021).

47 F. B. Adamson, 'Sending states'.

48 M. Sökefeld, *Struggling for Recognition: The Alevi Movement in Germany and in Transnational Space* (Oxford: Berghahn, 2008).

49 B. Şenay, *Beyond Turkey's Borders: Long-distance Kemalism, State Politics and the Turkish Diaspora* (London: I. B. Tauris, 2013).

50 Even today organisations operating abroad have to inform the Turkish state of their establishment to gain official recognition.

51 A. Yükleyen and G. Yurdakul, 'Islamic activism and immigrant integration: Turkish organisations in Germany', *Immigrants & Minorities* 29:1 (2011), 64–85.

52 L. Mügge, 'Managing transnationalism'.

53 This term has a derogatory undertone, dismissing Turkish immigrants as uneducated, low-skilled people.

54 Z. S. Artan, 'From Village Turks to Euro Turks'.

55 *Ibid.*

56 Z. Kadirbeyoğlu, 'Country report: Turkey,' *EUDO Citizenship Observatory 31* (2010).

57 Y. Aydın, 'Turkey's diaspora policy and the "DİTİB" challenge', *Turkeyscope: Insights on Turkish Affairs* 3:8 (2019), https://dayan.org/content/turkeys-dias-pora-policy-and-ditib-challenge#_ednref5

58 G. P. Freeman and N. Ögelman, 'Homeland citizenship policies and the status of third country nationals in the European Union', *Journal of Ethnic and Migration Studies* 24:4 (1998), 769–88.

59 'Constitution of the Republic of Turkey', *TBMM* (1982), https://global.tbmm.gov.tr/docs/constitution_en.pdf

60 Z. Öniş, 'Turgut Özal and his economic legacy: Turkish neo-liberalism in critical perspective', *Middle Eastern Studies* 40:4 (2004), 113–34.

61 Interview, TBB official, Berlin, 6 November 2013.

62 Interview, French Ministry of the Interior official, Paris, 14 January 2019.

63 G. Avcı, 'Religion, transnationalism and Turks in Europe', *Turkish Studies* 6:2 (2005), 201–13; Z. Çıtak, 'Between "Turkish Islam"'.

64 A. Kaya and A. Tecmen, 'The role of common cultural heritage in external promotion of modern Turkey: Yunus Emre Cultural Centres', *Bilgi University European Institute Working Paper No. 4* (2011).

65 Z. Kadirbeyoğlu and A. Okyay, 'Turkey: Voting from abroad in 2015 general elections', *Global Governance Programme Report* (2015), https://globalcit.eu/voting-from-abroad-in-turkey-s-general-elections-2015/

66 E. Østergaard-Nielsen, *Transnational Politics*.

67 Z. Kadirbeyoğlu, 'Country report: Turkey'.

68 B. Pusch, 'Legal membership on the side of the transnational German-Turkish space', in *Turkish Migration Policy*, eds I. Sirkeci and B. Pusch (London: Transnational Press London, 2016), pp. 205–27.

69 L. Mügge, 'Managing transnationalism'.

70 İ. Ö. Yener-Roderburg, 'Party organisations across borders: Top-down satellites and bottom-up alliances: The case of AKP and HDP in Germany', in *Political Parties Abroad: A New Arena for Party Politics*, eds T. Kernalegenn and E. van Haute (London: Routledge, 2020), pp. 218–37.

71 A. Arkilic and A. E. Gurcan, 'The political participation of Alevis'.

72 B. Baser, *Diasporas and Homeland Conflicts: A Comparative Perspective* (Farnham: Ashgate, 2015).

73 A. Yükleyen, *Localising Islam in Europe: Turkish Islamic Communities in Germany and the Netherlands* (New York: Syracuse University Press, 2012).

74 Z. Kadirbeyoğlu, 'National transnationalism: Dual citizenship in Turkey', in *Dual Citizenship in Europe: From Nationhood to Social Integration*, ed. T. Faist (Aldershot: Ashgate, 2007), pp. 127–47.

75 Z. S. Artan, 'From Village Turks to Euro Turks'.

76 TBMM Proceeding, Session 20, Volume 3, 24 March 1998.

77 Interview, YTB official, Ankara, 24 July 2013.

78 E. Østergaard-Nielsen, *Transnational Politics*.

79 A. Kaya and F. Kentel, *Euro-Türkler: Türkiye ile Avrupa Birliği Arasında Köprü mü, Engel mi?* (Istanbul: Bilgi University Press, 2005).

80 E. Østergaard-Nielsen, *Transnational Politics*, p. 116.

81 D. Aksel, *Home States*, p. 111.

82 For election results, see: www.ysk.gov.tr/doc/dosyalar/docs/2002Milletvekili-Secimi/gumrukdahil/gumrukdahil.pdf

83 Interview, YTB official, Ankara, 25 June 2019.

84 Interview, AKP deputy, Ankara, 26 June 2019.

85 E. Yeldan and B. Ünüvar, 'An assessment of the Turkish economy in the AKP era', *Research and Policy on Turkey* 1:1 (2016), 11–28; K. Kirişçi and A. Sloat, 'The rise and fall of liberal democracy in Turkey: Implications for the West', *Brookings Institution Policy Brief* (February 2019), www.brookings.edu/wp-content/uploads/2019/02/FP_20190226_turkey_kirisci_sloat.pdf

86 H. Kösebalaban, *Turkish Foreign Policy.*

87 Z. Öniş and M. Kutlay, 'Rising powers in a changing global order: The political economy of Turkey in the age of BRICs', *Third World Quarterly* 34:8 (2013), 1409–26.

88 Ö. Taşpınar, 'Turkey: The new model?', *Brookings Institution Report* (25 April 2012), www.brookings.edu/research/papers/2012/04/24-turkey-new-model-taspinar

89 M. Müftüler-Bac, 'Turkey's political reforms: The impact of the European Union', *Southeast European Politics and Societies* 10:1 (2005), 16–30.

90 K. Tambar, *The Reckonings of Pluralism: Political Belonging and the Demands of History in Turkey* (Stanford: Stanford University Press, 2014).

91 A. Arkilic and A. E. Gurcan, 'The political participation of Alevis'.

92 Ö. Kayhan-Pusane, 'Turkey's Kurdish opening: Long awaited achievements and failed expectations', *Turkish Studies* 15:1 (2014), 81–99.

93 A. İçduygu and D. Aksel, 'Turkish migration policies: A critical historical retrospective', *Perceptions* 18:3 (2013), 167–90; J. White, *Muslim Nationalism and the New Turks* (Princeton: Princeton University Press, 2013); A. Okyay, 'Diaspora Making as a State-led Project: Turkey's Expansive Diaspora Strategy and Its Implications for Emigrant and Kin Populations' (PhD dissertation, EUI, 2015); Y. Aydın, 'The New Turkish Diaspora Policy'.

94 A. Davutoğlu, 'Turkish foreign policy and the EU in 2010', *Turkish Policy Quarterly* 8:3 (2009), 11–17.

95 'Başbakandan üçüncü balkon konuşması', *Hürriyet*, 13 June 2011, www.hurriyet.com.tr/ gundem/18015912.asp

96 H. Yavuz, 'Introduction', in *The Emergence of a New Turkey*, ed. H. Yavuz (Utah: University of Utah, 2006), pp. 1–23.

97 Y. Aydın, 'Turkey's diaspora policy'.

98 M. Kaçar, 'Küresel "Girişim" Gücü: Türk Diasporası', *Artı 90* 1 (2012), 68–9.

99 R. Erzan and K. Kirişçi, *Turkish Immigrants in the European Union: Determinants of Immigration and Integration* (London: Routledge, 2008).

100 M. Erdoğan, 'Euro-Turks Barometer'.

101 F. Bel Air, 'Migration profile: Turkey', *European University Institute Robert Schuman Centre for Advanced Studies Paper 9* (2016), 4–5, https://cadmus.eui.eu/bitstream/handle/1814/45145/MPC_PB_2016_09.pdf?sequence=

102 L. Zanfrini, *The Challenge of Migration in a Janus-faced Europe* (Basingstoke: Palgrave Macmillan, 2018).

103 T. Escritt, 'German Parties Fret about Turkish Voters as Erdogan Makes Mark', *Reuters*, 14 September 2017, www.reuters.com/article/us-germany-election-turks/german-parties-fret-about-turkish-voters-as-erdogan-makes-mark-idUSKCN1BO1H1

104 Y. Aydın, 'Turkey's diaspora policy'.

105 T. Barfield, 'Over 100,000 Foreigners Get German Citizenship', *Local*, 6 August 2014, www.thelocal.de/20140806/100000-foreigners-get-german-citizenship

106 'Relations between Turkey and the Federal Republic of Germany', *Turkish Ministry of Foreign Affairs* (2021), www.mfa.gov.tr/relations-between-turkey-and-the-federal-republic-of-germany.en.mfa

107 Interview, Turkish Consulate official, Paris, 29 January 2019.

108 'Relations between Turkey and France', *Turkish Ministry of Foreign Affairs* (2021), www.mfa.gov.tr/relations-between-turkey-and-france.en.mfa

109 Y. Mamou, 'Islamisation of Europe: Erdogan's new Muslim political network', *Gatestone Institute* (2017), www.gatestoneinstitute.org/10509/france-islamic-party; 'Türk partisine binlerce tehdit', *Avrupa Sabah*, 8 February 2019, www.sabah.com.tr/avrupa/2019/02/08/almanlarin-korkulu-ruyasi-turk-partisine-binlerce-tehdit

110 Interview, Turkish Consulate official, Paris, 29 January 2019.

111 Interview, YTB official, Ankara, 27 June 2019.

112 İ. Ö. Yener-Roderburg, 'Party organisations across borders', p. 225.

113 'Yurtdışında Oy Kullanan Seçmen Sayısı Açıklandı', *Habertürk*, 5 April 2017, www.haberturk.com/gundem/haber/1451637-yurt-disinda-oy-kullanan-secmen-sayisi-aciklandi

114 Interview, YEE official, Ankara, 31 July 2013; Interview, UID official, Cologne, 27 November 2013; Interview, YTB official, Ankara, 25 June 2019.

115 M. Müftüler-Bac, 'Turkey's political reforms'.

116 E. Østergaard-Nielsen, 'Turkey and the "Euro-Turks"'.

117 Interview, İB (formerly known as the Office of Public Diplomacy) official, Ankara, 1 August 2013; Interview, Turkish Embassy official, Berlin, 13 February 2019.

118 D. Dombey, 'Six markets to watch', *Foreign Affairs*, January/February (2014), www.foreignaffairs.com/articles/turkey/2013-12-06/six-markets-watch-turkey

119 Interview, Turkish Ministry for EU Affairs official, Ankara, 25 July 2013; Interview, YTB official, Ankara, 25 June 2019.

120 Interview, İB (formerly known as the Office of Public Diplomacy) official, Ankara, 1 August 2013. Emphasis added by the author.

121 Erdoğan's full speech is available at: www.youtube.com/watch?v=1FLv8M-KrFXw

122 Interview, Turkish Embassy official, Paris, 24 January 2019.

123 A. Arkilic and L. Macdonald, 'The European Union's disintegration over refugee responsibility-sharing', *Women Talking Politics* (November 2019), 26–9; Interview, Directorate for EU Affairs official, Ankara, 26 June 2019.

124 A. Kaya, *Turkish-origin Migrants and Their Descendants*.

125 K. Shaheen, 'Turkey Threatens to End Refugee Deal in Row over EU Accession', *Guardian*, 25 November 2016, www.theguardian.com/world/2016/nov/25/turkey-threatens-end-refugee-deal-row-eu-accession-erdogan

126 F. Vermeulen, 'The paradox of immigrant political participation in Europe amidst crises of multiculturalism', in *The Oxford Handbook of Migration Crises*, eds C. Menjívar, M. Ruiz and I. Ness (Oxford: Oxford University Press, 2019), pp. 801–17.

127 Interview, Turkish Consulate official, Berlin, 26 February 2019.

128 'General Information', *YTB* (2021), www.ytb.gov.tr/en/abroad-citizens/general-information-2

129 Interview, Turkish Embassy official, Paris, 24 January 2019.

130 Interview, YTB official, Ankara, 25 June 2019.

131 'Turkey among Top 5 in Number of Diplomatic Missions', *Daily Sabah*, 8 February 2018, www.dailysabah.com/diplomacy/2018/02/09/turkey-among-top-5-in-number-of-diplomatic-missions

132 'Büyükelçiler sıkıntılı', *Cumhuriyet*, 16 January 2014, www.cumhuriyet.com.tr/haber/turkiye/30437/buyukelciler-sikintili.html

133 Interview, Turkish Consulate official, Berlin, 3 December 2013.

134 Interview, Turkish Embassy official, Berlin, 7 November 2013.

135 F. B. Adamson, 'Sending states', 224.

136 S. Akgönül, 'Turkish Islam in Europe: Political Activism and Internal Conflicts', *Oasis*, 18 July 2019, www.oasiscenter.eu/en/turkish-islam-in-europe-akp-vs-gulen

137 Z. Çıtak, 'Between "Turkish Islam" and "French Islam"'; C. Maritato, 'Addressing the blurred edges of Turkey's diaspora and religious policy: Diyanet women preachers sent to Europe', *European Journal of Turkish Studies* 27 (2018), doi: 10.4000/ejts.6020

138 Interview, *Diyanet* official, Ankara, 24 July 2013.

139 J. Gibbon, 'Religion, Immigration and the Turkish Government in Germany', Living Islam in Europe: Muslim Traditions in European Contexts Conference, Berlin, 7–9 May 2009.

140 İ. Gözaydın, *Diyanet*.

141 B. Bruce, 'Governing Islam Abroad: The Turkish and Moroccan Muslim Fields in France and Germany' (PhD dissertation, Sciences Po-Paris, 2015), p. 119; B. Bruce, *Governing Islam Abroad: Turkish and Moroccan Muslims in Western Europe* (Basingstoke: Palgrave Macmillan, 2018), p. 33.

142 'Diyanet'in 2020 bütçesi sekiz bakanlığı geride bıraktı', *BirGün*, 24 October 2019, www.birgun.net/haber/diyanet-in-2020-butcesi-sekiz-bakanligi-geride-birakti-273683

143 B. Bruce, 'Governing Islam Abroad', p. 191.

144 *Ibid.*, p. 192.

145 '2019–2023 Dönemi Stratejik Planı', *Diyanet* (2020), www.sp.gov.tr/tr/stratejik-plan/s/1844/Diyanet+Isleri+Baskanligi+2019–2023

146 '2018 İdare Faaliyet Raporu', *YTB* (2018), www.ytb.gov.tr/kurumsal/faaliyet-raporlari

147 M. Ekşi, *Kamu Diplomasisi ve AK Parti Dönemi Türk Dış Politikası* (Ankara: Siyasal Kitabevi, 2018).

148 The TİKA was founded in 1992 to organise economic, social and cultural activities in the Turkish-speaking countries of Central Asia and Caucasia. Since the 2000s, it has shifted its focus to technical infrastructure, developmental aid and corporate capacity improvement in the Middle East, Africa, Asia and Latin America. For more, see: www.tika.gov.tr/en/page/about_us-14650

149 This report can be accessed from the TBMM's website: https://acikerisim. tbmm.gov.tr/xmlui/handle/11543/2788?show=full

150 'Merve Kavakçı Muhtar Kentle aynı kurulda', *Anadolu Ajansı*, 29 December 2012, www.aa.com.tr/tr/turkiye/merve-kavakci-ve-muhtar-kent-ayni-kurulda/ 290815

151 '2019 İdare Faaliyet Raporu', *YTB* (2019), www.ytb.gov.tr/kurumsal/faaliyet-raporlari; A. Arkilic, 'Long-distance politics and diaspora youth: Analyzing Turkey's diaspora engagement policies aimed at post-migrant generations', in *Routledge International Handbook of Diaspora Diplomacy*, ed. Liam Kennedy (London: Routledge, 2022), pp. 214–29.

152 Y. Özdemir, 'Bir diaspora hayali', *Evrensel*, 23 June 2012, www.evrensel.net/ haber/31463/bir-diaspora-hayali

153 Interview, YTB official, Ankara, 24 July 2013.

154 'Sivil Toplum Destekleri', *YTB* (2021), www.ytb.gov.tr/destekler-ve-burslar/sivil-toplum-destekleri; A. Arkilic, 'Empowering a fragmented diaspora'.

155 '2017 İdare Faaliyet Raporu', *YTB* (2017), p. 50, www.ytb.gov.tr/kurumsal/ faaliyet-raporlari

156 '2019 İdare Faaliyet Raporu', p. 33.

157 '2015 İdare Faaliyet Raporu', *YTB* (2015), www.ytb.gov.tr/kurumsal/faaliyet-raporlari

158 Interview, YTB official, Ankara, 24 July 2013.

159 G. K. Muyan, 'Closer National Ties during the Pandemic: Turkey's Diaspora Engagement Policy', *Daily Sabah*, 10 April 2020, www.dailysabah.com/opinion/op-ed/closer-transnational-ties-during-pandemic-turkeys-diaspora-engagement-policy; A. Arkilic, 'What is the impact of the COVID-19 pandemic on Turkey and its "corona diplomacy"?', *University of Auckland Big Q Project* (2020), www.thebigq.org/2020/05/26/what-is-the-impact-of-the-covid-19-pandemic-on-turkey-and-its-corona-diplomacy/

160 'Diaspora COVID-19 Destek ve İş Birliği Programı Tamamlandı', *YTB* (2021), www.ytb.gov.tr/haberler/ytb-diaspora-covid-19-is-birligi-ve-destek-programi-tamamlandi

161 Interview, YEE official, Ankara, 31 July 2013.

162 'Yunus Emre Bülteni', *YEE* (September 2009), p. 7.

163 'Vision-Mission', *YEE* (2021), www.yee.org.tr/en/corporate/vision-mission

164 'Yunus Emre Institute', *YEE* (2021), www.yee.org.tr/en/corporate/yunus-emre-institute

165 'President's Message', *YEE* (2021), www.yee.org.tr/en/corporate/presidents-message

166 'Faaliyet Raporu', *YEE* (2018), www.yee.org.tr/tr/yayin/2018-faaliyet-raporu
167 *Ibid.*
168 Interview, YEE official, Ankara, 31 July 2013; Interview, YEE official, Paris, 23 February 2019.
169 Interview, YEE official, Paris, 5 March 2013.
170 'Yunus Emre Bülteni', *YEE* (September 2009), pp. 3–4, www.yee.org.tr/sites/default/files/yayin/eylul_2009.pdf
171 'Yunus Emre Bülteni', *YEE* (February 2011), p. 18, www.yee.org.tr/tr/yayin/2011-subat-bulteni
172 'Vizyon-Misyon', *İB* (2021), www.iletisim.gov.tr/turkce/vizyon-misyon
173 Interview, Ministry of Foreign Affairs official, Ankara, 1 August 2013; Interview, İB official, Ankara, 1 August 2013.
174 İ. Kalın, 'Soft power and public diplomacy in Turkey', *Perceptions* 16:3 (2011), 19.
175 Interview, UID official, Cologne, 27 November 2013.
176 'Avrupa Türk Diasporası ve Siyasal Katılım', *UID* (2016), http://u-i-d.org/avrupa-tuerk-diasporasi-ve-siyasal-katilim/
177 'Bölge Başkanları', *UID* (2021), http://u-i-d.org/bolge-ve-subeler/
178 S. Cornell, '"Weaponising" the Diaspora: Erdoğan and the Turks in Europe', *The Turkey Analyst*, 5 April 2017, www.isdp.eu/publication/weaponizing-diaspora/
179 Y. Aydın, 'The New Turkish Diaspora Policy'.
180 Interview, French Ministry of the Interior official, Paris, 11 January 2019.
181 Law No. 6721, https://turkiyemaarif.org/page/51-tmf-law-11
182 A. Ünal, 'Maarif Foundation Head: We Aim to Offer an Education that Reflects Turkish Vision, Promote Turkish Language', *Daily Sabah*, 13 February 2017, www.dailysabah.com/politics/2017/02/13/maarif-foundation-head-we-aim-to-offer-an-education-that-reflects-turkish-vision-promote-turkish-language
183 S. Kasap, 'Turkey's Maarif Teaches 300,000 Students in 35 countries', *Anadolu Ajansı*, 16 June 2019, www.aa.com.tr/en/education/turkeys-maarif-teaches-30–000-students-in-35-countries/1505698
184 *Ibid.*
185 'Tanıtım', *DEİK* (2021), www.dtik.org.tr/konsey-yapilanmasi-tanitim
186 'The Turkish Diaspora Will Be Organized in Over a 100 Countries within 2 Years', *TOBB* (June 2012), www.tobb.org.tr/Sayfalar/Eng/Detay.php?rid=1587&lst=MansetListesi
187 'Dünya Türk Girişimcileri Kurultayı', *TOBB* (April 2009), www.tobb.org.tr/Baskanimiz/Sayfalar/Konusmalari.php
188 S. Adar, 'Rethinking political attitudes of migrants from Turkey and their Germany-born children', *SWP Research Paper 7* (June 2019), www.swp-berlin.org/fileadmin/contents/products/research_papers/2019RP07_ada.pdf
189 Z. Sahin-Mencutek and S. A. Yılmaz, 'Turkey's experience with voting from abroad in the 2014 and 2015 elections', *Rethink Institute Paper* (2015), www.rethinkinstitute.org/turkeys-experience-with-voting-from-abroad-in-the-2014-and-2015-elections/

190 Another amendment came in 2012 (Law No. 6304), to improve the administration of the Blue Card and to extend the right to apply for a Blue Card to the descendants of former Turkish nationals who obtained Turkish citizenship by birth. See: B. Pusch and J. Splitt, 'Binding the Almanci to the Homeland', *Perceptions* 18 (2013), 148.

191 Interview, Ministry of Labour and Social Security official, Ankara, 25 July 2013.

192 D. Aksel, *Home States*, p. 123.

193 A. Nazeef, 'Erdogan's Tentacles: How Turkish Socio-religious Networks Influence Europe's Political Landscape', *Trends*, 7 January 2021, https://trendsresearch.org/insight/erdogans-tentacles-how-turkish-socio-religious-networks-influence-europes-political-landscape/

194 'President Erdogan Ratifies Law on Military Service', *Daily Sabah*, 26 January 2016, www.dailysabah.com/turkey/2016/01/26/president-erdogan-ratifies-law-on-military-exemption-fee

3

'You are our ambassadors': Turkey's changing relations with its diaspora in France

There are 620,000 Turks in France. Why don't you submit an application to become a French citizen? I am shouting out to my fellow citizens who have not obtained French citizenship yet. Apply for dual citizenship. Don't postpone this important task. Know your legal rights. You are our ambassadors in France ... Never feel desperate. Your country is a powerful country and it will continue to grow. We will always fight back when they [enemies] attack us. Be proud of your identity, language and religion. Don't forget to apply for French citizenship ... France needs people like you. But never assimilate and never let your children assimilate![1]

Large-scale Turkish emigration to France started in 1965 following a bilateral agreement signed by both governments and gained momentum in the 1970s when French companies systematically invited Turkish guest workers.[2] The Turkish exodus has continued into the new century in the form of legal family reunifications, brain drain of students and highly skilled individuals, and irregular entry.

Historically, immigrant political activism in France has been mainly driven by non-Turkish immigrant groups. For example, in 1983, young North Africans marched from Marseille to Paris to demand equal citizenship rights and anti-discriminatory measures.[3] Between 1983 and 1985, France witnessed three other mass demonstrations launched by North Africans: the March against Racism and for Equal Rights, Convergence 84 and the March for Civil Rights.[4] North African organisations also fostered immigrants' presence in local politics by initiating voter-registration campaigns and by lobbying political parties to include immigrant-origin politicians in their cadres.[5] North and Sub-Saharan Africans coordinated other mass protests throughout the 1990s and 2000s. They expressed their grievances during the 'without papers' (*sans-papiers*) movement in 1996, the 2004 headscarf ban and the 2005 *banlieue* riots that erupted in the suburbs of Paris and other French cities. Yet compared to these groups, Turks in France maintained relative silence during these protests.[6]

While Turkey-originated Alevi, Kurdish and secular immigrant organisations in France have formed solidarity networks with non-Turkish immigrant organisations since the 1980s, conservative Turkish immigrant organisations have been largely absent from political life in France.[7] Neither the *sans-papiers*, headscarf or *banlieue* protests in the 1990s and 2000s nor the recognition by France of the mass killings of Armenians in 1915 as genocide[8] in 2001 triggered political action among the conservative Turkish diaspora. Turkish-origin immigrants' disinterest in host country politics was puzzling given that all Muslim minority groups face similar challenges in France.

Yet from the mid-2000s onwards, the political apathy of Turkish Muslim leaders in France has transformed into active citizenship and begun to influence relations between France and Turkey. This recent engagement is striking given that Turks are overall the least integrated immigrant group in France in terms of language skills, enrolment and success in public schools, access to higher education, the number of university graduates, employment, upward mobility and mixed marriages.[9] Compared to emigrants from North and Sub-Saharan Africa, French Turks also have the lowest rate of naturalisation, electoral registration and participation and political representation in elected bodies.[10]

While Turkey's EU candidacy, the growing threat of Islamophobia and other host-state-related developments have served as key push factors, Turkey's diaspora engagement activities in France remain an important yet understudied element that has instigated a new sense of active citizenship among Turkish Muslim leaders. Turkey's new diaspora policy has restructured overseas Turks' previously marginalised identities and rendered them more self-confident by addressing them as hard-working, competent and harmonious people who contribute to their home and host states.

Ankara has also instilled feelings of collective identity by bringing like-minded conservative-nationalist and Sunni Islamic immigrant organisations in France together for various activities and meetings, by drawing attention to their similarities and by encouraging them to collaborate and form alliances with each other. The transformation of the image of certain immigrant organisations from one of stigmatisation into one of normalisation has helped organisations overcome past tensions and engage themselves in inter-organisational collaboration. By creating a common identity and purpose for the diaspora, Turkey has strengthened its conservative emigrants' group consciousness. Turkey has also empowered select Turkish diaspora organisations through the provision of capacity-development and know-how programmes. Such support has created a bridge for knowledge transfer between the homeland and conservative diaspora organisations and rejuvenated the organisational capacity of diaspora leaders. The homeland's projection of collective identity, combined with the provision of such support, has activated diaspora diplomacy conducted by Turkish conservative-nationalist and Sunni Islamic groups.

This chapter will first present the history of Turkish associations in France and examine their political mobilisation in the pre-2003 era. It will then shift the analysis to Turkey's diaspora engagement with French Turks since 2003. Through an examination of increased official correspondence with Turkish immigrant organisations, pro-Turkish diaspora rallies and various state institutions' activities in the transnational space, it will illustrate how such engagement has prompted diaspora diplomacy.

The history of Turkish organisational life in France

In earlier periods of Turkish emigration to France, Turks established small solidarity organisations (*amicales*) to meet their daily needs, assist newcomers and socialise. The first types of organisations focused on labour, student concerns and charity.[11] For example, the Intercultural Citizen Actions (previously the Association of Solidarity with Turkish Workers, ASTU) was established in Strasbourg in 1974 to fight against the maltreatment of immigrants in their workplaces and to foster solidarity.[12] Turkish immigrants also had religious needs and, therefore, converted hotel rooms, garages and warehouses into small prayer halls (*masjids*).[13] These early organisations were rudimentary, informal and loosely organised.[14] This was in part due to immigrants' socio-economic challenges and also to France's institutional obstacles, such as the obligation to secure prior authorisation from the French government to establish foreign associations.[15]

Ultranationalists linked to the MHP in Turkey opened the first political umbrella organisation founded by French Turks in 1978. For years, MHP-linked diaspora groups in France remained aloof from other conservative organisations and had their imams sent from nationalist support networks in Turkey. Even though they were previously poorly mobilised under different names – such as the Grey Wolves, Cultural Associations, Idealist Hearths and Idealist Associations – they united their branches under the Turkish Federation in 1995. By 2013, the Turkish Federation had fifty organisations across France.[16]

Although the Grey Wolves is not the most active Turkish diaspora organisation, it has become publicly visible, especially as a result of developments on the Armenian issue. The organisation's mobilisation increased after the formation of the political alliance between the AKP and the MHP in 2013 (see Chapter 2).[17] France barred the Grey Wolves in October 2020, citing its violent activities and discourse.[18] The decision came after the group defaced an Armenian genocide memorial near Lyon with pro-Turkish slogans and references to Erdoğan shortly after Turkish and Armenian nationalists attacked each other amid the September 2020 Nagorno-Karabakh conflict.[19] In response to the ban, the Turkish Ministry of Foreign Affairs denied the existence of the group (due to the absence of an official organisation named the Grey Wolves in France), and accused the French authorities of being under the influence of the Armenian lobby and of failing to 'protect the freedom of assembly and expression of Turks in France'.[20]

The 1970s also saw the incorporation of *masjids* into well-organised religious networks. Since the *Diyanet*-linked organisations did not arrive in France until the 1980s, 'alternative' religious currents dominated the Turkish Islamic field during the first two decades of Turkish immigration.[21] After the 1971 military coup in Turkey, leaders of the Union of Islamic Cultural Centres sought refuge in Europe. This organisation practises Islamic mysticism related to the Sufi Naqshibandiyya order and follows the teachings of Süleyman Hilmi Tunahan Efendi, a renowned Islamic scholar of his time (1888–1959).[22] The Union of Islamic Cultural Centres became the first Turkish immigrant organisation to inaugurate formal mosques in Europe. Its first mosque in France opened its doors in 1979, [23] and the organisation has remained a close-knit community providing space for daily religious practices in its mosques and Qur'anic education in its boarding schools. The Union of Islamic Cultural Centres has forty associations across France.[24]

The France-based *Millî Görüş* (*Communauté Islamique du Millî Görüş*) was formed in 1979 as an organisation closely tied to Necmettin Erbakan's *Millî Görüş* movement in Turkey.[25] Its activities were shaped by Islamic sharia law and focused on the management of Hajj visits, burial and repatriation of Muslims, the provision of halal food and the construction of mosques.[26] According to *Millî Görüş* officials, the organisation's current raison d'être is to increase Islam's role in the public sphere, to prevent the Turkish diaspora's assimilation and to promote Muslim identity in Europe.[27] The organisation pays specific attention to youth education: nearly 2,000 Turkish-origin French students attend classes related to Turkish culture, language and Islamic education in *Millî Görüş* mosques. It also has kindergartens as well as private primary, secondary and high schools, some of which are organised through an organisation called the European Union for Private Muslim Education.[28] The *Millî Görüş* is home to 300 mosques and associations across France.[29] Its gigantic Ottoman-style Eyyûb Sultan Mosque, which is set to be the largest in Europe, with a total price tag of about €32 million ($38 million), will open its doors by 2023 in the Meinau district of Strasbourg. The project has received financial assistance from the Mayor of Strasbourg.[30]

The 1980 military coup triggered another massive wave of Turkish emigration to France. Politically engaged newcomers settled mainly in

Paris, Rhône-Alpes, Alsace-Lorraine and Bretagne, and founded non-religious organisations.[31] In particular, many Turkish-origin immigrant associations settled in Strasbourg-Saint-Denis and Clichy-sous-Bois in Paris. The ACORT, created in 1980 by refugees linked to the left-wing Revolutionary Path movement in Turkey, is one of the oldest diaspora organisations in Strasbourg-Saint Denis. It is still active today, pursuing activities related to anti-discrimination and immigrants' equal participation.[32]

In the first decades of Turkish emigration to France, foreign associations had to obtain prior approval to be formed. In 1981, with the election of the leftist François Mitterrand to the presidency, this was abolished and Turkish associational life flourished.[33] The now defunct left-wing Democratic Association of Workers from Turkey began to operate in 1982. Similar to the ACORT, it included Alevi- and Kurdish-origin immigrants until these groups established their own ethnic and religious organisations.[34]

In 1983, Kurds formed their first umbrella organisation, the Kurdish Institute of Paris, as 'an independent, non-political secular organisation, embracing Kurdish intellectuals and artists from different horizons as well as Western specialists on Kurdish studies'.[35] Today the Kurdish Institute of Paris seeks 'to maintain in the Kurdish community a knowledge of [Kurdish] language, history and cultural heritage [and] to contribute to the integration of Kurdish immigrants … into their host societies'.[36]

Turks formed two other non-religious organisations in the 1980s. The secular-oriented ELELE came into being Paris in 1984. Until its closure in 2010, the ELELE developed successful projects on the integration of Turks, anti-discrimination and diversity. It also provided Turkish-language classes, concerts and film screenings. According to one of its representatives, it received the largest amount of funding from the French government among all Turkish immigrant associations, covering 80 per cent of its costs through governmental aid.[37] The Anatolian Cultural Centre, also founded in 1984, is another secular organisation offering Turkish-language courses to both young-generation Turks and foreigners while running exhibitions and events to promote Turkish culture in France.[38]

A year later, the COJEP was created to act as the youth wing of the *Millî Görüş*.[39] However, it separated from the *Millî Görüş* in 2000 and has established close links with the AKP. Over time, it has evolved into an influential political lobby group with twenty-five regional divisions in France and fifteen national branches across the rest of Europe. It holds participatory status at the European Parliament, and membership of the UN Economic and Social Council and the Conference of International Non-Governmental Organisations at the Council of Europe.[40] In 2010, the COJEP founded the European Muslim Initiative for Social Cohesion (EMISCO) to battle

Islamophobia in Europe and launched a media platform called *Medya Turk*, which targets French Turks.[41]

The 1980s marked the beginning of a period when Turkish authorities felt the need to marshal the Turkish community in France under the patronage of 'official Islam'. In order to isolate Turkish immigrants from 'dangerous' political and religious currents, such as the Union of Islamic Cultural Centres and the *Millî Görüş*,[42] Ankara formed the first *Diyanet*-linked DİTİB in France in 1986.[43] As an institution closely aligned with the Turkish state,[44] the DİTİB is the largest Turkish religious umbrella organisation in Europe, frequented by around 70 per cent of Turkish Muslims, most of whom are first-generation immigrants.[45] The DİTİB has headquarters in Paris, Strasbourg, Lyon and Bordeaux, and 267 mosque associations throughout the country.[46]

In the 1990s, two more Kurdish ethno-nationalist organisations became politically active in France. The Federation of Associations from Kurdistan (KOMKAR) separated itself from the PKK and denounced the use of violence for political ambitions. The KOMKAR coordinated political demonstrations, campaigns and hunger strikes as a reaction to political developments in Turkey.[47] The second organisation, the PKK-affiliated Federation of Cultural and Patriot Workers' Association of Kurdistan, evolved into the Federation of Kurdish Associations in France (FEYKA). In 2014, the FEYKA changed its name again, to the Democratic Kurdish Council in France (CDK-F).[48] Over time, the KOMKAR has lost power and the CDK-F has begun to control the Kurdish community in Europe against the backdrop of the PKK's increasing popularity within the diaspora.[49] During this period, KOMKAR and PKK supporters had numerous deadly clashes.[50] The Ahmet Kaya Kurdish Cultural Centre, founded in 2001, has also been involved in campaigns, petitions and demonstrations against the Turkish state since its establishment.[51] Kurds in France, like Kurds in other European countries, have been actively rallying support and lobbying the EU and other supranational organisations for their causes.[52]

Alevis have formed their own associations as well. The first Alevi Cultural Centre was created in Paris in 1992, then others followed in Strasbourg and Metz.[53] Like other Turkish-origin organisations, these were small and mainly focused on homeland problems. The FUAF, the largest Alevi umbrella organisation, came into existence in Strasbourg in 1998 and operates forty-one Alevi Cultural Centres.[54] It advocates for the preservation and recognition of Alevi culture and faith, and the integration of the Alevi community in France.[55]

Gülen-affiliated organisations emerged in Europe in the late 1990s. Even though Fethullah Gülen visited some French and German cities in the 1980s, the institutionalisation of the Gülen Movement only materialised a decade later. Following the collapse of the Soviet Union, Gülen opened private schools in Central Asia and other post-Soviet countries.[56] When Gülen entered the Islamic field in Europe, he built educational centres, high schools and 'intercultural dialogue' centres instead of mosques and Islamic schools.[57] One of the leaders of the Gülen Movement in Europe argued that the Movement's goal was 'to take initiatives to be useful to society through education and dialogue, and develop socio-cultural programmes, which promote mutual understanding and tolerance'.[58] Even though Gülen schools claim to prioritise secular education, the Movement remains a Turkish-Muslim, socio-religious institution unique to Anatolia.[59] In addition to its two private independent schools – the Collège Educ'Active in Villeneuve-Saint Georges near Paris and the Collège Selman Asan in Strasbourg – the Gülen Movement in France has twenty after-school learning centres called EtudePlus.[60]

The Gülen Movement owns many civil society, media, business and women's organisations as well. Founded in 2005, the Paris Platform is one of the most potent instruments of the Gülen Movement in France, with a focus on social cohesion and inter-faith activities.[61] *Zaman France*, a bilingual newspaper created in 2005 and shut down in 2016 in the post-coup period, was another arm of the Gülen Movement in France. The Movement is also represented by the Federation of Franco-Turkish Entrepreneurs (FEDIF) and the Waterlily Institute, a business and a women's organisation respectively. Gülen associations and followers in France have maintained a low public profile, particularly since 2016.

In addition to these diaspora organisations, the 2000s witnessed the establishment of Turkish party branches in Europe. The secular CHP opened its first office in Paris in 2015 with five others in Strasbourg, Bordeaux, Nantes, Lyon and Marseille. The HDP has also had an office in France since 2015.[62] Two years later, the AKP opened its first satellite office in the country to enhance its position in the transnational space and to counter the Gülenist threat.[63]

Political mobilisation of conservative Turkish organisations in France before 2003

The ACORT was the only diaspora organisation that turned its face to France instead of Turkey in the first three decades of Turkish emigration. ACORT members engaged in political activism to combat the institutional hurdles slowing down immigrants' socio-economic and political integration in French society. In 1983 and 1985 respectively, the ACORT co-founded the Council of Immigrant Associations in France (CAIF) and the Immigration Forum with North African, Portuguese and Spanish organisations. These platforms held marches to rally immigrants on the issues of family reunification, residence and work permits and anti-discrimination. In 1993, ACORT leaders even held a hunger strike to protest at legislation that banned non-citizen foreign residents from participating in local elections.[64]

Yet the ACORT rarely worked with other Turkey-originated immigrant organisations. Its only cooperation attempt came in 1991, when it formed the French Council of Turkish Immigrant Associations (CFAIT) along with fifteen other organisations (including the ASTU, the ELELE, the COJEP and some Alevi and Kurdish organisations). However, the CFAIT disbanded only a few years later. According to an ACORT official, these groups failed to unite at that time because they did not agree on common interests. Conservative Turkish organisations showed no interest in non-religious activities. Secular, Kurdish and Alevi organisations, on the other hand, were mired in homeland politics and narrow identity-related issues rather than broader host-state-related concerns. Internal divisions pitted these organisations against each other.[65]

I asked interviewees why Turks have traditionally been less visible in the French political arena than other immigrant groups. One argument voiced by a Turkish-origin municipal councillor was that North and Sub-Saharan Africans' colonial ties with France have familiarised them with the French language and political processes and, hence, improved their political-mobilisation prospects. In contrast, he suggested, Turkish immigrants have struggled with the French language and political system.[66] Another respondent advanced a different argument: Turks did not take an interest in the *banlieue* protests because they do not hold the same colonial resentments and they have always situated themselves in a superior category compared to other Muslim emigrant groups due to the Ottoman Empire's 'glorious history' and lack of colonial subordination to Western powers.[67] According to other Turkish diaspora representatives, the issue of Islam and immigration has never been a Turkish problem in France. France's first encounter with Islam was with Maghrebis, and its larger size put this immigrant group under the spotlight. In contrast, Turks have enjoyed a privileged 'invisibility' in the eyes of French policymakers, an argument that will be explored further in Chapter 6.[68]

According to the Trajectories and Origins Survey, Turks indeed perceive that they are less subject to discrimination than North and Sub-Saharan Africans in France, while, paradoxically, they experience discrimination at only slightly lower rates than these groups and, in reality, are less integrated.[69] As such, the lack of collective identity and organisational capacity across Turkish immigrant groups is more likely to explain Turkish Muslim leaders' absence from French politics until recently.

After the 1980 coup, the Turkish state showed some interest in uniting the Turkish expatriate community in France. However, this short-term interest was driven by surveillance purposes. Only those loyal to the Turkish state were granted consular protection, the right to return to the homeland and even financial support for associational activities. The entry of state Islam into France through the DİTİB also led to rivalry within the Turkish Islamic landscape as some of the older conservative-religious organisations felt threatened by the DİTİB.[70]

In the 1990s, the Turkish government attempted to coalesce the Franco-Turkish diaspora through various initiatives. The Union of Turkish Associations in France (UATF), founded in 1992 with the backing of the Turkish Consulate, was different from the DİTİB in that it was based on a shared understanding of Turkish identity and citizenship. It also engaged in a wide range of political activities aimed at the French state, including support for Turkey's admission into the EU.[71] As discussed in the previous chapter, another early initiative was the creation of the Advisory Board for Turkish Citizens Living Abroad in 1998 to address legal problems encountered by Turkish immigrants and to aid their integration. The Turkish Consulate nominated several appointees from France for this Advisory Board, including the founders of the ELELE and the Anatolian Cultural Centre. However, rather than embracing the broader Turkish diaspora community, these state-led attempts had a selective bias, supporting individuals and organisations that espoused the official ideology of state Kemalism. Ultimately they were met with suspicion and resentment by conservative diaspora members.[72]

Members of the Turkish Islamic community in France complained about secular Turkish governments' distant relations with them and their overall 'lack of attention and protection' (*ilgisizlik ve sahipsizlik*).[73] As a *Millî Görüş* representative explained, 'before 2002, we were ashamed of saying "we are Turkish". We lacked the right to vote, to engage in politics. Not anymore.'[74] According to an administrator from the *Millî Görüş*'s women's unit, Turkish consulates and embassies treated devout overseas citizens very badly in the pre-AKP period: 'The Turkish Consulate in Lyon almost did not let me marry my husband because of my headscarf. They insulted me and asked me to uncover my head. I refused and was forced to expose at least my ears. Only after that was our ceremony finalised. This strict secular state mentality is changing and we feel embraced and respected now.'[75] An official from the Union of Islamic Cultural Centres expressed similar problems with Turkish diplomats back then: 'We had to receive a document from the Turkish Consulate and provide it to the French municipality in Nancy to prove that our organisation was legal. The Turkish Consulate did not give it to us.'[76]

DİTİB leaders also complained about Turkish policymakers' historical neglect: 'Until the 2000s, no Turkish official cared about Turks in Europe. If they came to Strasbourg, they would visit the European Parliament and completely ignore us. Turkish ambassadors would never visit an Islamic organisation.'[77] According to another DİTİB representative, 'this normalisation period is very recent. Turkish consulates were excluding most members of the Turkish community. The monopolisation of the *Diyanet* fragmented the community. They used to say "if you are a Turkish citizen, you have to go to *Diyanet* mosques".'[78] An administrator from the Turkish Federation agreed that before the AKP there was no official engagement with the conservative segments of the Turkish diaspora: 'We had no visits, no meetings, there was no interest in us whatsoever. We had no political rights, we could only vote at the customs … Our bond to Turkey has solidified in the last fifteen years.'[79] COJEP representatives concluded that 'the tension between the state and the diaspora is over. Today Turkish officials visit every organisation, even Alevis, without any bias'.[80]

Turkey's diaspora engagement activities in France in the post-2003 era

Increased official correspondence and diaspora rallies

Following two directives issued in 2003 by the then Minister of Foreign Affairs, Abdullah Gül, to Turkish embassies and consulates in Europe, Turkish diplomats in France began to attend Ramadan dinners, visit conservative organisations, invite them to official ceremonies and seriously consider their lobbying potential. In 2005, the Turkish Consulate in Paris asked representatives of leading Turkish organisations in France to create a joint platform to discuss relevant issues facing the Turkish community. This request stemmed from the AKP's understanding of the new role of Turks in Europe.[81] Uğur Arıner, the Turkish Consul General in France between 2009 and 2012, suggested that Turkish organisations should unite under common goals and take action whenever national interests were at stake.[82] Echoing Arıner's remarks, Tahsin Burcuoğlu, Turkey's ambassador between 2010 and 2014, argued that Turkish diaspora associations should work collectively for the sake of national unity and interests, particularly regarding the 'Armenian issue'.[83] According to these diplomats, the Turkish state should create federations to give direction to immigrant organisations' political activities abroad.[84] A French bureaucrat from the Ministry of the Interior confirmed that Turkey's anti-Armenian position and EU bid had brought together conservative Turkish organisations.[85] Consequently, a new Advisory Board consisting of Turks living in France was established in 2012. Unlike the previous Advisory Board, which included secular Kemalist leaders from the ELELE and the Anatolian Cultural Centre, the new board consisted mostly of conservative-nationalist Turks, such as representatives of the DİTİB, the Turkish Federation and the *Millî Görüş*.[86] In the same year, conservative Turkish organisations also formed the Union of French-Turkish Cultural Associations as an overarching lobby organisation.[87]

Additionally, the UID opened its first branch in Paris in 2012 in a ceremony attended by AKP parliamentarians and Turkey's ambassador to France.[88] UID officials emphasised that the UID aims to strengthen diplomatic relations between Turkey and France and to boost the social status of Turks by encouraging their political participation in French elections.[89] For example, the UID publicised Turkish candidates on social media and connected them with French mayors prior to French elections.[90] It has also built close relationships with the AKP: the organisation's first director, Ahmet Oğraş, was simultaneously acting as a DİTİB representative in France.[91]

Mass rallies set up by the UID serve as the backbone of the Turkish state's diaspora engagement efforts in France. Since 2010, Erdoğan has addressed the Turkish community in stadiums to encourage their political participation. Erdoğan's messages demonstrate that the AKP sees Turks in the country as a political lobby that is expected to promote its interests in Europe. At these gatherings, Erdoğan has criticised France's policies concerning the Armenian issue and called for the French government to increase its efforts to welcome Turkey into the EU.[92] He has also applauded the AKP's achievements in order to attract diaspora votes.[93]

In France, 298,839 Turkish citizens were eligible to vote in the 2014 Turkish presidential elections but only 8.4 per cent of them cast their vote. Erdoğan received 66 per cent of Franco-Turkish diaspora votes in this election[94] compared to 51.7 per cent of votes cast in Turkey.[95] For the June 2015 Turkish parliamentary elections, 311,802 French Turks were eligible to vote and their turnout rate rose to 37 per cent. The AKP secured 50.6 per cent of French expatriate votes[96] as opposed to 40.8 per cent of votes cast in the homeland.[97] For the November 2015 Turkish parliamentary elections, 317,997 French Turks were eligible to vote and their turnout rate rose to 44.9 per cent. The AKP received 58.6 per cent of French expatriate votes[98] as opposed to 49.9 per cent of votes cast in the homeland.[99] In the 2017 Turkish constitutional referendum, of the 326,196 eligible voters, 43.7 per cent (142,766 French Turks) voted and 64.8 per cent of Franco-Turkish voters supported the proposed changes[100] compared to 51.4 per cent of Turkish voters.[101] In the 2018 Turkish presidential and parliamentary elections, of the 340,751 eligible French Turks, 47.3 per cent voted. Erdoğan and the AKP received 63.7 per cent and 55.1 per cent of the votes

Table 3.1 Expatriate turnout and voting behaviour in Turkish elections and referenda (France)

Election	Total number of registered voters	Voter turnout (percentage)	Votes cast for AKP/ Erdoğan (percentage)
2014 presidential	298,839	8.4	66
2015 parliamentary (June)	311,802	37	50.6
2015 parliamentary (November)	317,997	44.9	58.6
2017 referendum	326,196	43.7	64.8
2018 parliamentary and presidential	340,751	47.3	55.1 (AKP) 63.7 (Erdoğan)

Sources: Turkish Supreme Electoral Council, *Sabah*, and *Habertürk* election archives: www.ysk.gov.tr/tr/secim-arsivi/2612, www.sabah.com.tr/secim-sonuclari, www.haberturk.com/secim.

respectively, which was higher than the domestic votes for Erdoğan and the AKP (see Table 3.1).[102]

Diyanet *activities*

Turkey's growing diaspora engagement efforts are also evidenced by the increasing number of *Diyanet* religious personnel sent to France, particularly under AKP rule. In 1983, there were around twenty *Diyanet* imams serving in France; between 2003 and 2014, the number rose from approximately eighty to over 150.[103] Furthermore, since the early 2000s, the DİTİB's religious personnel have periodically met with other Turkish Islamic organisations and diplomats.[104]

A DİTİB official revealed that most mosques in France are DİTİB-administered (around 200) and that imams sent from Turkey to France are officially capped at 151 (half of the total number of foreign imams serving in France). He argued that this was a comparatively generous agreement because Algeria and Morocco, despite their deeper historical relations with France and larger emigrant population in the country, were allowed fewer imams[105] than Turkey. He cited this as an indication of how respected the DİTİB is in the eyes of French authorities.[106] The DİTİB in France was also the only Muslim organisation invited to the *Istichara* (consultation) process led by Jean-Pierre Chevènement in 1997, which served as the basis of the CFCM.[107] In addition, the *Diyanet* has engaged in negotiations with French policymakers to open up new religious service attaché positions in France.[108]

More importantly, the *Diyanet* initiated the International Theology Programme in 2006 to provide Islamic education to young diaspora Turks, including those from France, at Turkish theology institutes. The programme, which started at Ankara University, allows students residing in Europe to serve in their host countries as theology professors and imams upon completion of their training.[109] Fully funded by the *Diyanet*, the International Theology Programme signals Turkey's growing influence over the Turkish diaspora in Europe. Since 2010, graduating students have taken up key positions as teachers and religious leaders in their countries of residence. As Benjamin Bruce notes, in doing so, this programme 'constitutes a key component of Turkey's religious diaspora policies and seeks to ensure the continuity of the *Diyanet*'s influence in the transnational religious field while reinforcing home state conceptions of legitimate religious authority'.[110]

As a result of a 'declaration of intent' signed by Ankara and Paris, the *Diyanet* also established the Strasbourg Theology Institute in the Hautepierre district of Strasbourg in 2011. Financed by the Turkish state, the DİTİB in France had the final say in the design of the curriculum and the appointment of teachers.[111] Students who successfully completed this programme received an undergraduate degree from Istanbul University's Faculty of Theology. As a DİTİB official pointed out, this programme's central objective was to train religious personnel for DİTİB mosques who are fluent in Turkish and French and familiar with both cultures. Even though the Strasbourg Theology Institute closed its doors in 2014,[112] it was the most comprehensive theological training project initiated by an Islamic organisation operating on Western soil[113] and, therefore, a testament to Turkey's growing presence in France. The DİTİB five-acre site still exists, functioning as 'the largest Muslim site in Europe'[114] and as a European convention centre where regular workshops for DİTİB personnel from all around Europe take place.

What is more, in 2015, the DİTİB opened a religious high school (*imam hatip lisesi*), named the Lycée Yunus Emre, next to the DİTİB in Hautepierre.[115] Nineteen students graduated from the school in 2018, and it then expected to welcome 152 students given increasing demand from Turkish- as well as North African-origin families.[116] DİTİB officials reported that they were planning to open more theology institutes, kindergartens and private high schools in other parts of France and Europe.[117] In December 2020, the Lycée Yunus Emre also submitted an application for authorisation of a six-year imam-training programme.[118] Despite President Macron's October 2020 vow to limit the influence of foreign countries and adopt a stricter monitoring of schooling and funding of mosques, France has traditionally tolerated Turkey's leverage within its borders to a greater extent than most other western European countries, as analysed in detail in Chapter 6.

YTB activities

The empowerment of Turkish diaspora organisations lies at the heart of Turkey's diaspora agenda. Since the establishment of the YTB in 2010, Turkey has been able to reach out to conservative organisations more efficiently. The YTB regularly visits Turkish diaspora organisations operating in France[119] and runs brainstorming workshops to encourage their participation in French politics.[120] In addition, the institution has launched more than six capacity-development training programmes in Turkey and France.[121] Other training courses encourage civil society leaders to construct collaborative funding bids to French and European authorities and inform them about YTB financial aid programmes.[122] The YTB has also held brainstorming meetings with UID executives[123] and collaborated with the DİTİB in several projects.[124]

In June 2017, on a four-day visit to France, the YTB met seventy-five representatives of Turkish organisations and academics to discuss racism, xenophobia and Islamophobia in Europe.[125] A year later, YTB officials visited Lyon and Strasbourg to strengthen collaborations with Turkish diaspora organisations and to discuss their challenges.[126] In 2018, the YTB Communication Academy was launched as a media network to 'enhance relations with the Turkish diaspora, to combat racism and discrimination and to broadcast the YTB's activities [to] the Turkish diaspora'.[127] Similarly, the Anti-Discrimination Project and the Active Citizenship and Equal Participation Programme help Turkish organisations in France to stand against racism.[128]

Turkish civil society organisations operating in France also receive financial support from the YTB for their projects so that they can 'conduct more effective and professional activities' and 'make significant contributions to "societal development", "public opinion" and "active citizenship" in France'.[129] More than half of YTB funding is earmarked for lobbying, educational and capacity-development activities, with the remaining funds spent on activities related to cultural and family affairs.[130]

Since 2012, active citizenship has also been facilitated through the International Justice Programme,[131] which seeks to educate Turkish jurists living in France about their legal protections.[132] The YTB's legal-awareness activities seek to reach the broader Turkish community in France as well. For example, it published a booklet detailing France's legal system to help raise awareness among French Turks of their legal rights.[133] The institution is involved in other active citizenship projects, such as the Election Information Campaign, which advises Turkish immigrants of their electoral rights in Turkey and France. The campaign is publicised through brochures and posters, social media announcements and regular meetings with

immigrant-organisation leaders.[134] Lastly, the YTB conducts public awareness campaigns on the Armenian issue. In 2015, it published the book
*A Centennial Issue: New Approaches in the Democratisation Process
(1915–2015)* in six different languages to promote the Turkish state's foreign
policy stance regarding the issue.[135]

Political mobilisation of conservative Turkish organisations in France after 2003

As an official from the Turkish Consulate in Paris noted, political developments in both home and host states influence the Turkish diaspora's recent
political activism in France.[136] Uncompromising French opposition to
Turkey's EU membership triggered the first wide-ranging 'political awaken-
ing'.[137] This event prompted a sharp rise in the number of Turkish people
running for office in France.[138] In the 2008 elections, 200 Turkish-origin
French citizens ran in municipal-assembly and vice-mayoral races, and of
these, 107 were elected as councillors.[139] With only four Turks having been
elected to local councils in the 2001 elections, this was an unexpected political development.[140] Today there are 200 Turkish-origin councillors in
France, an increase encouraged by Ankara as it is seen as an opportunity not
only to enhance the integration of Turks in Europe but also to influence
local politics.[141] Since the 2000s, French Turks have also joined both right-
and left-wing political parties to shape national politics.[142]

Another groundbreaking development that led to significant collective
action from conservative Turkish organisations occurred in 2012 when the
French Senate passed a bill criminalising the denial of the 1915 mass killings
of Armenians by Ottoman Turks as genocide. The new bill mandated a
€450,000 fine and a year in jail for genocide deniers.[143] While 96.8 per cent
of French Turks closely followed the developments related to this bill, mainly
via Turkish media, only 3 per cent suggested that the mass killings of Armenians by Ottoman Turks should be recognised as genocide and only 6.9 per
cent concluded that the Turkish state owes Armenians an apology.[144] To
oppose the bill, conservative diaspora groups, including the DİTİB, the *Millî
Görüş*, the Union of Islamic Cultural Centres and the Turkish Federation,
formed the Coordination Council of Franco-Turkish Associations to hold
rallies across France. Secular, Kurdish and Alevi organisations did not accede
to this initiative.

In 2012, the Coordination Council arranged the largest ever collective
demonstration of Turks in France: 35,000 people gathered in Paris with
banners reading 'No to the Shame Law (*Utanç Yasasına Hayır*)'.[145] As one of
the event's masterminds explained, such political commitment and

cooperation among Turkish Islamic organisations was previously unheard of. A year later, France's Constitutional Council annulled the bill.[146] Another architect of this rally asserted that the event was an extension of the Turkish state's efforts to block the influence of Armenian lobby groups in France.[147] As such, it provides evidence of how the Turkish state's national interests in this matter have encouraged activism among the Turkish community in Europe. This demonstration led to the creation of the above-mentioned Union of French-Turkish Cultural Associations in 2012 and the Turkish Community High Council in 2014 – two Turkish umbrella organisations defending Turkish foreign policy interests relating to the 'Armenian' cause.[148]

Also in 2012, the DİTİB, the *Millî Görüş* and the COJEP coordinated another mass political campaign to mobilise the Turkish population in national and local elections in France. The 'Now or Never (*Ya Şimdi Ya Hiç*)' campaign started in Strasbourg and quickly spread to thirty-five French cities. These organisations co-sponsored a video inviting French Turks to turn out to vote and to run for office.[149] In an interview conducted shortly after campaign launch, a COJEP leader stated that 'in the 1960s and 1970s, we [French Turks] had to establish mosque associations to protect our national and religious identity. Today organised political action is the only way.'[150] This campaign evolved into a larger electoral operation that resulted in eight Turks running for mayor (a position superior to local councillor or vice mayor) for the first time, in the 2014 municipal elections.[151] Other electoral campaigns, including 'Do Something Now (*Şimdi Bir Şey Yap*)' and 'Time is Up (*Vakit Doldu*)', have been formed to encourage Turks' participation in local politics. As one of the initiators of these campaigns explained:

> French politicians now approach us [Turks in France] very differently. All the politicians I talk to mention Turkey's increasing power. They all want to visit Turkey. We feel more self-confident recently ... Turkish officials ... encourage us to apply for dual citizenship, participate in French politics and preserve Turkish culture and values. Not long ago, they ignored us completely. This attitude has changed with the AKP. New institutions, such as the YTB, provide us with both moral and financial support. This opens space for joint action.[152]

Another indicator of burgeoning Turkish Muslim politicisation is an increasing interest among Sunni Islamic organisations in the French state's mediation efforts with the Muslim community and their growing role within the CFCM. As stated above, in 1997 Chevènement convened the *Istichara* process, which ultimately led to the establishment of the CFCM in 2003 as a representative body that would create an Islam *of* France as opposed to an Islam *in* France.[153] The institution seeks to facilitate dialogue between French Muslims and state authorities regarding the regulation of Islamic worship and public ritual practices, the allocation of Muslim cemetery spaces, the training and accreditation of imams, halal certification and the construction of mosques.[154] While the French state designates the president and vice president of the CFCM, it is not a party to the CFCM, fulfilling only an observatory role.[155] In addition to its central body, the CFCM consists of the Regional Councils for the Muslim Faith, which also play an important role.[156]

An administrator from the CFCM stated that the institution does not speak for the entire Muslim population but rather gives voice only to observant Muslims and that its proposals and decisions are not binding.[157] The main organisations represented in the CFCM are: (1) the Coordination Committee of Turkish Muslims of France (CCMTF), founded in 2001 and linked to the DİTİB;[158] (2) the *Millî Görüş*; (3) the Algerian-linked National Federation of the Great Mosque of Paris; (4) the pro-Moroccan Assembly of Muslims in France; (5) the Muslim Brotherhood-affiliated Muslims of France (previously the Union of Islamic Organisations of France); (6) the National Federation of Islamic Associations of Africa; and (7) the Tabligh, a transnational South East Asian Islamist movement. According to an agreement signed between the French government and these organisations, each mosque has an electoral weight based on the square footage of their prayer spaces. Depending on how large their space is, mosques nominate grand electors to select two thirds of the CFCM's administrative committee, with the French Ministry of the Interior assigning the remaining spaces.[159]

The early years of the CFCM were characterised by a power struggle between Algerian and Moroccan organisations. Since these groups relied heavily on support from their embassies, foreign states had been involved in the formation of the CFCM. Although, initially, Algerian leaders, backed by the French state, secured more clout in the institution, Moroccan Islam emerged as the new dominant force after the first CFCM elections. Apart from the DİTİB-linked CCMTF, Turkish Islamic organisations were reluctant to engage in communication with the French government in this period. While some French officials considered attributing a role to the *Millî Görüş*, DİTİB leaders and the then Turkish Ambassador to France objected to this plan.[160]

Over time, Turks have begun to play a key role in the CFCM, largely outweighing the number and significance of the Turkish community in France. Particularly after 2007, the DİTİB, the *Millî Görüş* and the Union of Islamic Cultural Centres have sent their representatives to the CFCM's meetings and cooperated with Maghrebi organisations. For example, the *Millî Görüş* formed an alliance with Moroccan groups to secure more seats during CFCM elections.[161] Moreover, former UID and DİTİB affiliate Ahmet Oğraş served as the CFCM's president between 2017 and 2019 and is one of the leaders of Instance de Dialogue avec l'Islam de France, a platform established in 2015 to foster discussions between Muslim leaders and public authorities regarding radicalisation in France.[162] Given that all the previous CFCM leaders were of North African-origin, Oğraş's leadership in the CFCM is crucial.

A *Le Monde* reporter confirmed that, while in the past Algeria and Morocco played a dominant role in the CFCM, Turks are now the most decisive actor despite their smaller numbers. He explained that this is because of Turkey's growing influence in Europe, the increasingly organised nature of the Turkish diaspora, as opposed to the fragmented Maghrebi community, and France's softer stance towards Turks. According to the reporter, 70 per cent of all mosques in France are controlled by Turkey and most Friday sermons (*vaaz*) are delivered by Turkish imams sent by Ankara.[163] A former DİTİB official who was also involved in the CFCM informed me that at least half of Turkish Friday sermons in France are frequented by Arabs because they find their own mosques 'inadequate'. He added that in recent years Ankara has also formed close links with the Muslim Brotherhood-affiliated Muslims of France.[164] This observation is echoed by Samim Akgönül, who argued that 'Non-Turkish Muslim populations, descendants of other Muslim immigrant groups in western Europe and members of Muslim minorities or majorities in the Balkans are also targets of Turkish Islam, while Turkey wants to become the champion of Sunni Islam in Europe.'[165]

The DİTİB, the *Millî Görüş*, the UID, the COJEP and the Turkish Federation have come together on other occasions. In 2018, their joint press release urged the French government to boycott the genocide law and condemned the Coordination Council of Armenian Associations.[166] A representative from the Turkish Federation reported that Turkish diaspora organisations are in the process of forming an all-embracing commission to expedite the Turkish diaspora's lobbying efforts with respect to the Armenian issue.[167] He added that these organisations collaborated once again in 2018 to protest the Paris municipality's decision to allow a march by Kurdish separatists and to support Turkey's fight against Kurdish terrorism in Syria.[168] Some conservative Turkish organisations even criticised certain municipalities in Paris for endorsing Kurdish[169] and Gülenist groups.[170] Most recently, in February 2021, the DİTİB and the *Millî Görüş* refused to sign Macron's ten-point charter proposed to reaffirm Islam's compatibility with French values on the basis that such decisions should be taken after 'a broad, democratic and participatory consultation' and that such top-down impositions would wreak havoc in the Islamic community by undermining trust.[171] The COJEP also confronted the French media's negative coverage of the Turkish state's activities in France.[172]

A DİTİB official in France noted that major shifts in Turkey's diaspora policy have directly affected their political engagement: 'It feels good to have Turkey backing us ... Our people are no longer reluctant to obtain French citizenship. Erdoğan's words encourage us.'[173] Another DİTİB leader agreed:

> Before the 2000s, Turks were an introverted and fragmented community ... Turkey's growing strength has empowered us. Even the way French policy-makers look at us has changed recently. We owe this to the AKP government ... Now Turkish officials get together with civil society leaders. They reassure us by saying: 'You aren't alone.' Our government looks after us. In turn, our position here has strengthened ... Fifteen years ago we were antagonistic towards each other. Today we work together.[174]

According to a third DİTİB leader:

> Turks in France are representatives of Turkey. If Turkey invests in our capacity and skills, both sides win ... The YTB was established with this goal in mind. It aims to boost our resources and gives us direction. It teaches us how to write projects, how to prepare press speeches, how to engage French politicians and how to take action together despite our differences.[175]

A *Millî Görüş* board member in Paris insisted that the homeland's policies have lifted collective Turkish-Muslim spirit and pride in France, and was satisfied with the capacity-building activities designed for them: 'We lean upon Turkey; we are no longer alone ... In diaspora meetings and capacity-development seminars, we discuss how we can reinforce our position in Europe.'[176] Another administrator suggested that YTB officials ask Turkish Muslim organisations to form joint political platforms so that they can speak with one voice while defending Turkish interests in France.[177] Other *Millî Görüş* representatives confirmed that conservative-nationalist and Sunni Islamic organisations no longer see each other as enemies but as allies. For example, the *Diyanet* now sends imams to the *Millî Görüş*'s mosques for a period of two years. The *Millî Görüş* has also floated project partnerships with the YTB and established an umbrella organisation with the DİTİB and the Turkish Federation in Strasbourg and Metz.[178]

Union of Islamic Cultural Centres representatives in France have also discussed partnership opportunities with the YTB and met with other conservative Turkish organisations to embark on joint activities, such as Holy Birth Week celebrations commemorating the birth of Prophet Mohammad. Once unthinkable, such partnerships stress that the 'common consciousness and synergy' created by Turkish diaspora organisations in France is a positive development.[179]

Turkish Muslim leaders in France have even formed their own political parties. The PEJ was founded in Strasbourg in 2015 as the first ever party established by Franco-Turks. The PEJ participated in the Provincial General Assembly elections in the same year but was eliminated in the first round. Party officials noted that they were nonetheless proud of this performance since the party garnered the support of thousands of people in four cities and ten cantons across France within only two months of its foundation. According to its chairperson, the PEJ was established to defend the rights of Muslims experiencing discrimination in France and it reached its current potential with efforts from Turkish associations.[180] According to many critics, the PEJ is an anchor of the AKP as its leaders are actively involved in the COJEP[181] and the AKP seeks to influence Europe and hunt down dissidents in the diasporic space through these actors.[182]

Conclusion

The recent surge in collective political action among conservative Turkish diaspora organisations in France reflects the conscious efforts of Turkish policymakers to empower these organisations in the post-2003 era. Turkey has differentiated its diaspora policies based on the loyalty of organisations within the broader diaspora. An ideologically proximate and loyal diaspora group would be visible and assertive in terms of political action and, therefore, would serve the political interests of the homeland more effectively. Accordingly, the Turkish government has favoured conservative-nationalist and Sunni Islamic diaspora organisations over others, an argument that will be explored further in Chapters 4 and 5.

Turkey's new diaspora policies have bolstered conservative diaspora leaders' self-confidence and collective identity, and enhanced their organisational capacity against the rising backdrop of Islamophobia in France. By presenting select organisations, such as the DİTİB, the *Millî Görüş*, the Turkish Federation and the COJEP, as Turkey's ambassadors and representatives abroad, Turkey's new diaspora policy has initiated a process of 'identity work' and restructured Turkish Muslims' previously marginalised identities. The creation of a common identity and purpose for the diaspora has also helped overseas Turks surmount their past tensions and engage in inter-organisational collaboration. Furthermore, Ankara has empowered conservative Turkish diaspora organisations through the provision of capacity-development and know-how programmes channelled by Turkish institutions. The homeland's projection of collective identity combined with the provision of such support has given rise to diaspora diplomacy in France. Given that around 350,000 French Turks are eligible to vote in Turkish elections, Turkey's new diaspora policy has also sought to attract expatriate votes from France for domestic elections and to extend the reach of the AKP's authority into transnational space.

Notes

1 For more on Erdoğan's address to the Turkish diaspora in Lyon in 2014, see: 'Başbakan Erdoğan Fransa'daki Türklere Seslendi', *Hürriyet*, 21 June 2014, www.hurriyet.com.tr/gundem/basbakan-erdogan-fransadaki-turklere-seslendi-26657828

2 A. Kaya and F. Kentel, *Euro-Türkler*, p. 28; U. Manço, 'La dimension démographique et les caractéristiques sociales et économiques de l'émigration turque en Europe', *Anatoli* 3 (2012), 121–30.

3 S. Bonnafous, 'La presse française et les 'événements immigrés' de 1974 à 1984', *L'Homme et la société* 87:1 (1988), 53–62.

4 M. Poinsot, 'Competition for political legitimacy at local and national levels among young North Africans in France', *Journal of Ethnic and Migration Studies* 20:1 (1993), 79–92.

5 M. Tribalat, *Faire France: Une enquête sur les immigrés et leurs enfants* (Paris: La Découverte, 1995); A. Hargreaves, 'The political mobilisation of the North African immigrant community in France', *Ethnic and Racial Studies* 14:3 (1991), 350–67; A. Hargreaves, *Immigration, Race and Ethnicity in Contemporary France* (London: Routledge, 1995).

6 In February 1980, seventeen illegally employed Turks in textile industries in Paris began a hunger strike seeking legal employment and better working conditions. Apart from the political participation of these individual workers in the protests, no Turkish immigrant organisation participated in the *sans-papiers* movement on a larger scale. See: J. Freedman, 'The French "sans-papiers" movement: An unfinished struggle', in *Migration and Activism in Europe since 1945*, ed. W. Pojmann (Basingstoke: Palgrave Macmillan, 2008), pp. 81–96; E. Yalaz, 'Immigrant Political Incorporation'.

7 S. Akgönül, 'Turks in France: Religion, Identity and Europeanness', in *Turks in Europe: Culture, Identity, Integration*, eds T. Küçükcan and V. Güngör (Amsterdam: Türkevi Research Center, 2009), pp. 35–65; S. Akgönül, *La Turquie 'nouvelle' et les Franco-Turcs: Une interdépendance complexe* (Paris: L'Harmattan, 2020).

8 'France Dedicates First Armenian Genocide Commemorations', *Deutsche Welle*, 29 April 2019, www.dw.com/en/france-dedicates-first-armenian-genocide-commemorations/a-48467494

9 A. Hargreaves, *Multi-ethnic France: Immigration, Politics, Culture and Society* (London: Routledge, 2007); Z. Çıtak, 'Between "Turkish Islam" and "French Islam"'; F. Baskin, 'Turkish women in Alsace: Language maintenance and shift in negotiating integration', in *Turkish Migration, Identity and Integration*, eds İ. Sirkeci, B. D. Şeker and A. Çağlar (London: Transnational Press London,

2015), pp. 77–85; C. Beauchemin, C. Hamel and P. Simon (eds), *Trajectories and Origins*.

10 E. Yalaz, 'Immigrant Political Incorporation'.

11 Interview, ELELE official, Paris, 20 February 2013.

12 'Historique', *ASTU* (2021), www.astu.fr/historique/

13 V. Amiraux, *Acteurs de l'Islam entre Allemagne et Turquie: Parcours militants et expériences religieuses* (Paris: L'Harmattan, 2001).

14 G. Kepel, *Les banlieues de l'Islam: Naissance d'une religion en France* (Paris: Le Seuil, 1987); Interview, ELELE official, Paris, 20 February 2013.

15 C. Wihtol de Wenden, 'Generational change and political participation in French suburbs', *Journal of Ethnic and Migration Studies* 21:1 (1995), 69–78.

16 Interview, Turkish Federation official, Paris, 1 March 2013.

17 S. Akgönül, 'Turkish Islam in Europe'.

18 'Grey Wolves: Far-right Group to Be Banned in France', *BBC*, 3 November 2020, www.bbc.com/news/world-europe-54787028

19 *Ibid.*

20 'France Bans Turkish Ultra-Nationalist Grey Wolves Movement', *Deutsche Welle*, 4 November 2020, www.dw.com/en/france-bans-turkish-ultra-national-ist-grey-wolves-group/a-55503469

21 S. Akgönül, 'Millî Görüş: Institution religieuse minoritaie et nouvement poli-tique transnational', in *Islamismes d'Occident, les voies de la renaissance*, ed. A. Samir (Paris: Lignes de Repères, 2006), pp. 63–89.

22 G. Jonker, *Eine Wellenlange zu Gott: der 'Verband der Islamischen Kulturzen-tren' in Europa* (Bielefeld: Transcript, 2000).

23 T. Lemmen, *Islamische Organisationen in Deutschland* (Bonn: Friedrich Ebert Stiftung, 2000); B. Caymaz, *Les mouvements islamiques turcs à Paris* (Paris: L'Harmattan, 2002).

24 B. Balcı, 'Situating the Gülen Movement in France and in Europe', *Politics, Religion and Society* 19:1 (2018), 69–80.

25 Interview, *Millî Görüş* official, Paris, 17 May 2013.

26 D. Aksel, *Home States*.

27 Interview, *Millî Görüş* official, Paris, 17 May 2013.

28 Interview, *Millî Görüş* official, Paris, 17 January 2019.

29 'Qui sommes-nous?', *Millî Görüş* (2021), https://cimgfrance.fr/qui-sommes-nous/

30 'In Strasbourg the Power of Erdogan Weaves Its Web', *World News Today*, 9 February 2021, www.world-today-news.com/in-strasbourg-the-power-of-erdo-gan-weaves-its-web/; L. Bryant, 'Strasbourg Mosque a Lightning Rod for Broader Turkish–English Tensions,' *Voice of America*, 8 April 2021, www.voanews.com/europe/strasbourg-mosque-lightning-rod-broader-french-turkish-tensions

31 G. Petek-Şalom, 'Les ressortissants turcs en France et l'évolution de leur projet migratoire', *Revue hommes et migrations* 1212 (1998), 14–23; U. Hüküm, G. Petek and D. Gürsoy, *Turcs en France* (Paris: Saint-Pourçain-sur-Sioule, 2007).

32 Interview, ACORT official, Paris, 22 January 2019.

33 C. Wihtol de Wenden, 'Generational change'.
34 Interview, ACORT official, Paris, 12 December 2013.
35 'Who Is the Kurdish Institute?', *Kurdish Institute of Paris* (2021), www.institut-kurde.org/en/info/who-is-the-kurdish-institute-s-1232550990
36 *Ibid.*
37 Interview, ELELE official, Paris, 20 February 2013.
38 Interview, Anatolian Cultural Centre official, Paris, 25 February 2013.
39 Interview, COJEP official, Strasbourg, 16 March 2013.
40 'About Us', *COJEP* (2021), http://cojep.com/about-us/?lang=en
41 Interview, *Le Monde* reporter, Paris, 17 January 2019.
42 A. Yükleyen, *Localising Islam in Europe*.
43 In the 1970s, the *Diyanet* sent temporary religious personnel to Europe for the month of Ramadan. See: İ. Gözaydın, *Diyanet*.
44 DİTİB presidents serve as the counsellor for religious services at Turkish embassies abroad. They hold diplomatic status and receive their salary from the *Diyanet*. Hence, DİTİB presidents have both religious and administrative duties. See: B. Bruce, *Governing Islam Abroad*.
45 Interview, DİTİB official, Paris, 23 May 2013.
46 Interview, DİTİB official, Paris, 23 May 2013; Interview, *Millî Görüş* official, Paris, 15 January 2019.
47 Z. Karagöz, 'The Kurdish diasporic mobilisation in France', *Journal of Mediterranean Knowledge* 2:1 (2017), 79–100.
48 'Qu'est-ce que le Conseil démocratique kurde en France?', CDK-F (2021), https://cdkf.fr/a-propos/
49 B. Baser, 'KOMKAR: The unheard voice in the Kurdish diaspora', in *Dismantling Diasporas: Rethinking the Geographies of Diasporic Identity, Connection and Development*, eds A. Christou and E. Mavroudi (Farnham: Ashgate, 2015), pp. 113–28.
50 *Ibid.*
51 B. Baser, 'The Kurdish diaspora in Europe'.
52 L. Hintz, *Identity Politics Inside Out: National Identity Contestation and Foreign Policy in Turkey* (Oxford: Oxford University Press, 2018), p. 146.
53 D. Koşulu, 'The Alevi quest in Europe through the redefinition of the Alevi movement: Recognition and political participation, a case study of the FUAF in France', in *Muslim Political Participation in Europe*, ed. J. Nielsen (Edinburgh: Edinburgh University Press, 2013), pp. 255–76.
54 Interview, FUAF official, Paris, 9 December 2013.
55 *Ibid.*
56 E. Demir, 'New Religious Sociabilities in Euro-Islam: The Organisational Logics and Recognition Politics of Gülen Movement in France and Germany', *Proceedings of The International Conference on Peaceful Coexistence: Fethullah Gülen's Initiatives for Peace in the Contemporary World* (November 2007), pp. 355–70.
57 J. Irvine, 'Gülen Movement and Turkish integration in Germany', in *Muslim Citizens of the Globalised World: Contributions of the Gülen Movement*, eds R. Hunt and Y. Aslandogan (Somerset: The Light Publication, 2006), p. 59.

58 M. de la Baume and G. Paravicini, '"Sleepless" Nights for Gülen's Supporters in Europe', *Politico*, 24 August 2016, www.politico.eu/article/sleepless-nights-for-fetullah-gulen-supporters-in-europe-erdogan-turkey-coup/

59 B. Balcı, 'Situating the Gülen Movement in France and in Europe'.

60 A. Bonzon, 'How Strong is the Gülen Movement in France?', *Hizmet Movement News Archive*, 20 May 2014, https://hizmetnews.com/12363/strong-gulen-movement-france/#.Xy9eKhMzagS

61 For more information, see: www.plateformedeparis.fr/presentation/

62 Interview, CHP official, Paris, 18 January 2019.

63 'AK Parti'den 7 ülkede temsilcilik', *Anadolu Ajansı*, 29 December 2017, www.aa.com.tr/tr/politika/ak-partiden-7-ulkede-temsilcilik/1017851

64 Interview, ACORT official, Paris, 12 December 2013.

65 Interview, ACORT official, Paris, 22 January 2019.

66 Interview, Turkish-origin municipal councillor, Paris, 10 May 2013.

67 Interview, ACORT official, Paris, 12 December 2013.

68 Interview, Union of Islamic Cultural Centres official, Paris, 1 June 2013.

69 S. Brouard and V. Tiberj, *As French as Everyone? A Survey of French Citizens of Maghrebin, African and Turkish Origin* (Philadelphia: Temple University Press, 2011); Y. Brinbaum, M. Safi and P. Simon, 'Les discriminations en France: entre perception et experience', *INED Documents de Travail 183* (2012), www.ined.fr/fr/publications/document-travail/discriminations-france-perception-experience; E. Yalaz, 'Immigrant Political Incorporation'; Y. Brinbaum, M. Safi and P. Simon, 'Discrimination in France: Between perception and experience', in *Trajectories and Origins: Survey on the Diversity of French Population*, eds C. Beauchemin, C. Hamel and P. Simon (Berlin: Springer, 2018), p. 199.

70 D. Aksel, *Home States*.

71 I. Rigoni, 'Mobilisations, actions et recompositions: migrants de Turquie et réseaux associatifs en France, en Allemagne et en Belgique' (PhD dissertation, Université Paris 8, 2000).

72 B. Şenay, *Beyond Turkey's Borders*.

73 Interview, DİTİB official, Strasbourg, 28 May 2013.

74 Interview, *Millî Görüş* official, Paris, 17 May 2013.

75 Interview, *Millî Görüş* official, Paris, 17 May 2013.

76 Interview, Union of Islamic Cultural Centres official, Paris, 12 December 2013.

77 Interview, DİTİB official, Strasbourg, 23 May 2013.

78 Interview, DİTİB official, Paris, 4 March 2013.

79 Interview, AKP official, Paris, 17 January 2013.

80 Interview, COJEP official, Strasbourg, 16 March 2013.

81 Interview, DİTİB official, Strasbourg, 28 May 2013.

82 'Türk Dernekleri Bir Çatıda Toplanıyor', *Haberler*, 26 March 2012, www.haberler.com/paris-te-turk-kultur-dernekleri-bir-cati-altinda-3480721-haberi/

83 *Ibid.*

84 *Ibid.*

85 Interview, French Ministry of the Interior official, Paris, 11 January 2019.

86 D. Aksel, *Home States*, p. 140.

87 Interview, Anatolian Cultural Centre official, Paris, 21 January 2019.

88 'UETD Fransa Merkezi Paris'te Açıldı', *Anadolu Ajansı*, 1 May 2012, 'www. merhaba.info/article,22097,uetd-fransa-merkezi-paris-te-a-ld-.html

89 Interview, UID official, Paris, 27 March 2013.

90 D. Aksel, *Home States*, p. 145.

91 Interview, CFCM official, Paris, 25 May 2013.

92 'Fransa'daki Türklere Anayasa Değişikliğini Anlattı'.

93 Erdoğan's Strasbourg speech is available at: www.youtube.com/watch?v=1X4_JeCD9no

94 '2014 Cumhurbaşkanlığı Seçimleri Fransa', *Habertürk*, 11 August 2014, www. haberturk.com/secim/secim2014/cumhurbaskanligi-secimi/ilce/yurtdisi-fransa-1123

95 '2014 Cumhurbaşkanlığı Seçimleri', *Habertürk*, 11 August 2014, www.haber-turk.com/secim/secim2014/cumhurbaskanligi-secimi

96 '2015 Haziran Genel Seçimleri Fransa', *Sabah*, 7 June 2015, www.sabah.com.tr/secim/7-haziran-2015-genel-secimleri/fransa-secim-sonuclari?utm_campaign=secim_2015_haziran&utm_source=refresh_other&utm_medium=refresh_other

97 '2015 Haziran Genel Seçimleri', *Sabah*, 7 June 2015, www.sabah.com.tr/secim/7-haziran-2015-genel-secimleri/

98 '2015 Kasım Genel Seçimleri Fransa', *Sabah*, 2 November 2015, www.sabah.com.tr/secim/1-kasim-2015-genel-secimleri/fransa-secim-sonuclari?utm_campaign=secim_2015_kasim&utm_source=menu_ulke&utm_medium=menu_ulke

99 '2015 Kasım Genel Seçimleri', *Sabah*, 2 November 2015, www.sabah.com.tr/secim/1-kasim-2015-genel-secimleri/

100 '2017 Referandum Fransa', *Sabah*, 17 April 2017, www.sabah.com.tr/secim/16-nisan-2017-referandum/fransa-referandum-sonuclari

101 '2017 Referandum', *Sabah*, 17 April 2017, www.sabah.com.tr/secim/16-nisan-2017-referandum/

102 '2018 Cumhurbaşkanlığı Seçimleri Fransa', *Sabah*, 25 April 2018, www.sabah.com.tr/secim/24-haziran-2018-secim-sonuclari/fransa-secim-sonuclari

103 B. Bruce, *Governing Islam Abroad*, p. 412.

104 *Ibid.*, p. 426.

105 According to Benjamin Bruce, there has never been a hard limit for Algerian or Moroccan imams, and financing mosques has been the more controversial issue between the French state and the Maghrebi organisations. See: B. Bruce, *Governing Islam Abroad*.

106 Interview, DİTİB official, Strasbourg, 23 May 2013.

107 Interview, CFCM official, Paris, 25 May 2013.

108 B. Bruce, *Governing Islam Abroad*.

109 Interview, DİTİB official, Strasbourg, 28 May 2013; 'Uluslararası İlahiyat Programı Tanıtım ve Başvuru Kılavuzu', *Diyanet* (2021), https://disiliskiler.diyanet.gov.tr/Documents/U%C4%B0P%20PROGRAM%202020%20ONAYpdf

110 B. Bruce, 'Imams for the diaspora: The Turkish state's International Theology Programme', *Journal of Ethnic and Migration Studies* 46:6 (2020), 1167.

111 Interview, DİTİB official, Strasbourg, 28 May 2013.

112 According to Benjamin Bruce, one of the main reasons why the Strasbourg Theology Institute closed down so quickly and easily was because of the expectation that the International Theology Programme could attract all the students. See: B. Bruce, 'Imams for the diaspora'.

113 Interview, DİTİB official, Strasbourg, 28 May 2013.

114 J. Laurence, *Coping with Defeat: Sunni Islam, Roman Catholicism, and the Modern State* (Princeton: Princeton University Press, 2021), p. 298.

115 D. Aksel, *Home States*, p. 145.

116 'Fransa'da DİTİB'e bağlı açılan Yunus Emre Lisesi ilk mezunlarını verdi', *Artı33*, 5 July 2018, www.arti33.com/fransada-ditibe-bagli-acilan-yunus-emre-lisesi-ilk-mezunlarini-verdi/

117 Interview, DİTİB official, Paris, 12 December 2013.

118 'In Strasbourg the Power of Erdogan Weaves Its Web'.

119 '2012 İdare Faaliyet Raporu', *YTB* (2012), p. 43, www.ytb.gov.tr/kurumsal/faaliyet-raporlari

120 '2014 İdare Faaliyet Raporu', *YTB* (2014), p. 32, www.ytb.gov.tr/kurumsal/faaliyet-raporlari

121 '2013 İdare Faaliyet Raporu', *YTB* (2013), pp. 46–9, www.ytb.gov.tr/kurumsal/faaliyet-raporlari

122 '2014 İdare Faaliyet Raporu', p. 46; 'Fransa Faaliyet Raporu', *YTB* (2015), https://ytb.gov.tr/ytbadmin/assets/uploads/files/FRANSA.pdf;

123 *Ibid.*, p. 33; 'Fransa Faaliyet Raporu'; '2016 İdare Faaliyet Raporu', *YTB* (2016), pp. 31–2, www.ytb.gov.tr/kurumsal/faaliyet-raporlari

124 '2019 İdare Faaliyet Raporu', *YTB* (2019), p. 69, www.ytb.gov.tr/kurumsal/faaliyet-raporlari

125 '2017 İdare Faaliyet Raporu', *YTB* (2017), p. 53, www.ytb.gov.tr/kurumsal/faaliyet-raporlari

126 '2018 İdare Faaliyet Raporu', *YTB* (2018), p. 28, www.ytb.gov.tr/kurumsal/faaliyet-raporlari

127 *Ibid.*, p. 78.

128 'Fransa Faaliyet Raporu', pp. 10–13, 38.

129 *Ibid.*, pp. 56–7.

130 *Ibid.*

131 '2012 İdare Faaliyet Raporu', p. 28.

132 '2015 İdare Faaliyet Raporu', *YTB* (2015), p. 31, www.ytb.gov.tr/kurumsal/faaliyet-raporlari

133 'Fransa Faaliyet Raporu', p. 41.

134 *Ibid.*

135 *Ibid.*, p. 50.

136 Interview, Turkish Consulate official, Paris, 28 January 2019.

137 Interview, ACORT official, Paris, 12 December 2013.

138 Interview, DİTİB official, Strasbourg, 28 May 2013.

139 'Yerel Seçimlerde 130 Türk Aday Var', *Hürriyet*, 22 March 2014, www.hurriyet.com.tr/gundem/yerel-secimlerde-130-turk-aday-var-26061465

140 Interview, Turkish Consulate official, Paris, 28 January 2019.
141 *Ibid.*
142 D. Aksel, *Home States*, p. 145.
143 'Le Parlement adopte la loi sur le génocide arménien', *Le Monde*, 23 January 2012, www.lemonde.fr/europe/article/2012/01/23/lle-parlement-adopte-la-loi-sur-le-genocide-armenien_1633536_3214.html
144 M. Erdoğan, 'Fransa'daki Türkiye Kökenlilerin Güncel Konulardaki Görüş ve Düşüncelerinin Araştırması', *Hacettepe University Migration and Politics Research Center Report* (2012), http://fs.hacettepe.edu.tr/hugo/dosyalar/duyuru_190412.pdf
145 'Turks Stage Mega March in Paris'.
146 'French Genocide Law "Unconstitutional" Rules Court'.
147 Interview, Anatolian Cultural Centre official, Paris, 25 February 2013.
148 Interview, Anatolian Cultural Centre official, Paris, 21 January 2019.
149 This video is available at: www.youtube.com/watch?v=SyYmDu0ydyQ
150 Interview, COJEP official, Strasbourg, 20 April 2012, www.haberler.com/fransa-da-yasayan-turklere-sandik-cagrisi-3554013-haberi/
151 'Yerel Seçimlerde 130 Türk Aday Var'.
152 Interview, COJEP official, Strasbourg, 16 March 2013.
153 B. Godard and S. Taussig, *Les musulmans en France: Courants, institutions, communautés: Un état des lieux* (Paris: Hachette, 2007); B. Bruce, *Governing Islam Abroad*.
154 Interview, CFCM official, Paris, 25 May 2013.
155 *Ibid.*
156 B. Bruce, *Governing Islam Abroad*, p. 129.
157 Interview, CFCM official, Paris, 25 May 2013.
158 DİTİB officials established the CCMTF to show that the DİTİB is an independent organisation with no organic ties to Turkey. Interview, former CCMTF representative in the CFCM, Paris, 4 March 2013.
159 R. Kılınç, *Alien Citizens: The State and Minorities in Turkey and France* (Cambridge: Cambridge University Press, 2019), p. 70.
160 B. Bruce, *Governing Islam Abroad*.
161 Z. Çıtak, 'Between "Turkish Islam" and "French Islam"'.
162 'Instance de dialogue avec l'Islam de France', *French Ministry of the Interior* (2016), www.interieur.gouv.fr/Archives/Archives-des-actualites/2016-Actualites/Instance-de-dialogue-avec-l-Islam-de-France; Interview, French Ministry of Justice official, Paris, 24 January 2019.
163 Interview, *Le Monde* reporter, Paris, 17 January 2019.
164 Interview, former DİTİB and CFCM official, Paris, 4 March 2013.
165 S. Akgönül, 'Turkish Islam in Europe'.
166 Interview, Turkish Consulate official, Paris, 28 January 2019.
167 Interview, Turkish Federation official, Paris, 17 January 2019.
168 *Ibid.*

169 'Fransa'da Türk dernekleri ortak bildiri hazırladı, o senatöre sert tepki gösterdi', *Artı33*, 3 March 2018, www.arti33.com/fransada-turk-dernekleri-ortak-bildiri-hazirladi-o-senatore-sert-tepki-gosterdi/

170 'Fransa'daki Türklerden Fransız belediyesine "FETÖ" tepkisi', *Sabah*, 25 March 2018, www.sabah.com.tr/dunya/ 2018/03/26/fransadaki-turklerden-fransiz-belediyesine-feto-tepkis

171 '3 French Muslim groups reject Islamic charter', *Anadolu Ajansı*, 21 January 2021, www.aa.com.tr/en/europe/3-french-muslim-groups-reject-islamic-charter/2118761

172 A. Nazeef, 'Erdogan's Tentacles'.

173 Interview, DİTİB official, Paris, 14 May 2013.

174 Interview, DİTİB official, Strasbourg, 28 May 2013.

175 *Ibid.*

176 Interview, *Millî Görüş* official, Paris, 17 May 2013.

177 Interview, *Millî Görüş* official, Paris, 19 March 2013.

178 Interview, *Millî Görüş* official, Paris, 15 January 2019.

179 Interview, Union of Islamic Cultural Centres official, Paris, 28 January 2019.

180 'French Muslim Party to Contest By-election', *Anadolu Ajansı*, 14 April 2016, www.aa.com.tr/en/todays-headlines/french-muslim-party-to-contest-by-election/555264

181 A. Esman, 'Europe's Rising Islam-based Political Parties', *The Investigative Project on Terrorism* (2017), www.investigativeproject.org/6038/europe-rising-islam-based-political-parties

182 Y. Mamou, 'Islamisation of Europe'.

4

'The creation of a new Turkey will start in Germany': Turkey's changing relations with its diaspora in Germany

> You are our power outside our country ... For us you are not guest workers.
> You are our strength in foreign countries ... The ballot box is your weapon ...
> The creation of a new Turkey will start in Germany.[1]

Germany admitted its first Turkish immigrant workers in small numbers through private initiatives in the mid-1950s. During these first years, the majority of guest workers – semi-skilled, literate men aged between twenty and thirty-nine from urban parts of Turkey – were based in shipbuilding plants;[2] labourers from rural Anatolia constituted only 17.2 per cent of the Turkish population in Germany. But from the 1960s, the heavy-industry sectors demanded unskilled labour through short-term bilateral guest-worker agreements (*Anwerbeabkommen*).[3] This demographic shift had a long-lasting impact on the socio-economic, religious and political fabric of the Turkish diaspora in Germany. Like France, Germany experienced economic recession in 1973, caused by the oil crisis, and halted labour recruitment from abroad. Despite this, the Turkish population in Germany grew throughout the 1970s. The 1973 family-reunification law allowed dependents of Turkish workers to reunite with their spouses. This period also witnessed a swell in asylum applications from Turkey.[4]

Similar to their counterparts in France, despite their long history in the country, conservative Turkish organisations were largely absent from the political life of Germany until the mid-2000s. Their recent political activism is surprising given that, as in France, Turks constitute the least integrated immigrant community in Germany in terms of employment, language skills, attendance in school, naturalisation and electoral participation and representation.[5] While some Turkey-originated German politicians have gained stronger political representation since the late 1980s, the majority of politicians elected to the Bundestag do not have any links to conservative Turkish organisations.[6] Therefore, non-religious Turkish politicians' growing political clout does not explain the unprecedented political activism of conservative Turkish Muslims over the last two decades.

The groundbreaking political moments in Germany alone cannot explain this transformation either. Turkish Muslim leaders in Germany were relatively silent during the horrendous Neo-Nazi attacks that killed scores of Turks in Berlin, Mülheim, Solingen and Mölln between 1990 and 1996, and the implementation of the contentious 2000 Nationality Act. The Act reformed the old citizenship law (*Reichs- und Staatsangehörigkeitsgesetz*) by introducing three main changes: (1) it reduced the residency requirement for citizenship from fifteen to eight years; (2) it replaced *jus sanguinis* (right of blood) with *jus soli* (right of soil), stipulating that children whose parents were foreigners would acquire automatic German citizenship if born in Germany and if at least one of the parents had lived in Germany for eight years or had held an unlimited residential permit for three years; and (3) the new law introduced the option model (*Optionsmodell*), where, at the age of twenty-three, children obtaining German citizenship through the *jus soli* model would decide which citizenship they preferred to hold. If they failed to choose one nationality, their German nationality would be rescinded.[7] EU and Swiss citizens, and citizens of some Middle Eastern and Latin American countries that do not allow dual citizenship are exempt from this rule.[8] As will be discussed in Chapter 7, although the option model was abolished in 2014, dual citizenship for Turks is still not automatic as certain conditions must be fulfilled.[9] Given the salience of this issue for the Turkish community, conservative Turkish immigrant organisations' disinterest in the citizenship reform process in the 1990s was surprising.[10] In fact, these organisations' leaders voiced their first political claims regarding dual citizenship only after 2010 and organised their largest collective political action as late as 2013.

Turkey's recent diaspora outreach activities in Germany have built greater capacity among conservative diaspora organisations. The growing presence of Turkish diplomats and *Diyanet* personnel in the country, the YTB's financial and know-how support, and diaspora rallies have instilled self-confidence and collective identity in organisation leaders, resolved their collective action problems and strengthened their mobilisation skills. Turkey's engagement with the Turkish community in Germany follows deliberate political goals (such as increasing the political lobbying potential of German Turks in favour of the Turkish government's foreign policy interests and canvassing expatriate votes for Turkish elections). With its large population, the Turkish community's lobbying activities in Germany do not go unnoticed. The AKP channels resources to conservative diaspora organisations in Germany because these organisations are ideologically closer to the incumbent government and thus are more inclined to support AKP interests abroad and in Turkish elections.

This chapter will first present the history of Turkish organisational life in Germany and examine Turkish political mobilisation in the country prior to

2003. The second part of the chapter will explore the role of increased official correspondence with Turkish immigrant organisations, pro-government diaspora rallies and various state institutions' activities and programmes, and diaspora diplomacy activities conducted by conservative-nationalist and Sunni Islamic leaders in Germany.

The history of Turkish organisational life in Germany

During the first three decades of Turkish immigration in Germany, Turkish workers experienced isolation from German society. Since Germany had no integration efforts at that time, most newcomers lacked language skills and Turkish workers lived collectively in immigrant settlements and dormitories (*Heime*), socialising in mosques with minimal contact with locals.[11] German bureaucrats referred to Turks as 'guest workers' (*Gastarbeiter*), 'foreigners' (*Ausländer*) and 'residents' (*Mitbürger*) rather than 'immigrants', to highlight their sojourner status.[12]

Turkish immigrant-organisational life in Germany was marked by class-based claims in the 1960s and 1970s, which later became increasingly ethnic and religious in the 1980s.[13] The first types of organisations founded by German Turks were small labour unions, student organisations and local solidarity networks.[14] In this period, Islam was effectively seen as a 'guest religion' that Germany had no legal obligation to accommodate. Consequently, Germany failed to meet the religious needs of its expanding Turkish population. The *Diyanet* was not sufficiently networked to address the religious concerns of Turkish Muslims either.[15] In the DİTİB's absence, Turks set up temporary prayer rooms and backyard mosques, which later evolved into religious associations.[16] In 1973, the Union of Islamic Cultural Centres became the first religious Turkish organisation founded in Germany. Having turned into a federation in 1983, the organisation is now headquartered in Cologne but has more branches in other cities.[17]

The second Turkish Islamic organisation established in Germany was the *Millî Görüş*. Evolving from an informal network in the early 1970s, the *Millî Görüş* opened its first mosque in the country in 1976.[18] In 1983, Cemalettin Kaplan split from the *Millî Görüş* and founded a revolutionary Islamist organisation named *Kaplancılar*. Although it was very active within and beyond Germany, the organisation broke up into different factions following Kaplan's death in 1995. Six years later, Germany outlawed *Kaplancılar*.[19] In 1995, the *Millî Görüş* obtained its current name, *Islamische Gemeinschaft Millî Görüş*. While the association's main base is in Cologne, it has 340 branches and more than 30,000 followers across Germany.[20]

To respond to the increasing suspicion of Islamic groups in Germany in the post 9/11-era, the *Millî Görüş* strived to separate itself from the *Millî*

Görüş movement in Turkey and embrace a new discourse that emphasised transnational reference to the global *ummah*. The organisation also coordinated activities and programmes relating to Turkish integration in Germany and disseminated a pro-integrationist, cooperative and moderate official message.[21] Despite this reform process, it was included on the Federal Office for the Protection of the Constitution's blacklist.[22] The *Millî Görüş*'s direct link to Turkey and religious activities are still seen as a threat to Germany's democratic and secular regime.[23] For example, the organisation was charged with money laundering and criminal association, and experienced extensive raids in 2009.[24] Although charges were later dropped, the organisation was barred from attending the DIK, a decision challenged by the *Millî Görüş* and other Turkish Muslim organisations.[25] In 2019, a court in Cologne ruled that the *Millî Görüş* had committed tax evasion while arranging pilgrimage trips to Mecca for Turkish Muslims and should be watched carefully.[26] According to a *Millî Görüş* administrator, German officials are aware of the positive changes taking place inside the organisation but they turn a blind eye to them.[27] In the early 1980s, Turkish immigrants also formed two Berlin-based Islamic organisations: the IFB and the TGB. Today the TGB serves as the largest Turkish religious umbrella organisation in Berlin and is tied to the *Millî Görüş*.[28]

The Kurdish exodus to Germany started in the 1960s. While initially Kurds were part of Turkish student or worker associations, they formed their own organisations in the 1970s. Founded in 1978, the KOMKAR is the oldest federative organisation of Kurds in Germany.[29] It emerged from the worker-oriented Kurdish Migrant Association, which had been established in 1974.[30] However, in the early days of Kurdish immigration, Germans perceived Kurds as a subgroup of the Turkish diaspora and paid little attention to their ethno-cultural differences. Kurdish emigrants who left Turkey due to repression and persecution experienced invisibility in Germany: Kurdish stores had to have Turkish names and Kurdish children's names had to be approved by Turkish and German authorities, creating double exclusion.[31] While Kurds experienced deeper marginalisation, the situation was not favourable for Turks, either. Germany's processes of ethnicisation and racialisation socially constructed all emigrants from Turkey, including Alevis, as foreigners rather than immigrants or citizens.[32]

The DİTİB entered the religious field much later than many other Turkish organisations. The first DİTİB was created in Cologne in 1984 with 135 member associations, although it had sent temporary imams to Germany during Ramadan in earlier years.[33] When the DİTİB opened its first branch, it sought to prevent the development of 'heretic' religious organisations, such as the *Millî Görüş*. However, these organisations had far more appeal to the Turkish community than the DİTİB. The DİTİB is the largest Turkish umbrella organisation in Germany: it has 960 mosque associations[34] (out of a total of approximately 2,500 mosques[35]) and nearly 1,100 imams.[36]

Until recently, the DİTİB was an important point of contact and a key partner in religious affairs for German authorities. The organisation received funds from the German government for its counter-extremism and refugee aid programmes,[37] and acted in partnership with Germany in Islamic education in various states (*Länder*).[38] However, as will be explained in subsequent chapters, since the 2017 espionage scandal concerning their personnel, the DİTİB's relations with Germany have soured significantly. The DİTİB once again came under fire in 2018 when its imams allegedly called on congregants to pray for a Turkish military victory against Kurds,[39] organised a military re-enactment presenting Turkish children in combat uniforms as 'martyrs' ready to combat Kurds[40] and inaugurated a mega mosque in Cologne.[41] Although Germany has granted €5.8 million ($6.9 million) to the organisation since 2012, its partnership with the DİTİB halted in 2019.[42] Moreover, the Federal Office for the Protection of the Constitution decided that the activities of the DİTİB should be scrutinised.[43]

The Alevi mobilisation in Germany also intensified in the 1980s.[44] Similar to the process in France, Alevis in Germany had initially been part of various left-wing organisations established by workers and formed their own organisations later. In 1986, German Alevis established cultural associations in Mainz, Frankfurt, Dortmund, Cologne, Hamburg and Berlin. In 1989, they published a declaration that defined the Alevi identity as different from Sunni Islam and called for the recognition of Alevi rights in Turkey and Europe.[45] This declaration precipitated the establishment of the AABF in the same year:[46] with 160 member organisations and 700,000 members, the AABF is the largest Alevi umbrella organisation in Germany.[47] It shares the same approach with the Pir Sultan Association, the largest Alevi umbrella association in Turkey.[48] In addition to the AABF, the Alevi diaspora in Germany has been represented by the Cem Foundation since 1997 and the Ahlal Bayt Alevi Federation in Europe since 2001, two other organisations that do not define Alevism as a religion in its own right but as part of Sunni Islam.[49]

While Alevis' collective political action was gaining speed in the 1980s, ultranationalists affiliated with the MHP and the Grey Wolves also institutionalised: they formed the Turkish Federation in Frankfurt in 1978[50] and the ATİB in Mainz in 1987.[51] The ATİB's founders emphasised as the reasons behind their formation German Turks' transition from temporary to permanent settlement, the discriminatory and divisive attitudes of previous Turkish governments and the top-down and exclusionary practices of German policymakers.[52] Shortly after its creation, the ATİB began to experience violent conflicts with Kurdish diaspora groups.[53] Today the organisation is in command of twenty-four branches across Germany and focuses on

Qur'anic education and the preservation of Turkish identity, culture and language in Europe.[54] There are around 20,000 ultranationalists affiliated with the Grey Wolves on German soil, some of whom have infiltrated German political parties, such as the Christian Democrats.[55] Osmanen Germania also operates as an ultranationalist boxer gang, with 300 members, although, in 2018, the Federal Ministry of the Interior banned the group due to its violent activities and strong connections to the AKP.[56] In November 2020, Germany decided to outlaw the Grey Wolves as well on the basis that it contradicts Germany's constitution and harms societal harmony.[57]

Another prominent Kurdish diaspora organisation, the Federation of Kurdish Associations in Germany (YEK-KOM), opened its doors in 1994 after Germany banned all PKK-affiliated organisations. Street fights between Kurds and Turkish nationalists, vandalism and arson attacks against Turkish buildings as well as pressure exerted by Turkish authorities on the German government led to this ban. PKK-led violence endured in Germany throughout the 1990s and seriously damaged the image of Kurds in the eyes of the German public and policymakers. In 1993, Germany recognised the PKK as a terrorist organisation and, six years later, Turkish intelligence arrested PKK leader Abdullah Öcalan in Kenya, deepening Kurdish–Turkish tensions.[58]

Currently the YEK-KOM is the largest Kurdish organisation in Germany with forty-six branches.[59] In 2014, it changed its name to the Democratic Society of Kurdish People in Germany (NAV-DEM).[60] The Federal Office for the Protection of the Constitution sees the NAV-DEM as the political arm of the PKK and reported that, with its 14,000 followers, the PKK is the most powerful political Kurdish network in Germany. The NAV-DEM focuses on Kurdish identity, politics and culture, and continues to lobby local, national and supranational actors (mainly the EU) for the Kurdish cause. However, its relations with the German state have been turbulent, characterised by raids, detentions and deportations.[61]

Secular Turks have also formed their own associations in Germany. In 1995, the TGD was created in Hamburg as a federation operating at the national level. Today it represents 267 individual associations.[62] The TGD encapsulates the secular TBB, an umbrella organisation founded in Berlin in 1991. The TBB has thirty-seven member associations and eighty-six individual members.[63] Both organisations prioritise the fight against racism and xenophobia, minority rights and the equal participation of emigrants from Turkey in all areas of German life.

The 1990s saw the institutionalisation of the Gülen Movement in the country. Similar to their counterparts in France, Gülen followers in Germany refrained from building mosques and sponsoring Qur'anic education, and opened schools, 'intercultural dialogue' centres and business and women's associations instead.[64] The first Gülen-affiliated institution in Germany, the BIL Learning House, was inaugurated in Stuttgart in 1995 and turned into a private school in 2003.[65] Over the years, the Gülen Movement has established other institutions, such as the Intercultural Dialogue Centre in Munich and the Foundation for Dialogue and Education in Berlin.[66]

By the mid-2000s, the Gülen Movement in Germany had erected more than 100 learning centres and three private high schools. These high schools offered the same curriculum as public college preparatory high schools, with the addition of Turkish as an optional language. Unlike other Islamic organisations, Gülen networks in Germany are loosely organised and decentralised, with each city or town administering its own schools and associations. That said, the Gülen Movement's main media network, *Zaman*, was instrumental in promoting the Movement's activities across Europe from its German headquarters.[67] In 2016, following the aborted coup, many Gülen institutions and *Zaman* closed down.[68] Yet in 2018, the Gülen Movement still had around 100,000 Gülen supporters, 150 learning centres, thirty private high schools and twelve dialogue centres in Germany, many of them funded through private donations.[69]

In addition to diaspora organisations, Turkish political parties have established overseas offices in Germany since the mid-2000s. Even though the CHP began to court migrant worker organisations and hold political campaigns in the country as early as the 1970s,[70] it only opened its first office in 2014.[71] The AKP's first office in Germany came three years later in order to connect with diasporans from Turkey, to mobilise its constituency and political allies in Europe and to combat Gülenists.[72] However, before opening its German branch, the AKP had established Election Coordination Centres in 2014 to encourage voting through traditional campaigning methods.[73] Since the 2000s, the HDP and the MHP have opened offices in Germany as well.[74]

Political mobilisation of conservative Turkish organisations in Germany before 2003

In the first few decades of emigration from Turkey to Germany, most diaspora organisations focused on religious services and/or homeland-oriented political activities. For example, while some AABF political activities focused on debates on the provision of mandatory religious education in German public schools, much AABF activism was aimed at Ankara, such as its claim for the constitutional recognition of Alevism and against the *Diyanet* freezing the appointment of Alevi socio-religious leaders (*dedes*) to Europe.[75]

By the same token, critical junctures and key political developments in Turkey triggered mass protests by the Kurdish diaspora in Germany. Various diaspora groups came together systematically to condemn the violation of Kurdish rights in the homeland. The march that took place in Bonn in the 1990s was one the largest demonstrations ever held by the Kurdish diaspora: eight different Kurdish organisations, including PKK sympathisers, organised the march.[76] Also in the 1990s, Kurds plotted a series of protests against Turkey following the capture of PKK leader Öcalan by Turkish authorities. As discussed previously, in this period German authorities defined Kurds as 'Turks' and blocked their mobilisation channels. For this reason, in addition to combating discrimination and xenophobia, Kurds were struggling to gain ethno-cultural recognition in the country.[77]

The secular TGD distinguished itself from other organisations from Turkey by engaging more in activities directed at Germany:[78] it organised press releases and public conferences to advocate for the replacement of the German policy on foreigners with a policy of equality and dual citizenship for Turks.[79] However, homeland-related developments significantly influenced the TGD's mobilisation. The organisation's constitution stressed that most TGD members were Turkey-originated citizens of Germany and demanded further protection and support from the German state 'as a cultural minority'.[80] TGD leaders declared that the association's central goal was to form 'better communication between the German and Turkish nation by supporting a cultural exchange, youth welfare as well as education and occupational training'.[81]

The DİTİB, on the other hand, initially immersed itself in religious service by covering three aspects of Islamic religiosity: *ibadet* (rite), *itikat* (religious belief) and *ahlak* (morality). Its political activities were mostly marginal as the organisation 'did not initially formulate a political catalogue of demands directed to the German public'.[82] While 9/11 was a turning point that propelled the organisation's participation in politics, its mobilisation did not go beyond press statements that denounced terrorist attacks carried out in the name of Islam.[83] Similar to the DİTİB, the Union of Islamic Cultural Centres and the ATİB restricted their activities to the religious realm.[84]

Unlike these organisations, the *Millî Görüş* was politically active in the pre-2003 era. The deep connection between the *Millî Görüş* in Germany and in Turkey necessitated the organisation's heavy involvement in homeland-related political activities seeking the reorganisation of the political order in Turkey along Islamic lines. For example, one of its most significant mass demonstrations took place in 1997 in response to the closure of religious preacher schools in Turkey.[85]

A paralysing disharmony within the conservative Turkish community was also responsible for limiting Turkish organisations' participation in

German politics in the past. Two examples are telling: in 1978, several Turkish Muslim organisations, including the *Millî Görüş* and the Union of Islamic Cultural Centres, formed a temporary alliance to apply for the provision of Islamic education in North Rhine-Westphalia. Yet these conservative organisations could not agree on the curriculum and the project failed.[86] A second defining event happened in 1988 when the DİTİB, the *Millî Görüş* and the Union of Islamic Cultural Centres came together with other influential local Muslim organisations to lobby for Islamic education. Yet within five years, their platform had collapsed completely.[87] The de facto dominance of the DİTİB in the Turkish transnational landscape was one of the factors fragmenting inter-organisational cooperation.[88] Other Islamic organisations needed to work with the DİTİB to create unity in the Turkish organisational field. However, the interests of the DİTİB contrasted with those of other conservative diaspora groups.

The institutionalisation of hierarchical relations between the German government and immigrant organisations further suppressed political activism among German Turks. Turkish immigrant organisations had very limited independent representation at parliamentary committee meetings. For example, they were not even invited to the 1999 Hearing of Experts during the 2000 German citizenship reform process.[89] Many observers have argued that the implementation of the 2000 reform did not improve Turks' integration prospects. The German citizenship regime remained replete with 'material and symbolic barriers', onerous naturalisation tests and a prevailing mistrust of Muslims.[90] By viewing emigrants from Turkey as 'migrant workers' until the 1980s, 'Turks' until the 1990s and 'Muslims' today, Germany has undermined the self-esteem and political potential of this community.[91] Put differently, Turkish organisations' internal problems and Germany's institutional, legal and discursive barriers have shattered German Turks' self-confidence, collective identity and organisational capacity and, therefore, hindered their collective political engagement for some time.

Turkish governments also fell short in developing a robust policy towards Turks in Germany until the 2000s. Two officials from the Turkish Embassy[92] and Consulate[93] in Berlin explained that, before 2003, Turkish diplomats remained at arm's length from Islamic organisations as they were seen as a threat to the secular state. This is no longer the case. As discussed further below, a *Diyanet* representative also indicated that, in the post-2003 era, once frosty relations between the Turkish government and conservative immigrant organisations in Germany have blossomed due to the *Diyanet*'s willingness to dispatch imams to different Islamic organisations.[94]

A *Millî Görüş* delegate attributed the recent reconciliation process of religious Turkish organisations to the AKP's electoral victory in 2002: 'In the past, even if we wanted to work together with other organisations, this was not possible ... The AKP is not taking any sides. It says: "We are in favour of brotherhood". They are promoting our cooperation in the field.'[95] In a similar vein, Union of Islamic Cultural Centres leaders linked conservative immigrant organisations' growing collective political activism to the AKP's rise to power in 2002.[96]

Ultranationalist ATİB officials also suggested that the YTB's support for Turkish diaspora organisations has played a key role in their empowerment: 'Our name was on European diplomats' blacklist in the 1980s and 1990s. But now we are treated with respect ... Turkey has changed a lot since 2002. Today it is much more self-confident. So are we.'[97] Another ATİB adminis-trator proclaimed: 'There was a vacuum in the organisational field until the 2000s. We were in a cocoon. But then the AKP looked out for us ... We left our cocoon ... Our mosques represent the Turkish state. We are a big, influ-ential lobby group. It does not matter if Turkey joins the EU. We [the Turkish diaspora] are already in the EU.'[98]

Turkey's diaspora engagement activities in Germany in the post-2003 era

Increased official correspondence and diaspora rallies

Since 2003, Turkish diplomatic personnel in Germany have become increas-ingly involved in the organisational life of Turks in Germany. As summarised in Chapter 2, one of the most concrete indicators of this policy change was the issuing of two directives by the Turkish Ministry of Foreign Affairs in 2003 that mandated Turkish bureaucrats serving in Europe to support and collaborate with Islamic organisations that were seen in the past as harmful to the secular Turkish state. These directives shook the de facto dominance of the DİTİB and thawed the ice between Turkish diplomats and Turkish Muslim leaders in Germany. The creation of the UID also initiated a process of rapprochement among conservative Turkish organisations.

Since the early 2000s, representatives of the DİTİB, the *Millî Görüş*, the Union of Islamic Cultural Centres, the ATİB and the UID have come together on many occasions. The increased correspondence between Turkish bureau-crats and these organisations reflects Turkey's increasing interest in its diaspora. For example, in 2014 and 2015, YTB officials met with Turkish citizens in Heidelberg, Mannheim, Cologne and Dortmund, accompanied by Turkey's then vice prime minister. During these official trips, AKP depu-ties and ministers also visited Turkish mosques that had been attacked by Neo-Nazi groups, including the Mevlana Mosque in Berlin and the Yunus Emre Mosque in Mannheim, to emphasise that 'Turkish Muslims living in Germany are not alone'.[99]

Another effective way to reach out to Turkey's diasporas in Germany is through massive rallies. In 2008, 20,000 individuals attended a rally at Cologne's Lanxess Arena to hear Erdoğan address the gathering. The rally was not part of Erdoğan's official visit to Germany but was run by the UID as a private event. Three years later, at a rally in Düsseldorf with 10,000 Turks, Erdoğan exclaimed:

> Turkey is proud of you! I am here to feel your yearning with you, I am here to enquire about your welfare. I am here to show that you are not alone! ... They call you guest workers, foreigners or German Turks. It doesn't matter what they all call you: You are my fellow citizens, you are my people, you are my friends. You are my brothers and sisters! You are part of Germany, but you are also part of our great Turkey.[100]

In his speech, Erdoğan urged Merkel to drop her opposition to Turkey's accession to the EU. He repeated the point that German language was key to Turkish integration: 'I want you and your children to learn German. They must study and obtain their master's degrees. I want you to become doctors, professors and politicians in Germany.'[101] He also lauded the AKP's specific accomplishments in diaspora affairs, such as the introduction of the Blue Card programme.[102] This speech was integral to electoral campaigning for the June 2011 Turkish general election. The rally sought to attract indirect electoral support since at that time Euro-Turks were still required to travel to Turkey in order to vote in Turkish elections. However, the main motivation for the rally was to 'foster a dialogue of inclusion and a sense of extra-territorial citizenship, and generally maintain a Turkish identity among citizens and heritage members abroad' since diaspora Turks have the power to 'facilitate the access of Turkish business to Europe, provide grassroot support for Turkey's accession to the EU, and send considerable financial transfers and investments back to Turkey'.[103]

Later, Erdoğan held other diaspora rallies in Germany. Prior to the August 2014 presidential elections, the UID attracted 4,000 supporters to Berlin's Tempodrom:

> I thank all our brothers and sisters, all our citizens who filled this big stadium in Berlin today. I thank [you] for your love, for your loyalty (*ahde vefa*), for your affection. I once again brought you the greetings of your siblings and relatives back in Turkey ... I know that you are following your homeland from here day by day. Turkey is safe. Turkey is secure. Turkey is developing exponentially and peacefully, and marching towards 2023 [the Republic's centennial] ... We asked German authorities to extend dual citizenship rights to Turks. We initiated a dialogue with the EU on visa liberalisation. Don't cut your ties to Turkey. Don't let our youth to turn their back to our religion and roots.[104]

Most rally attendees were followers of conservative Turkish immigrant organisations.[105] Some of my respondents noted that these organisations are key drivers of attendance at such rallies, chartering buses and providing free meals.[106] Erdoğan's declaration that Turkish expatriates constitute an intrinsic part of the Turkish nation marks a drastic change from the rhetoric of the past and resonates well with a significant segment of the Turkish diaspora. His political discourse, charismatic leadership and references to 'a powerful Turkey' embody and reflect the emotions, needs and desires of Turkish expatriates in Europe who have been grappling with exclusion for decades.[107] A Turkish immigrant-organisation leader reported that Erdoğan referred to him and other diaspora representatives as 'raiders' (akıncılar) in a meeting held in Germany.[108] When asked by journalists to explain Erdoğan's appeal, other rally participants argued that he was a source of pride for them. For example, one 2011 Düsseldorf rally-goer affirmed Erdoğan's image as a champion of diaspora Turks' welfare: 'Germany will never accept us, but we have Erdoğan.' Another added: 'at last someone feels responsible for us; for the first time a Turkish Prime Minister [president] isn't forgetting his compatriots abroad'.[109]

Erdoğan assembled more rallies in Germany than in any other European country. Two factors prompted this: first, German Turks are a stronger lobby group than other segments of the Turkish diaspora due to their large population base. Accordingly, Erdoğan's government desires that they advocate for Turkey's interests in Europe. Second, Turks living in Germany are a vital voter base in Turkish domestic elections. Germany is the fourth largest constituency after Istanbul, Ankara and Izmir and, therefore, is the country where the AKP mobilises Turkish voters ahead of Turkish elections most visibly. In addition to the UID, the Election Coordination Centres serve as an important arm of the AKP's extraterritorial organisational structure.[110]

In Germany, 1,383,042 Turkish citizens were eligible to vote in the 2014 Turkish presidential elections but only 8.2 per cent of them cast their vote, with Erdoğan receiving 68.6 per cent of the German expatriate votes[111] compared to 51.7 per cent of the votes cast in Turkey.[112] In the June 2015 Turkish parliamentary elections, 1,405,015 German Turks were eligible to cast their vote and the turnout rate rose to 34.3 per cent, with the AKP garnering 53.6 per cent of the votes in Germany[113] compared to 40.8 per cent of the votes in Turkey.[114] In the November 2015 Turkish parliamentary elections, 1,411,198 German Turks were eligible to cast their vote and the turnout rate rose to 40.7 per cent, with the AKP receiving 59.7 per cent of the votes in Germany[115] compared to 49.9 per cent of the votes in Turkey.[116] In the 2017 Turkish constitutional referendum, of the 1,429,492 eligible Turkish voters in Germany, 46.2 per cent voted and 63 per cent supported the constitutional changes[117] as opposed to 51.4 per cent of the population in

Table 4.1 Expatriate turnout and voting behaviour in Turkish elections and referenda (Germany)

Election	Total number of registered voters	Voter turnout (percentage)	Votes cast for AKP/ Erdoğan (percentage)
2014 presidential	1,383,042	8.2	68.6
2015 parliamentary (June)	1,405,015	34.3	53.6
2015 parliamentary (November)	1,411,198	40.7	59.7
2017 referendum	1,429,492	46.2	63
2018 parliamentary and presidential	1,443,585	45.7	55.7 (AKP) 64.8 (Erdoğan)

Sources: Turkish Supreme Electoral Council, *Sabah* and *Habertürk* election archives: www.ysk.gov.tr/tr/secim-arsivi/2612, www.sabah.com.tr/secim-sonuclari, www. haberturk.com/secim.

Turkey.[118] Finally, in the 2018 Turkish presidential and parliamentary elections, of the eligible 1,443,585 German Turks, 45.7 per cent participated in the elections, with Erdoğan and the AKP receiving 64.8 per cent and 55.7 per cent of German Turkish votes respectively.[119] Turkish voters' support for Erdoğan and the AKP back in the homeland was only 52.6 per cent and 42.6 per cent respectively (see Table 4.1).[120]

Diyanet *activities*

The *Diyanet*'s largest body of overseas personnel resides in Germany.[121] In the past, long-term *Diyanet* personnel stayed in Germany for a maximum period of four years, and this increased to five years in 2002.[122] The number of long-term *Diyanet* personnel has also climbed rapidly since the AKP's rise to power: there were around 150 religious personnel serving in Germany in 1983, 480 in 2002 and more than 800 by 2014.[123] In addition, the *Diyanet* has begun to collaborate with the Goethe Institute in Turkey to familiarise its imams with German language and culture before the start of their tenure in Germany. Up to sixty *Diyanet* imams now take 'integration' courses at the Goethe Institute each year.[124]

Over the last two decades, the *Diyanet*'s religious counsellors and attachés have met more frequently with bureaucrats from the Turkish Ministry of Foreign Affairs and the TBMM, and almost every month, high-ranking AKP deputies attend DİTİB mosques and events. Recent years have also brought increasing dialogue between the *Diyanet* and other religious organisations[125] and improved mobilisation efforts on the part of the *Diyanet* to boost Turkish diaspora participation in homeland elections. Since 2014, *Diyanet* imams have helped staff at Turkish voting booths although some of them have been criticised for their discriminatory behaviour towards individuals supporting opposition parties.[126]

The *Diyanet*'s activities in Germany expanded when it endowed two Islamic theology professorships at Goethe University Frankfurt in 2004. Professors teaching at this university are sent from Turkey, and students registered in this programme visit Turkey during the academic year to attend lectures taught by Turkish theology professors in Istanbul.[127] Since 2010, Islamic centres have been established in Münster, Frankfurt, Osnabrück, Tübingen and Erlangen-Nuremberg to train academics in Islamic theology.[128] However, unlike the situation in France, the entire funding for these programmes comes from Germany.[129] In fact, the German government has excluded the DİTİB from these programmes and added its own local imam civic-training programmes in Munich, Berlin, Frankfurt and Stuttgart.[130] In 2019, Germany proposed a new law that would require Turkish imams to learn German[131] and launched another pilot project at the University of Osnabrück to train local imams, with start-up funding from the Federal Ministry of the Interior.[132]

While Turkey's involvement in the theology institutes in Germany is minimal, the *Diyanet* has gained some leverage on European soil through the International Theology Programme, as discussed in the previous chapter. However, as a DİTİB official asserted, Germany is reluctant to appoint this programme's graduates as teachers of religious education in public schools even though there is an urgent need for teachers who can speak both Turkish and German. According to this official, German policymakers think that graduates of their own theology institutes would make better candidates for these positions.[133] The *Diyanet*'s International Theology Programme has grown since its establishment and now trains around 600–700 students from fifteen different countries, most of whom come from Europe.[134] German Turks form the largest group and constitute roughly half of the enrolled students in any given year.[135]

YTB activities

Active citizenship is the most important issue for the YTB. The institution launched the Civil Society Workshops as a flagship activity to empower the leaders of diaspora organisations and facilitate their participation in

Germany's economic and political life. Brainstorming workshops held in both Germany and Turkey act as another important activity to foster civic engagement among German Turks. In 2019, Erdoğan and YTB officials met with the representatives of Turkish diaspora organisations in Berlin for similar purposes.[136]

The YTB is active on media fronts, too. In 2016, the Western Europe Local Media Workshop in Frankfurt sought to identify the weaknesses of the Turkish diaspora's media channels.[137] Similarly, the YTB Communication Academy brought together Turkish-origin academics, journalists and experts in 2019 to generate 'a strong media and strong diaspora' awareness.[138]

Between 2011 and 2014, Turkish civil society organisations in Germany submitted 296 project applications to the YTB, which provided financial assistance to 113 projects (38 per cent).[139] The YTB granted this financial assistance to diaspora organisations so that they could 'conduct more effective and professional activities, and make significant contributions to "societal development", "public opinion" and "active citizenship"',[140] and 78 per cent of YTB support went to lobbying, educational and capacity-development activities.[141] Furthermore, the YTB holds systematic meetings with representatives of civil society organisations to inform them of funding opportunities[142] and has run other special empowerment programmes aimed at DİTİB leaders.[143]

The AKP also promotes the active citizenship of Turkish Muslim leaders: the International Justice Programme aims to educate Turkish citizens living in Germany about their legal rights through 'justice seminars', and the Fight against Discrimination Project seeks to equip Turkish Muslim leaders with the necessary tools to combat Islamophobia and to publish reports that document the extent of discrimination German Turks face.[144] Moreover, the YTB has initiated Consultation Meetings (*İstişare Toplantıları*) for Turkish expatriates in Germany to discuss anti-discrimination, human rights, racism and Islamophobia with them.[145] In one such meeting, held in Munich in 2017, representatives of Turkish diaspora organisations met with prominent Turkish politicians, including Binali Yıldırım, Turkey's then prime minister.[146]

The YTB has initiated public awareness campaigns as well to boost German Turks' participation in elections. Its Election Information Campaign informed German Turks of their electoral rights in Turkey and Germany. A related project based in Hamburg in 2015 sought to encourage the political participation of 90,000 Turkish German residents in local council elections.[147]

Finally, the YTB strives to improve Turkish diaspora organisations' lobbying capacity surrounding the Armenian issue. In 2015, as noted in the previous chapter, the YTB published a book to 'enlighten the Turkish and

German society regarding the Armenian issue in the most accurate manner'.[148] The book was distributed to German universities, public libraries and civil society organisations.[149]

Political mobilisation of conservative Turkish organisations in Germany after 2003

As in France, Turkish Muslim leaders' political activism in Germany has grown spectacularly from 2003 onwards. An early sign of the changing political behaviour of conservative organisations came in 2004 when they entered the headscarf debate by organising a demonstration.[150] Afterwards, Turkish Muslims held public forums and public hearings in state parliaments, issued press statements and conducted lobbying activities to oppose the headscarf ban. Although only five years had passed between the 1999 Nationality Act debate and the headscarf disagreement, Turkish immigrant organisations' claims-making throughout the latter was substantially higher than their claims-making in the former.[151]

In 2006, the German government formed the DIK under the leadership of Wolfgang Schäuble, the former Federal Minister of the Interior, who sought to institutionalise dialogue between the German state, Sunnis and Alevis at national level.[152] Today in the DIK, Turkish Muslims are represented by the DİTİB, the Union of Islamic Cultural Centres, the AABF, the TGD, the *Millî Görüş*[153] and the Central Council of Muslims in Germany (ZMD). In addition, influential individuals not affiliated with any immigrant organisations are invited to the DIK.[154]

The establishment of the Coordination Council of Muslims in Germany (KRM) in 2007 is another example of conservative Turkish organisations' political activism. The DİTİB, the *Millî Görüş*, the Union of Islamic Cultural Centres and the ZMD[155] joined forces to establish the KRM as an umbrella organisation that would speak with one voice when negotiating with policymakers on important issues affecting Muslims. This was a remarkable achievement for the Turkish Muslim community despite the ethnic divisions within these organisations that have made decision-making difficult.[156]

Following the formation of the Christian Democrat–Liberal coalition in 2009, Germany's incoming Minister of the Interior, Thomas de Maizière, commenced the second phase of the DIK (2010–13) and announced three major areas of focus: (1) the promotion of institutionalised cooperation between the state and Muslims; (2) gender equality as a common value; and (3) the prevention of extremism, radicalisation and social polarisation.[157] The third legislative period (2013–17) emphasised new areas, including pastoral care in public facilities, Islamic welfare provision and the training of Muslim and Alevi clerics.[158] The DIK is currently in its fourth phase (2018–present) and focuses on integration, Islam and German law.[159]

In order to secure further recognition, in 2011 the DİTİB initiated the Muslim Community Registry (*Müslüman Cemaat Kütüğü*) campaign to count and list the members of the Turkish Muslim community in Germany.[160] As Chapter 7 will explain, to achieve the status of a corporation under public law (*Körperschaft des öffentlichen Rechts*), which extends certain subsidies and privileges to Christian, Jewish, Baha'i, Ahmadiyya and Alevi communities, Islamic organisations must reach a high threshold of followers. The Muslim Registry Campaign's main goal was thus to prove that the Turkish Muslim population in Germany is sufficiently large.[161]

Turkish Muslims' political activity surrounding citizenship also changed in the mid-2000s. While conservative-organisation leaders had mostly ignored the earlier citizenship debates, some began to voice political claims regarding dual citizenship after 2010. In March 2012, the TGB initiated a signature campaign that called for the government to grant dual citizenship to Turks.[162] The *Millî Görüş* and the DİTİB joined the campaign and collected 40,000 signatures in Berlin, which were later submitted to political parties.[163] Months later, the *Millî Görüş*, the DİTİB and the ATİB launched another signature campaign, 'Do Not Meddle with Our Language (*Türkçemize Karışma*)', advocating for the instruction of Turkish language as an optional language course in public schools.[164]

The largest collective political action led by conservative Turkish organisations in Germany came right before the September 2013 federal elections.[165] The *Millî Görüş*, the DİTİB, the Union of Islamic Cultural Centres, the ATİB and the TGB initiated the nationwide 'Go to the Ballot Box (*Sandığa Git*)' campaign.[166] This represented the first major effort by conservative diaspora groups to enhance electoral participation among Turks in Germany. They launched a media campaign, distributed booklets and arranged seminars and workshops on how to vote. They also issued a manifesto calling for: (1) the preservation of Turkish language and the promotion of bilingualism; (2) stronger Turkish opposition against discrimination and Islamophobia; (3) the cancellation of the German language test required for Turkish immigrants' family reunification; (4) the abolition of the option model for Turkish nationals; (5) the extension of the status of corporation under public law to Turkish Islamic organisations; (6) the promotion of multiculturalism; and (7) the acceleration of accession negotiations between Turkey and the EU.[167]

Anti-discrimination is another important action area for conservative Turkish organisations. In 2015, the *Millî Görüş* and the ATİB challenged the Patriotic Europeans against the Islamisation of the Occident (PEGIDA) movement and criticised populist German politicians and the media for encouraging these anti-immigrant groups.[168] They also protested in Cologne in 2019 to condemn the murder of eight Turks by the Neo-Nazi National Socialist Underground (NSU).[169] In the same year, officials from the major Turkish Islamic associations met with the German president, Frank-Walter Steinmeier, to express their concern about rising hate crimes and mosque attacks in Germany.[170] In 2020, the UID and the *Millî Görüş* once again came together with hundreds of thousands of Turks to protest against the armed assaults that killed four Turks at a café in Hanau.[171] My interviews with individuals representing the DİTİB,[172] the *Millî Görüş*,[173] the ATİB[174] and the TGB[175] also revealed that Turkish Muslim leaders are worried about systematic racism and Islamophobia in Germany, and German authorities favouring anti-AKP immigrant organisations. For them, this explains the increasing rapprochement between Ankara and Turkish Muslims.

Conservative organisations have worked to defend Turkey's national interests concerning the Armenian issue as well. In 2015, the *Millî Görüş*, the DİTİB, the TGB, the Union of Islamic Cultural Centres and the UID held a joint press conference to announce their challenge against a German parliamentary motion that labelled the 1915 mass killings of Ottoman Armenians as 'genocide'.[176] Together, these organisations initiated the 'Peace and Friendship March against Genocide Allegations (*Soykırım İftiralarına Karşı Barış ve Dostluk Buluşması*)' in Cologne.[177] A similar demonstration took place a year later just before the resolution passed almost unanimously in the Bundestag.[178]

A DİTİB leader in Germany suggested that this unprecedented rapprochement among conservative organisations was a promising development.[179] Others noted that their recent collective mobilisation was a reflection of Ankara's support: as one DİTİB administrator in Berlin remarked, 'economic and political changes in Turkey have had tremendous repercussions for us. Finally, we can proudly declare that we are Turkish. Our self-esteem has increased.'[180] Another added: 'Erdoğan's rally messages are very supportive and constructive. They unite us. In the past, we used to bow our heads. We were weak. His messages gave us power ... His firm stance ... gave us group consciousness ... Another important development is the YTB's support. They help us draft project proposals, so we are more successful with funding applications.'[181]

Millî Görüş representatives in Germany also feel newly empowered:

> Developments in Turkey directly influence the organisational landscape here ... We receive both moral and financial assistance [from Turkey] ... We are no longer alone ... Our activities and projects are now far more geared towards political participation and collective action. For example, we held an extensive

election campaign with other Turkish organisations, including the DİTİB and the Union of Islamic Cultural Centres, for the 2013 German federal elections. We showed local authorities that we are a powerful group.[182]

Another official surprisingly concluded that the *Millî Görüş* might even be disbanded in the future for the sake of common ideals.[183] *Millî Görüş* leaders also attributed conservative organisations' recent reconciliation and empowerment process to the efforts of the AKP government: 'In the past, even if we wanted to work together with other organisations, this was not possible ... The AKP doesn't take sides. It says: "We support brotherhood". They promote our cooperation.'[184] A third representative praised the YTB's support of their projects and added that 'when Erdoğan visits us in Berlin, we feel very happy, protected and motivated, especially against the back-drop of the rise of racism and Islamophobia in Europe'. He also maintained that conservative Turkish organisations' diaspora diplomacy has occurred only recently, coinciding with the AKP's rise to power and its inclusive atti-tude towards conservative immigrant organisations.[185] The *Millî Görüş*'s partnership with the AKP became evident again with the election of Mustafa Yeneroğlu, the organisation's former chairperson in Germany, as an AKP deputy in 2015.[186] However, Yeneroğlu's resignation in 2019 signals that the *Millî Görüş* remains a separate entity despite its rapprochement with the AKP and the DİTİB.[187]

Like their counterparts in France, Union of Islamic Cultural Centres rep-resentatives in Germany concurred with other Muslim leaders that Turkey's new diaspora policy had paved the way for heightened collaboration among Turkish Muslim organisations and improved their capacity to act together: 'Before the 2000s, Turkish Muslim leaders from different organisations did not even say hi to each other. Now we co-organise *iftar* dinners during Ramadan. We campaign together. We lobby together.'[188] Another declared: 'we no longer feel vulnerable'.[189]

The formation of political parties by German Turks with close links to the AKP is another indication of Turkey's diaspora diplomacy in Germany. The BIG – a local party established in Cologne in 2010 with the slogan 'We Are Germany'[190] – became the first 'Turkish' party in Germany. It advocates for access to education in Turkish, dual citizenship, the fight against Islam-ophobia and the preservation of ethnic and cultural identity and family val-ues. While the BIG's emphasis on Muslim immigrants attracts criticism for reinforcing their marginalisation, its founder claimed that, to the contrary, their goal is to improve immigrant integration in Germany by placing exist-ing parties under duress.[191] Since its establishment, the BIG has had limited impact in the regional elections in North Rhine-Westphalia, and it won only 17,000 votes in the 2013 federal elections.[192] While the party decided not to run in the 2017 federal elections as a protest against the anti-Turkish and populist political atmosphere, it did open branches in forty cities across Germany and mobilised for the 2019 European Parliament elections and the 2020 regional elections. The BIG's leader has strong aspirations: within eight years, the party seeks to have representatives in six state parliaments as well as in the Bundestag.[193]

A similar party, the ADD, was created in 2016 in response to the Bundestag's controversial motion that described the deaths of Ottoman Armenians in 1915 as genocide. The ADD's founder said that the motion turned a blind eye to the Turkish population's feelings: 'None of the eleven ethnic Turkish lawmakers from the mainstream parties opposed this motion. Just for the sake of their political career, they wouldn't dare to contradict their party line … After all that, we have said "enough is enough" and decided to found our party.'[194] The ADD won 14,000 votes in the 2017 regional elections in North Rhine-Westphalia.[195] The party used images of Erdoğan in its election campaign: 'Cast your vote for the friends of Turkey and empower them,' the poster read in Turkish, echoing recent remarks by Erdoğan, who asked German Turks to protest mainstream German parties ('the enemies of Turkey') and to vote instead for smaller parties ('the friends of Turkey').[196] Today the ADD is actively mobilised in seven states in Germany, under the slogan 'United Instead of Divided', and aims to bring the Turkish diaspora together.[197]

In 2019, a former spokesperson of the UID, Fatih Zingal, formed another Turkish party, the AfM, that sought to counter the extreme right-wing, anti-immigrant Alternative for Germany (AfD),[198] which had become the third largest party in the Bundestag.[199] Zingal said that within weeks of its creation the AfM had received 3,000 threats from Neo-Nazis and Gülenists, and that Turks are forming new parties because the existing German parties are not sufficiently protecting the Turkish community.[200] When asked whether he had any links to the AKP, Zingal said: 'Of course we have a bond of affection (*gönül bağı*). We are not hiding this anyway. We always stand by our state, country and president. That's why we receive so many threats and are excluded from German society.'[201]

Conclusion

Turkish conservative-nationalist and Sunni Islamic organisations in Germany, like their French counterparts, have engaged in political activism in earnest despite their belated start. Turkey's recent diaspora outreach activities in Germany have played a key role in prompting conservative German Turks' shift from political apathy to active citizenship to defend

Turkish foreign policy interests. The growing interaction between Turkish bureaucrats and immigrant-organisation leaders and the increased frequency of Turkish government-sponsored political rallies held in large German cities have paved the way for unprecedented Turkish diaspora diplomacy in Germany. The rising number of *Diyanet* personnel sent to Germany and the flow of financial assistance and organisational support from the newly formed diaspora institutions in Ankara to conservative organisations in Europe have also played an important role in sparking political mobilisation. Turkey's recent diaspora outreach activities in Germany have alleviated conservative diaspora groups' collective action problems by rendering them more self-confident and organisationally capable.

In addition to increasing the political lobbying potential of German Turks in favour of the Turkish government's interests, Turkey's engagement with its diaspora in Germany has followed other deliberate political goals, such as amassing expatriate votes for Turkish elections. Germany is home to a significant body of eligible voters for Turkish elections. In the 2018 Turkish presidential and parliamentary elections, around 1.5 million German Turks were eligible to vote. This means that their electoral participation has the potential to significantly influence the outcome of domestic elections. Consequently, Germany has become a key target for AKP officials and the party's extraterritorial branches.

Notes

1   For more on Erdoğan's address to the Turkish diaspora in Karlsruhe in May 2015, see: www.youtube.com/watch?v=1WdOl1wyZHI
2   G. Yurdakul, *From Guest Workers into Muslims*.
3   A. Kaya and F. Kentel, *Euro-Türkler*, p. 28.
4   E. Østergaard-Nielsen, *Transnational Politics*.
5   M. Anil, 'Explaining the naturalisation practices of Turks in Germany in the wake of the citizenship reform of 1999', *Journal of Ethnic and Migration Studies* 33:8 (2007), 1363–76; 'Study Shows Turkish Immigrants Least Integrated in Germany', *Deutsche Welle*, 26 January 2009, www.dw.com/en/study-shows-turkish-immigrants-least-integrated-in-germany/a-3975683l; E. Yalaz, 'Immigrant Political Incorporation'; S. W. McFadden, 'German citizenship law and the Turkish diaspora', *German Law Journal* 20:1 (2019), 72–88.
6   A. Guardia, 'Eleven German MPs under Police Protection over Armenian Vote', *Politico*, 12 June 2016, www.politico.eu/article/eleven-german-turkey-mps-under-police-protection-over-armenian-vote-genocide-bundestag-erdogan/; 'Fourteen Turkish-origin Germans Elected to Bundestag', *Hürriyet Daily News*, 25 September 2017, www.hurriyetdailynews.com/fourteen-turkish-origin-germans-elected-to-bundestag-118363

7   M. M. Howard, *The Politics of Citizenship in Europe* (Cambridge: Cambridge University Press, 2009).

8   N. Conrad, 'Dual Citizenship Law Takes Effect in Germany', *Deutsche Welle*, 19 December 2014, www.dw.com/en/dual-citizenship-law-takes-effect-in-germany/a-18143002; S. W. McFadden, 'German citizenship law and the Turkish diaspora'.

9   *Ibid.*

10 A. Boucher, 'The political participation of Berlin's Turkish migrants in the dual citizenship and headscarf debates: A multilevel comparison', in *Migration and Activism in Europe since 1945*, ed. W. Pojmann (Basingstoke: Palgrave Macmillan, 2008), p. 216.

11 N. Abadan-Unat, *Bitmeyen Göç*.

12 A. Kaya and F. Kentel, *Euro-Türkler*, p. 18.

13 N. Ögelman, 'Directing Discontent: Turkish-origin Associations in Germany' (PhD dissertation, University of Texas at Austin, 2003); G. Yurdakul, *From Guest Workers into Muslims*.

14 B. C. Zırh, 'Euro-Alevis: From *gastarbeiter* to transnational community', in *The Making of World Society: Perspectives from Transnational Research*, eds R. G. Anghel, E. Gerharz, G. Rescher and M. Salzbrunn (London: Transaction, 2008), pp. 103–33.

15 A. Yükleyen, *Localising Islam in Europe*.

16 *Ibid.*

17 'Organisation', *Union of Islamic Cultural Centres* (2021), http://vikz.de/index.php/organisation.html

18 A. Yükleyen, *Localising Islam in Europe*, p. 60.

19 A. Yükleyen, 'Compatibility of "Islam" and "Europe": Turkey's EU accession', *Insight Turkey* 11:1 (2009), 115–31; T. Veldhuis and E. Bakker, 'Muslims in the Netherlands: Tensions and violent conflict', in *Ethno-religious Conflict in Europe: Typologies of Radicalisation in Europe's Muslim Communities*, ed. M. Emerson (Brussels: Centre for European Policy Studies, 2009), pp. 81–109.

20 Interview, *Millî Görüş* official, Berlin, 27 February 2019.

21 A. Yükleyen, 'State policies and Islam in Europe: Milli Görüs in Germany and the Netherlands', *Journal of Ethnic and Migration Studies* 36:3 (2010), 445–63.

22 A. Amelina and T. Faist, 'Turkish immigrant associations in Germany: Between integration pressure and transnational linkages', *Revue Européenne des Migrations Internationales* 24:2 (2008), 91–120.

23 Interview, Federal Ministry of the Interior official, Berlin, 7 November 2013.

24 C. Bolsover, 'Investigations into Muslim Organisation Milli Gorus Dropped', *Deutsche Welle*, 21 September 2010, www.dw.com/en/investigations-into-muslim-organization-milli-gorus-dropped/a-6027213

25 *Ibid.*

26 'Milli Görüş eski yöneticilerine vergi kaçırmaktan tecilli hapis cezası', *Deutsche Welle*, 21 March 2019, www.dw.com/tr/milli-g%C3%B6r%C3%BC%C5%9F-eski-y%C3%B6neticilerine-vergi-ka%C3%A7%C4%B1rmaktan-tecilli-hapis-cezas%C4%B1/a-48013999

27 Interview, *Millî Görüş* official, Cologne, 19 November 2013.

28 Interview, IFB official, Berlin, 27 February 2019.

29 E. Østergaard-Nielsen, *Transnational Politics*.

30 'Selbstdarstellung', *Kurdistan Kultur und Hilfsverein* (2021), www.kkh-ev.de/seite/221133/selbstdarstellung.html

31 J. M. Mushaben, *The Changing Faces of Citizenship: Social Integration and Political Mobilisation among Ethnic Minorities in Germany* (New York: Berghahn, 2008); B. Baser, 'The Kurdish diaspora in Europe'.

32 R. Mandel, *Cosmopolitan Anxieties: Turkish Challenges to Citizenship and Belonging in Germany* (Durham: Duke University Press, 2008), p. 80.

33 Interview, DİTİB official, Paris, 4 March 2013.

34 'Kuruluş ve Teşkilat Yapısı', *DİTİB* (2021), www.ditib.de/default1.php?id=5&sid=8&lang=en

35 S. Serdar and D. Akal, 'Almanya artık Türkiye'den imam istemiyor', *Deutsche Welle*, 6 April 2019, www.dw.com/cda/tr/almanya-art%C4%B1k-t%C3%BCrkiyeden-imam-istemiyor/a-48235412

36 'DİTİB Launches Education Program to Train Imams in Germany', *Daily Sabah*, 10 January 2020, www.dailysabah.com/politics/2020/01/10/ditib-launches-education-program-to-train-imams-in-germany

37 'Germany Cuts Funding to Largest Turkish-Islamic Organization, DITIB', *Deutsche Welle*, 30 August 2018, www.dw.com/en/germany-cuts-funding-to-largest-turkish-islamic-organization-ditib/a-45297763

38 'Hessen eyaleti DİTİB ile İslam dersi işbirliğini sonlandırdı', *Deutsche Welle*, 28 April 2020, www.dw.com/tr/hessen-eyaleti-ditib-ile-islam-dersi-i%C5%9F-birli%C4%9Fini-sonland%C4%B1rd%C4%B1/a-53272949

39 C. Winter, 'German Intelligence Mulls Putting Largest Turkish-Islamic Group under Surveillance', *Deutsche Welle*, 21 September 2018, www.dw.com/en/german-intelligence-mulls-putting-largest-turkish-islamic-group-under-surveillance/a-45586282

40 *Ibid.*

41 K. Jennings and R. Heath, 'Erdogan's Messy Mega Mosque Opening', *Politico*, 29 September 2018, www.politico.eu/article/turkish-president-recep-tayyip-erdogan-mosque-mega-mess-cologne-germany-merkel-turkey/

42 'Germany Cuts Funding to Largest Turkish-Islamic Organization, DITIB'; 'Turkey's Erdogan Opens a Mosque in German City of Cologne', *BBC*, 29 September 2018; www.bbc.com/news/world-europe-45692666

43 'DİTİB Launches Education Program to Train Imams in Germany'.

44 D. Halm and S. Söylemez, 'Positionen von Migrantenorganisationen in grenzüberschreitenden politischen Debatten: Das Beispiel der "Armenien-Resolution" des Deutschen Bundestags', *Leviathan* 45:2 (2017), 221–54.

45 M. Sökefeld and S. Schwalgin, 'Institutions and their agents in diaspora', *Transnational Communities Working Papers Series, WPTC-2K-11* (2000), www.transcomm.ox.ac.uk/working%20papers/schwal.pdf

46 *Ibid.*

47 'Alevi Federations Germany: Together for Diversity', *AABF* (2021), https://alevi.com/en/home/

48 'Hakkımızda', *Pir Sultan Abdal Kültür Derneği* (2021), www.pirsultan.org/
49 A. Arkilic and A. E. Gurcan, 'The political participation of Alevis'.
50 'Hakkımızda,' *Almanya Türk Federasyon* (2021), http://turkfederasyon.com/almanya-t%C3%BCrk-federasyonu/hakk%C4%B1m%C4%B1zda
51 'Über Uns', *ATİB* (2021), www.atib.org/ueber-uns?lang=de
52 *Ibid.*
53 B. Baser, 'The Kurdish diaspora in Europe'.
54 'Über Uns'.
55 'The Grey Wolves Conquering Europe', *MENA Research Center* (2020), https://mena-studies.org/the-grey-wolves-conquering-europe/
56 'German Interior Ministry Bans Biker Gang Osmanen Germania BC', *Deutsche Welle*, 10 July 2018, www.dw.com/en/german-interior-ministry-bans-biker-gang-osmanen-germania-bc/a-44595773
57 C. Dalaman, 'Almanya'da Ülkücü Dernekler Yasaklanıyor', *Voice of America*, 18 November 2020, www.amerikaninsesi.com/a/almanyad-ulkucu-dernekler-yasaklaniyor/5667645.html
58 E. Østergaard-Nielsen, *Transnational Politics*; B. Baser, 'The Kurdish diaspora in Europe'.
59 'Arbeiterpartei Kurdistans (PKK) strukturiert Vereine in Europa um', *The Federal Office for the Protection of the Constitution Newsletter No. 3, Thema 6* (2014), www.verfassungsschutz.de/de/oeffentlichkeitsarbeit/newsletter/news-letter-archive/bfv-newsletter-archiv/bfv-newsletter-2014–3/bfv-newsletter-2014–03–06.html
60 İ. Ö. Yener-Roderburg, 'Party organisations across borders', p. 229.
61 B. Baser, *Diasporas and Homeland Conflicts*.
62 'Wer wir sind?', *TGD* (2021), www.tgd.de/tr/ueber-uns/
63 'Wir über uns', *TBB* (2021), https://tbb-berlin.de//ueber_den_tbb/selbstdarstel-lung
64 J. Irvine, 'The Gülen Movement and Turkish Integration in Germany', Second International Conference on Islam in the Contemporary World: The Fethullah Gülen Movement in Thought and Practice, University of Oklahoma (2006), www.gulenmovement.com/the-gulen-movement-and-turkish-integration-in-germany.html
65 A. I. Aydın, 'Dynamiques religieuses et logiques éducatives: Les Centres d'éducation du mouvement de Fethullah Gülen en France' (MA Thesis, Institut d'Etudes Politiques de Strasbourg, 2004).
66 J. Irvine, 'The Gülen Movement'; 'Turkey's Gulen Movement on the Rise in Germany', *Deutsche Welle*, 13 July 2018, www.dw.com/en/turkeys-gulen-movement-on-the-rise-in-germany/a-44652895
67 E. Demir, 'New Religious Sociabilities in Euro-Islam', pp. 355–70.
68 'Turkish Newspaper "Zaman" Shuts Down in Germany amid "Threats"', *Deutsche Welle*, 9 September 2016, www.dw.com/en/turkish-newspaper-zaman-shuts-down-in-germany-amid-threats/a-19540340; 'Turkey's Gulen Movement on the Rise in Germany'.
69 M. de la Baume and G. Paravicini, '"Sleepless" Nights for Gülen's Supporters in Europe'.

70 K. Burgess, *Courting Migrants*, p. 94.
71 'CHP'nin Münih ofisi açıldı', *Hürriyet*, 5 December 2014, www.hurriyet.com. tr/avrupa/chpnin-munih-ofisi-acildi-27711689
72 'AK Parti'den 7 ülkede temsilcilik', *Anadolu Ajansı*, 29 December 2017, www. aa.com.tr/tr/politika/ak-partiden-7-ulkede-temsilcilik/1017851
73 İ. Ö. Yener-Roderburg, 'Party organisations across borders', p. 225.
74 Turkish Consulate official, Berlin, 26 February 2019.
75 A. Amelina and T. Faist, 'Turkish immigrant associations in Germany', 101–2.
76 B. Baser, 'The Kurdish diaspora in Europe'.
77 B. Baser, 'Diaspora politics and Germany's Kurdish question', *University of Kent Diasporas and Security CARC Working Papers* (2014), https://citeseerx. ist.psu.edu/viewdoc/download?doi=10.1.1.658.7599&rep=rep1&type=pdf
78 Interview, TGD official, Berlin, 13 September 2013.
79 A. Amelina and T. Faist, 'Turkish immigrant associations in Germany', 104–5.
80 *Ibid.*, 104.
81 *Ibid.*
82 *Ibid.*, 96.
83 *Ibid.*, 97.
84 Interview, Union of Islamic Cultural Centres official, Berlin, 30 October 2013; Interview, ATİB official, Cologne, 18 November 2013.
85 A. Amelina and T. Faist, 'Turkish immigrant associations in Germany', 98–9.
86 M. Peucker and S. Akbarzadeh, *Muslim Active Citizenship in the West* (London: Routledge, 2014).
87 *Ibid.*
88 A. Yükleyen and G. Yurdakul, 'Islam, conflict and integration'.
89 A. Boucher, 'The political participation of Berlin's Turkish migrants', p. 217.
90 S. Green, *The Politics of Exclusion: Institutions and Immigration Policy in Contemporary Germany* (Manchester: Manchester University Press, 2004); K. Schönwalder and T. Triadafilopoulos, 'A bridge or barrier to incorporation? Germany's 1999 citizenship reform in critical perspective', *German Politics and Society* 30:1 (2012), 52–70.
91 G. Yurdakul, *From Guest Workers into Muslims*; A. Kaya, *Turkish-origin Migrants and Their Descendants*.
92 Interview, Turkish Embassy official, Berlin, 7 November 2003; Interview, Turkish Embassy official, Berlin, 13 February 2019.
93 Interview, Turkish Consulate official, Berlin, 3 December 2013; Interview, Turkish Consulate official, Berlin, 26 February 2019.
94 Interview, *Diyanet* official, Ankara, 24 July 2013.
95 Interview, *Millî Görüş* official, Cologne, 19 November 2013.
96 Interview, Union of Islamic Cultural Centres official, Cologne, 27 November 2013.
97 Interview, ATİB official, Cologne, 18 November 2013.
98 Interview, ATİB official, Berlin, 30 October 2013.
99 'Almanya Faaliyet Raporu', *YTB* (2015), p. 40, https://ytb.gov.tr/ytbadmin/ assets/uploads/ files/ALMANYA.pdf

100 'Erdogan Urges Turks Not to Assimilate', *Der Spiegel*, 28 February 2011, www. spiegel.de/international/europe/erdogan-urges-turks-not-to-assimilate-you-are-part-of-germany-but-also-part-of-our-great-turkey-a-748070.html
101 *Ibid.*
102 *Ibid.*
103 C. Thibos, 'Imputing diaspora: An examination of Turkish political rhetoric in Germany', *Diaspora*, 19: 2–3 (2017), 177.
104 'Artık o devirler kapandı', *Habertürk*, 4 February 2014, www.haberturk.com/ gundem/haber/918581-artik-o-devirler-kapandi
105 'Erdoğan'ın Köln Çıkarması', *Deutsche Welle*, 11 February 2008, www. dw.com/tr/erdo%C4%9Fan%C4%B1n-k%C3%B6ln-%C3%A7%C4%B-1karmas%C4%B1/a-3119307
106 Interview, FUAF official, Paris, 18 January 2019.
107 S. Adar, 'Rethinking political attitudes of migrants from Turkey and their Germany-born children'; N. Tokdogan, 'Emotional Motives of Erdoganism in the Turkish Diaspora', Max Planck Institute for Human Development (2021), www.mpib-berlin.mpg.de/research/research-centers/history-of-emotions/ citizenship-and-nationbuilding/emotional-motives-of-erdoganism
108 Interview, *Millî Görüş* official, Cologne, 22 November 2013.
109 'Erdogan Urges Turks Not to Assimilate'.
110 İ. Ö. Yener-Roderburg, 'Party organisations across borders', pp. 222–5.
111 '2014 Cumhurbaşkanlığı Seçimleri Almanya', *Habertürk*, 11 August 2014, www.haberturk.com/secim/secim2014/cumhurbaskanligi-secimi/ilce/yurtdi-si-almanya-1124
112 '2014 Cumhurbaşkanlığı Seçimleri', *Habertürk*, 11 August 2014, www.haber-turk.com/secim/secim2014/cumhurbaskanligi-secimi
113 '2015 Haziran Genel Seçimleri Almanya', *Sabah*, 7 June 2015, www.sabah. com.tr/secim/7-haziran-2015-genel-secimleri/almanya-secim-sonuclari?utm_ campaign=secim_2015_haziran&utm_source=refresh_other&utm_ medium=refresh_other
114 '2015 Haziran Genel Seçimleri', *Sabah*, 7 June 2015, www.sabah.com.tr/sec-im/7-haziran-2015-genel-secimleri/
115 '2015 Kasım Genel Seçimleri Almanya', *Sabah*, 2 November 2015, www.sabah. com.tr/secim/1-kasim-2015-genel-secimleri/almanya-secim-sonuclari?utm_ campaign=secim_2015_kasim&utm_source=menu_ulke&utm_medium= menu_ulke
116 '2015 Kasım Genel Seçimleri', *Sabah*, 2 November 2015, www.sabah.com.tr/ secim/1-kasim-2015-genel-secimleri/
117 '2017 Referandum Almanya', *Sabah*, 17 April 2017, www.sabah.com.tr/sec-im/16-nisan-2017-referandum/almanya-referandum-sonuclari
118 '2017 Referandum', *Sabah*, 17 April 2017, www.sabah.com.tr/secim/16-ni-san-2017-referandum/
119 '2018 Cumhurbaşkanlığı Seçimleri Almanya', *Sabah*, 25 April 2018, www. sabah.com.tr/secim/24-haziran-2018-secim-sonuclari/almanya-secim-son uclari

120 '2018 Cumhurbaşkanlığı Seçimleri', *Sabah*, 25 April 2018, www.sabah.com.tr/secim/24-haziran-2018-secim-sonuclari

121 B. Bruce, *Governing Islam Abroad*.

122 *Ibid.*

123 *Ibid.*, p. 412.

124 *Ibid.*, p. 403.

125 *Ibid.*, pp. 426–7.

126 B. Bruce, 'Imams for the diaspora', 1175.

127 J. Gibbon, 'Religion, Immigration and the Turkish Government in Germany'.

128 A. Schenk, 'Islamic theology: A bridge to Muslim life', *Goethe Institute* (2021), www.goethe.de/en/kul/wis/20779487.html?forceDesktop=1

129 Interview, DİTİB official, Berlin, 27 November 2013.

130 J. Laurence, *The Emancipation of Europe's Muslims: The State's Role in Minority Integration* (Princeton: Princeton University Press, 2012), p. 234.

131 'İmamlara Almanya şartı yürürlülüğe giriyor', *Deutsche Welle*, 20 December 2019, www.dw.com/tr/imamlara-almanca-%C5%9Fart%C4%B1-y%C3%BCr%C3%BCrl%C3%BC%C4%9Fe-giriyor/a-51755816

132 S. Serdar, 'Germany Set to Take Charge of Imam Education Locally', *Deutsche Welle*, 21 November 2019, www.dw.com/en/germany-set-to-take-charge-of-imam-education-locally/a-51271908

133 *Ibid.*

134 B. Bruce, 'Imams for the diaspora', 1167.

135 *Ibid.*

136 'Almanya Faaliyet Raporu', pp. 46–8; '2019 İdare Faaliyet Raporu', p. 33.

137 '2016 İdare Faaliyet Raporu', p. 32.

138 '2019 İdare Faaliyet Raporu', p. 57.

139 'Almanya Faaliyet Raporu', pp. 56–7.

140 *Ibid.*

141 *Ibid.*

142 '2016 İdare Faaliyet Raporu', p. 31.

143 '2017 İdare Faaliyet Raporu', p. 50.

144 'Almanya Faaliyet Raporu', pp. 49, 71.

145 '2017 İdare Faaliyet Raporu', p. 34.

146 *Ibid.*, p. 48.

147 'Almanya Faaliyet Raporu', pp. 39, 70.

148 *Ibid.*, p. 50.

149 *Ibid.*

150 '100 Prozent Baumwolle, 0 Prozent Terror', *Taggesspiegel*, 18 January 2004, www.tagesspiegel.de/berlin/100-prozent-baumwolle-0-prozent-terror/482804.html

151 A. Boucher, 'The political participation of Berlin's Turkish migrants', pp. 221–2.

152 A. Arkilic and A. E. Gurcan, 'The political participation of Alevis'.

153 The Islamic Council for the Federal Republic of Germany (IR) represents the *Millî Görüş* in the DIK. The IR was established in 1986 to convene Islamic organisations under one roof. Since the IR's biggest member is the *Millî Görüş*,

it is regarded by Germany as the 'sister organisation' of the *Millî Görüş*. In recent years, German authorities have objected to the *Millî Görüş*'s participation in the DIK. Interview, IRD official, Cologne, 18 November 2013.

154 S. Haug, S. Müssig and A. Stichs, *Muslimisches Leben in Deutschland* (Nürnberg: Bundesamt für Integration und Flüchtlinge, 2009); 'Overview: The DIK 2014–2016', *DIK* (2016), www.deutsche-islam- konferenz.de/DIK/EN/DIK/ArbeitDIK/DIK2014ueberblick/dik-2014-ueberblick-node.html;jsessionid=0E-30AB5CBA0BBFE0148A7C15D26A16B0.1_cid286

155 The ZMD was founded in 1994 as an Islamic federation based in Cologne. Unlike the IR, it does not have substantial Turkish membership. Interview, ZMD official, Cologne, 29 November 2013.

156 Interview, IRD official, Cologne, 18 November 2013.

157 'The German Islam Conference's Programme of Work – Ambitious and with a Practical Focus', *DIK* (2021), www.deutsche-islam-konferenz.de/DIK/EN/DIK/UeberDIK/Arbeitsprogramm/arbeitsprogramm-node.html

158 'Overview: Recent Events in the DIK', *DIK* (2021), www.wir-sind-bund.de/DIK_nmiv/EN/DIK/dik-node.html

159 C. Strack, 'German Islam Conference Reconvenes Search for German Islam', *Deutsche Welle*, 27 November 2018, www.dw.com/en/german-islam-conference-reconvenes-search-for-german-islam/a-46479656

160 'DİTİB'den Kampanya: Müslüman Cemaat Kütüğü', *Hürriyet*, 16 December 2014, www.hurriyet.com.tr/ditib-ten-kampanya-musluman-cemaat-kutugu-27782385

161 Interview, DİTİB official, Berlin, 27 November 2013.

162 Interview, TGB official, Berlin, 17 September 2013.

163 'Çifte Vatandaşlık İçin İmza Kampanyası Hızlandı', *Hürriyet*, 19 December 2012, http://avrupa.hurriyet.com.tr/haberler/gundem/1347501/cifte-vatandaslik-icin-sonbin-imza

164 'Türkçe İçin 2.541 İmza', *Hürriyet*, 26 August 2012, http://avrupa.hurriyet.com.tr/haberler/gundem/1273655/turkce-icinimza

165 E. Yalaz, 'Immigrant Political Incorporation'.

166 The TGD participated in this campaign later.

167 These claims can be seen at: www.sandigagit.com/index.html

168 'Irkçıya Karşı Haydi Sokağa', *Hürriyet*, 4 January 2019, www.hurriyet.com.tr/irkciya-karsi-haydi-sokaga-27883649

169 'DİTİB: Almanya'da Müslümanlara yönelik nefret kaygı verici', *Deutsche Welle*, 10 June 2019, www.dw.com/tr/ditib-almanyada-m%C3%BCsl%C3%BCmanlara-y%C3%B6nelik-nefret-kayg%C4%B1-verici/a-49129415

170 'Steinmeier Müslüman Dernek Temsilcilerini Kabul Etti', *Anadolu Ajansı*, 25 January 2018, http://aa.com.tr/tr/ dunya/steinmeier-musluman-dernek-temsilcilerini-kabul-etti-/1042589

171 'Hanau'da terör ve İslamofobi karşıtı yürüyüş', *Haberler*, 23 February 2020, www.haberler.com/hanau-da-teror-ve-islamofobi-karsiti-yuruyus-12947016-haberi/

172 Interview, DİTİB official, Cologne, 27 November 2013.

173 Interview, *Millî Görüş* official, Berlin, 27 February 2019.
174 Interview, ATİB official, Berlin, 30 October 2013.
175 Interview, TGB official, Berlin, 27 February 2019.
176 'Armenian Killings Were Genocide – German President', *BBC*, 23 April 2015, www.bbc.com/news/world-europe-32437633
177 'Almanya'da Soykırım Iddialarına Karşı Yürüyüş', *Hürriyet*, 22 April 2015, www.hurriyet.com.tr/avrupa/almanyada-soykirim-iddialarina-karsi-yuruyus-28797560
178 'Almanya'daki Türklerden Büyük Protesto', *Sabah*, 2 June 2016, www.sabah.com.tr/dunya/2016/06/02/almanyadaki-turklerden-buyuk-protesto; S. Sanderson, 'Bundestag Passes Armenian "Genocide" Resolution Anonymously, Turkey Recalls Ambassador', *Deutsche Welle*, 2 June 2016, www.dw.com/en/bundestag-passes-armenia-genocide-resolution-unanimously-turkey-recalls-ambassador/a-19299936
179 Interview, DİTİB official, Cologne, 27 November 2013.
180 Interview, DİTİB official, Berlin, 28 October 2013.
181 Interview, DİTİB official, Berlin, 9 October 2013.
182 Interview, *Millî Görüş* official, Berlin, 10 September 2013.
183 Interview, *Millî Görüş* official, Cologne, 22 November 2013.
184 Interview, *Millî Görüş* official, Cologne, 19 November 2013.
185 Interview, *Millî Görüş* official, Berlin, 27 February 2019.
186 'Mustafa Yeneroğlu AKP'den istifa etti', *Deutsche Welle*, 30 November 2019, www.dw.com/tr/mustafa-yenero%C4%9Flu-akpden-istifa-etti/a-51053719
187 *Ibid.*
188 Interview, Union of Islamic Cultural Centres official, Berlin, 30 October 2013.
189 Interview, Union of Islamic Cultural Centres official, Cologne, 27 November 2013.
190 This is in reference to the controversial 'You Are Germany (*Du Bist Deutschland*)' campaign. See: J. Ruchatz, 'Du bist Deutschland und die Popularität des Stars', in *Das Populäre der Gesellschaft*, eds C. Huck and C. Zorn (Cham: VS Verlag für Sozialwissenschaften), pp. 168–94.
191 Interview, BIG founder, Berlin, 17 September 2013.
192 A. Arkilic, 'An Immigrant Party in the German Elections', *Hürriyet Daily News*, 7 December 2013, www.hurriyetdailynews.com/an-immigrant-party-in-the-german-elections-59157
193 M. Topçu, 'Big Partisi Kurucu Genel Başkanı Haluk Yıldız'la Röportaj', *Uluslararası Politika Akademisi*, 9 February 2018, http://politikaakademisi.org/2018/02/09/big-partisi-kurucu-haluk-yildizla-roportaj/
194 A. Simşek, 'Turkish Immigrant Party Gets Ready for German Election', *Anadolu Ajansı*, 22 September 2017, www.aa.com.tr/en/europe/turkish-immigrant-party-gets-ready-for-german-election/916590.
195 *Ibid.*
196 'Party Founded by Turks in Germany Uses Erdogan's Posters in Campaign', *Hürriyet Daily News*, 7 September 2017, www.hurriyetdailynews.com/party-founded-by-turks-in-germany-uses-erdogan-posters-in-campaign-117697

197 M. Topçu, 'Alman ADD Partisi Yönetim Kurulu Üyesi Seyhan Acu ile Röportaj', *Uluslararası Politika Akademisi*, 14 February 2018, http://politikaakademisi. org/2018/02/14/alman-add-partisi-yonetim-kurulu-uyesi-seyhan-acu-ile-ropor-taj/

198 'Almanların korkulu rüyası!', *Sabah*, 8 February 2019, www.sabah.com.tr/ avrupa/2019/02/08/almanlarin-korkulu-ruyasi-turk-partisine-binlerce-tehdit

199 P. Kirby, 'German Election: Why This Is a Turning Point', *BBC*, 25 September 2017, www.bbc.com/news/world-europe-41094785

200 'Almanların korkulu rüyası!'

201 *Ibid.*

5

'Selective engagement': Mobilising a fragmented diaspora and the limits of diaspora diplomacy

Members of the Turkish diaspora in France, and imams and teachers sent from Turkey act as militants of the AKP and are encouraged to spy on political opponents with the support of Turkish embassies and consulates. The establishment of pro-Turkish political parties in Europe ... which promote the AKP's agenda, attests to this change. Pressure on us is mounting day by day.[1]

Turkey's selective diaspora policy displays a reversal of the official secularist bias of previous Turkish governments. Against the backdrop of Turkey's democratic backsliding and authoritarian turn, the AKP has increasingly pitted the 'loyal' and the 'dissenting' segments of the diaspora against one another (for instance, Turks vs Kurds, the AKP vs Gülenists, Sunnis vs Alevis). The AKP government's ongoing clashes with the Alevi, secular, Kurdish and Gülenist diaspora groups contrast with its robust relations with the conservative diaspora associations. The AKP's extraterritorial surveillance and suppression of dissident diasporans, particularly during and after the 2013 Gezi Park protests, the 2014 presidential elections, the 2016 failed coup and the 2017 constitutional referendum have generated fear and resentment in the diasporic space and rendered the already heterogeneous diaspora even more disunited. Divisions within the Turkish émigré community and deepening tension between Ankara and the non-conformist diaspora groups weaken Turkey's diaspora diplomacy, generate unrest within European host states and negatively affect Turkey–EU relations.

This chapter will first consider Turkey's growing authoritarian practices since 2011. This section provides some historic and political background to the responses of various diaspora groups to the AKP and unravels the linkages between the democratic downturn – and the consequences thereof – for Turkey's diaspora diplomacy. The chapter will then outline specific Alevi, secular, Kurdish and Gülenist organisations' perceptions of and responses to Turkey's authoritarian regime under the AKP and Erdoğan's increasing sway over Turkey's diasporas in Europe.

Turkey's authoritarianism since 2011

Turkey undertook groundbreaking reforms in human rights, minority rights and the rule of law after its acceptance as an EU candidate country in 1999. Turkey's Europeanisation process was driven by the EU's conditionality as well as pressure from pro-EU Turkish civil society organisations. While the coalition government of the DSP, the ANAP and the MHP was only partly committed to all the reforms demanded by the ruling parties' differing political agendas, it embraced a 'moderated hard-Eurosceptic' approach that criticised the EU but not Turkey's accession journey.[2] When the AKP entered the political arena in 2002, it presented itself as the champion of EU reforms. Following the 2002 elections, the AKP formed a pro-EU coalition with the CHP, as well as with the military and select civil society organisations.[3]

Between 1999 and 2004, Turkey passed nine packages amending the 1982 Constitution. The most important reforms of this period included the abolition of the death penalty, the improvement of freedom of expression, press freedom, women's rights and the introduction of broadcasting in minority languages. In addition, the prioritisation of supranational treaties over domestic law, the curtailment of the role of the military in politics and the abolition of the State Security Courts (established by the military junta of the 1980s), served as the harbinger of a new era for Turkish politics.[4]

Between 2005 and 2010, Turkey's Europeanisation reforms slowed yet continued in accordance with the AKP's domestic interests. The party still needed EU reforms to 'legitimise its rule in a Kemalist state' and to stay in power, because its popular support base was not fully consolidated.[5] Moreover, even though full accession negotiations with the EU began in 2005, the credibility of EU conditionality dwindled in Turkey when Austria, France and Germany offered Ankara privileged partnership in lieu of EU membership on the basis that the country was not compatible with the EU.[6] Such discouraging remarks and the EU's growing criticism of Turkey due to Ankara's maltreatment of Kurdish citizens weakened the pro-EU coalition in Turkey. 'Cherry-picking' of reforms by the AKP was evident on many occasions. For example, although the government launched broadcasting in Kurdish at the TRT, it prohibited the use of minority languages in political life and was reluctant to provide a complete overhaul of civil–military relations and minority reforms.[7]

The pro-EU coalition in Turkey was debilitated further in 2006 by the growing sensitivities of the CHP, the MHP and some civil society organisations about Cyprus and Kurdish issues, and the replacement of General Hüsamettin Özkök, a pro-reform chief of staff, with General Yaşar Büyükanıt, who disapproved of the AKP's plans to minimise the role of the military in politics. The 2008 appointment of General İlker Başbuğ briefly eased tensions between the AKP and the military,[8] although the 2008 *Ergenekon* and the 2010 *Balyoz* cases that accused some factions of the military of plotting a coup against the AKP government stalled Turkey's EU-accession process.[9] In this period, the AKP also began to attack Kurdish nationalists, leftists and secular groups, politicise the bureaucracy and the judiciary and dominate the media with the assistance of the Gülen Movement.[10]

The AKP's reframing of Alevism within a Turkish Islamic framework and its reluctance to grant full religious freedom to the Alevi community – in order to protect the party's Sunni-voting base – further deepened the rupture between the AKP and Alevis.[11] The Alevi Opening, examined in Chapter 2, broke down in 2010 when the AKP failed to respond to Alevi demands, such as the legal recognition of Alevi *cemevis*, a state apology for the Sivas massacre, the abolition of compulsory Sunni Islamic religious classes in public schools and the transformation of the *Diyanet* so that it would no longer cater solely to the needs of Sunni citizens.[12] The Kurdish Opening also lost momentum amid an escalating war between the Turkish military and the PKK. The 2011 Uludere incident (thirty-four Kurdish smugglers were killed by the Turkish military's air strikes due to inaccurate intelligence), hunger strikes by PKK-linked prisoners and dissenting voices within the AKP and the Kurdish community regarding the course of the Kurdish Opening ended the peace process between the government and Kurds.[13]

Furthermore, the alliance between the AKP and the Gülen Movement turned into a power struggle in 2010 as their common enemy, the Kemalist factions and the Turkish military, lost power. That year, Turkey sent an aid flotilla to breach the Israeli blockade of Gaza.[14] When the AKP spoke against the killing of ten Turkish activists on board by Israeli commandos, the Gülen Movement criticised the convoy itself as an unlawful transgression of Israeli authority. In 2011, the two sides traded further acrimony when Erdoğan refused to place pro-Gülenists on the AKP party list.[15] A year later, Erdoğan ordered the termination of Gülen operations when Gülenist prosecutors carried out an investigation into Hakan Fidan, the head of Turkish intelligence and one of Erdoğan's closest advisors.[16] This rivalry was heightened with the 2013 corruption investigations targeting Erdoğan, his son and three AKP ministers. Erdoğan deemed the investigations a 'judicial coup' by the Gülen Movement, replacing prosecutors on the cases and subsequently closing them.[17] The 'witch-hunt' against the Gülen Movement continued with the closure of Gülen schools and organisations inside and outside Turkish borders.[18]

Significantly, the AKP's ambitious political reforms have taken a back seat since 2011, with the violation of political rights and civil liberties. In contrast to the party's first and second terms in office, the third period is seen as a turning point, marking the beginning of the AKP's transition to 'authoritarian' rule.[19] Securing 49.8 per cent of the votes in the 2011 parliamentary elections, the AKP started to promote itself as the only democratising actor in Turkey, turning a blind eye to its former domestic partners as well as to the EU.[20] In this era, Turkey's EU-accession negotiations proceeded very slowly, with almost half of the chapters remaining open and only one chapter provisionally closed.[21] EU Progress Reports continuously remarked that Turkey's Europeanisation process had reached a stalemate.[22] As de-Europeanisation became a dominant trend in the political arena, the EU's role as a transformative power was permanently thrown into sharp relief.[23]

The AKP's authoritarianism became even more visible during the Gezi Park protests, 'the biggest spontaneous revolt in Turkish history', which lasted between May and July 2013.[24] The uprising emerged as an environmentalist demonstration against the AKP's controversial plan to demolish the Gezi Park in Istanbul's historic Taksim Square and quickly spread to other cities at home and abroad, becoming a medium to show dissatisfaction with the government's increasing Sunni-Muslim nationalism and diminishing freedom of press and expression.[25] Often labelled 'marauders' by AKP officials, an estimated 3.5 million Turks and hundreds of thousands of diasporans (particularly in Germany, the Netherlands and Belgium) participated in the demonstrations.[26] By 'turning into a symbol of repressed demands', the demonstrations brought together a diverse group of people, including secularists, leftists, students, Kurds, Alevis, feminists, the urban poor, the LGBTQ community and devout Muslims who were disappointed with AKP policies. However, due to the lack of a unified leadership and deadly police brutality, the demonstrations soon disintegrated.[27]

The Gezi Park protests brought additional tensions to the Turkish transnational landscape, exacerbating disagreements between AKP supporters and critics.[28] While individuals from all walks of life participated in the protests, the majority of those killed and detained were Alevis: one Alevi representative suggested that the Gezi Park protests resembled the 1978 Kahramanmaraş and the 1993 Sivas massacres in that sense.[29] The remarkable rate of Alevi involvement in the Gezi events was a reflection of heightening Alevi frustration under the AKP government.[30]

The 2014 elections, when Erdoğan became Turkey's first directly elected president, also triggered a new wave of discontent in Turkey and Europe. Particularly since 2015, the AKP has succumbed to a democratic breakdown as the party has put the fairness of elections under threat, systematically curtailed civil liberties and imposed its policies on the public rather than engage in deliberation.[31] As Chapter 2 explained, the AKP lost its parliamentary majority in the June 2015 elections and called for a snap general election in November, which was followed by the declaration of emergency rule. Following the regaining of the parliamentary majority in November, the AKP espoused a religious ultranationalist discourse and joined forces with the MHP.[32] The *Diyanet*'s new role as the face of Turkish nationalism and the Islamisation of society and politics through debates around the headscarf, religious schools and Alevism, together representative of this new alliance, have contributed to Turkey's democratic breakdown and societal polarisation.[33]

The infringement of political rights and civil liberties intensified after the 2016 coup attempt that killed 250 people and wounded more than 2,000.[34] In the post-coup term, the AKP detained at least 160,000 allegedly Gülen-affiliated people, of whom around 77,000 have been imprisoned on terrorism charges.[35] The party extended the state of emergency seven times between 2016 and 2018 and announced thirty-six executive orders.[36] In 2017, over 100,000 public sector employees with alleged Gülen-connections were sacked, which included approximately 3,500 judges, military and police officers, teachers, doctors and academics working at all levels of central and local government. The persecuted employees were replaced with those loyal to the AKP regime.[37] During this period, the AKP also ordered the arrest of Selahattin Demirtaş and Figen Yüksekdağ, the co-leaders of the HDP, and other HDP politicians.[38] The 2017 constitutional referendum, which introduced eighteen groundbreaking changes, including equipping the newly elected president with unparalleled power at the expense of the TBMM,[39] is the final straw of Turkey's authoritarianism. In early 2021, a new wave of protests swept Turkey and Europe in response to shrinking academic freedom at Turkish universities and Erdoğan's appointment of Melih Bulu,[40] a businessman known for his close ties to the AKP, to Turkey's prestigious Boğaziçi University as rector. These protests marked the largest display of civil uprising within and beyond Turkey's borders since the 2013 Gezi events.[41]

Alevi organisations

Over the last two decades, the transnational Alevi movement has made strides towards recognition and equal citizenship rights in Europe through Alevi political mobilisation aimed at host countries and EU institutions.[42] As outlined in the previous chapter, and discussed further below, there is no unity within the Alevi community in Europe; some Alevis support the AKP. That said, the leading Alevi organisations, like the AABF and the FUAF, have long been ardent critics of the AKP's policies. In the past, Alevis in Europe arranged rallies to make generic identity-based demands. However, the AKP's post-2011 political rule has sparked targeted demonstrations for the first time in the Alevi diaspora movement's history.[43]

According to Alevi representatives in France, the long-standing Sunni–Alevi rift has deepened under AKP rule, and Alevis in Turkey and Europe feel more suppressed now than ever before.[44] Alevi resentment under the AKP regime has resulted in many demonstrations in France. At a FUAF-led rally organised in Strasbourg in 2012, around 10,000 people, most of whom were Alevis, came together to protest the AKP's discrimination against Alevi and Kurdish minorities and the AKP's mishandling of the Turkish economy. The rally also attracted ten Alevi organisations and twenty leftist and Kurdish organisations from fourteen different countries across Europe. Armand Jung, then a member of the National Assembly of France, and Hüseyin Aygün, a CHP deputy, were also in attendance. FUAF official Erdal Kılıçkaya stated:

> When we look at Turkey from France, we see a dark picture. Recent developments, such as the AKP's reluctance to grant legal recognition to our *cemevis*, mandatory religious classes and various discrimination examples compel us to raise our voice. We, Alevis, the defenders of secularism, democracy and equality, say no to repression, injustice, assimilation and discrimination. We are marching on the streets of Strasbourg today to change the dark picture in Turkey.[45]

The Gezi Park protests reminded Alevis once again, as in the 1993 Sivas and the 1995 Gazi massacres, that their homeland was 'lost'.[46] The FUAF organised another rally in Lyon in 2014 to oppose Erdoğan's scheduled visit to France and the AKP's 'authoritarian' and 'oppressive' policies. Politicians from the French Communist Party attended in support.[47]

In addition, in 2015, the FUAF coordinated the 'Recep Tayyip Erdoğan Is Not Welcome in Strasbourg' rally, which allowed hundreds of thousands of individuals to collectively stand up to the AKP's 'dictatorship' and to call for solidarity with the HDP.[48] The mass meeting attracted leftist, secular and Kurdish organisations, as well as French and Turkish politicians, including Francis Wurtz, a member of the French Communist Party, and Fayik Yağızay, an HDP deputy.[49]

Other far-reaching FUAF events took place in the ensuing years. In 2016, 10,000 demonstrators convened in front of the European Parliament to denounce increasing sectarianism and authoritarianism in Turkey.[50] A year later, the FUAF launched a press conference in Paris to invite Turkish citizens in France to vote 'no' in the 2017 constitutional referendum.[51] The FUAF leadership saw these protests as an opportunity to galvanise the Alevi movement and to distinguish themselves from the AKP's 'Salafist' policies and 'identity engineering' in Europe.[52] In 2020, in seven different French cities, the FUAF organised additional demonstrations for the legal protection of Turgut Öker, the European Alevi Association Federation chairperson and HDP deputy, who had been convicted of insulting Erdoğan.[53]

Alevis set up a series of anti-AKP demonstrations in Germany as well. For example, in 2012, the AABF organised a Berlin rally to challenge the rise of Sunni-Muslim nationalism, authoritarianism and human rights violations in Turkey.[54] In Cologne in 2013, an AABF mass gathering of 40,000 people was held to support Gezi protestors in Turkey.[55] In 2014, with supporting speeches from German parliamentarians from the CDU, the Green Party and the Left Party, the AABF assembled 50,000 protesters to rally against AKP corruption scandals, police brutality and democratic backsliding.[56] In 2016, 30,000 people united at an AABF rally in Cologne with Left Party deputies and demanded the release of Selahattin Demirtaş and Figen Yüksekdağ.[57] The most recent large-scale AABF protest challenged the encroachment on Turkey's academic freedom and the swearing-in of the new Boğaziçi rector in January 2021.[58]

Alevi leaders in France argued that Turkey's new diaspora institutions discriminate against them, favouring Sunni organisations instead.[59] For example, an administrator from the Paris Alevi Cultural Centre claimed that the organisation receives no financial support for its projects from the YTB and that no Alevi leader from France serves on the YTB's Advisory Board.[60] This official cited the lack of Alevi participation in YTB committees and meetings as an indication of how much Turkey's diaspora policy neglects Alevis. Other FUAF representatives noted that even if they were invited to official meetings, they would not attend as they 'oppose the AKP's Sunnification agenda'.[61]

Alevi representatives in Germany also complained that the current Turkish diaspora policy undermines their integration. One AABF official argued that diaspora mobilisation should be bottom-up rather than top-down and that Alevis must create and mobilise their own diaspora. Yet he added that diasporans' feelings of exclusion and marginalisation due to pervasive racism and discrimination in Germany account for why the AKP's policies appeal to Turkish citizens in the country.[62] Another AABF representative claimed that the AKP government ignores the needs of the Alevi community and provides no financial or moral support. In his view, being excluded has its own benefits since it allows Alevis to distance themselves from the 'brutal and assimilationist Turkish state' and form firmer relations with German authorities that see them as 'good immigrants'.[63]

While select Alevi officials in Germany had initially been invited to some YTB events, they refused to attend them. An AABF delegate explained the reasoning behind their reluctance to become involved:

We attended the YTB's first summit in 2010 after receiving an invitation from them. However, once the meeting was over, we got together and decided that these meetings do not enable our participants to express their views and are designed to promote AKP interests. The German government holds similar civil society meetings. Unlike the Turkish case, in Germany, the government lets us speak. We believe that these meetings are a manifestation of Turkey's new political agenda targeting the diaspora. The sole aim of this agenda is to manipulate Turkish citizens in Europe. The AABF does not wish to be a part of these policies and we invite other diaspora organisations to stay away from these events.[64]

It is important to note that there is discord within the Alevi diaspora as not every Alevi association espouses an anti-AKP position.[65] In fact, as noted in the previous chapter, there are Alevi expatriate organisations, such as those linked to the Cem Foundation and the Ahlal Bayt Alevi Federation of Europe, which do not define Alevism as a religion in its own right and have opted for a close alliance with the AKP. For example, the Cem Foundation-linked organisations in Europe have collaborated with the *Diyanet* to send Alevi *dede*s to Europe 'to inform the Alevi community regarding the Alevi faith and to unite the Turkish diaspora community'.[66] According to Turkish authorities, this initiative shows that the *Diyanet* serves not only Sunnis but also other sects and communities from Turkey.[67] In a similar vein, a representative from the Ahlal Bayt Alevi Federation of Europe proclaimed that he is in full support of AKP policies:

If Alevism means love for Ali, then I am an Alevi. Islam does not differentiate between Alevis and Sunnis. Alevism should not be recognised as a faith outside Islam. Unfortunately, some Alevis interpret Alevism very differently ... The AKP is the only government in the Turkish Republic's history that approaches Alevis with good intentions. This government organised seven Alevi workshops. This means that Turkish officials accept Alevis as a unique group and that they are ready to listen to Alevis' problems. This is a historical development. It would be too naïve to expect [them] to resolve complicated problems overnight. We will support every step our government takes.[68]

This official maintained that Turkey's growing rapprochement with its émigré community in Europe is a reflection of Turkey's expanding economic and political power. He added that his organisation would gladly accept YTB funding for its projects,[69] and showed his support for the AKP by joining various state meetings as a speaker, including the YTB's '50th Anniversary of Turkish Emigration to Germany' symposium, held in Berlin in 2011. In this meeting, he condemned Germany's racist practices and underlined the importance of forming a unified Turkish lobby overseas.[70] In contrast, Alevi leaders in France and Germany view such Alevi organisations as AKP pawns that have no legitimacy in the eyes of the majority of the Alevi community due to their limited representation and flawed definition of Alevism.[71]

Secular organisations

Officials from secular organisations also confirmed that the rise of Sunni-Muslim nationalism and the emergence of a selective diaspora policy in Turkey impact them negatively.[72] An ACORT administrator in France stressed the unevenness in Turkey's diaspora agenda:

> In the early 2000s, we backed a political campaign to promote Turkey's EU membership. We met with the Turkish Ambassador and Consul General in Paris but they blocked us. Instead, they backed a different organisation controlled by Turkish officials. Turkey does not support ideologically non-conformist organisations like ours. Yes, the Turkish government has provided resources to empower diaspora organisations here – but only like-minded ones. We receive no financial or organisational support for our activities.[73]

This representative suggested that Turkey has ramped up its attempts to silence dissident voices in the diaspora and stopped sponsoring the ACORT's cultural activities since the eruption of the Gezi Park protests: this is in stark contrast to French municipalities, which continue to provide generous funding. Mirroring the statements of Alevi leaders, he argued that growing Islamophobia targeting emigrants from Turkey in the post-9/11 era has set the ground for Ankara's deepening relations with the diaspora.[74]

The Gezi Park protests opened a window of opportunity for solidarity among adversaries of the AKP. Yet these groups failed to form a strong network in France. The ACORT marshalled three major demonstrations with Alevi, Kurdish and other left-wing and secular groups in France in the wake of the 2013 Gezi Park events and the 2017 constitutional referendum.[75] It held another rally in 2015 with Alevi and Kurdish association representatives to commemorate the centennial of the massacre of Armenians by Ottoman Turks.[76] While these groups joined the ACORT's protests, their partnership receded quickly since each of them had become preoccupied with their own political agendas and causes.[77] In 2021, the ACORT also started a petition campaign criticising Erdoğan's appointment of the new rector to Boğaziçi University.[78]

Other secular organisations in France, such as the ELELE and the Anatolian Cultural Centre, are similarly concerned with Turkey's paternalistic diaspora outreach initiatives. An ELELE official informed me that her organisation used to receive funding from both the Turkish and French governments, but the inflow of financial support from Turkey halted under AKP rule.[79] In her view, 'the Turkish Embassy and Consulate in Paris have become increasingly politicised and focused on espionage activities ... They are no longer interested in dialogue but seek to monopolise us [alternative voices within the diaspora] via different state agencies.'[80] She maintained that the AKP government did not invite her to the YTB's Advisory Board, despite her credentials, because she is secular. Echoing ACORT leaders, this representative argued that it is difficult to bring together Kurds, Alevis, left-wing and secular groups from Turkey on a permanent basis because they are inward-looking and suspicious of each other. In other words, the anti-AKP front in France remains divided even after the Gezi protests.[81]

An official from the Anatolian Cultural Centre, who also serves on the YTB Advisory Board, likened the diasporic space in France to a 'microcosmos', where all the major Turkish political movements and parties have a 'satellite'.[82] He suggested that it is unsurprising that the AKP dominates the Turkish diaspora given that Turks have the worst educational, economic and political integration records among all minority groups in France and Germany. He too argued that the AKP uses Turkish expatriates as an apparatus to promote its political interests and that pro-Turkish rallies and the introduction of external voting have further balkanised the Turkish diaspora. According to him, the AKP's diaspora engagement has put ethnic diaspora Turks in a disadvantaged position by demanding their absolute loyalty and attachment to Turkey regardless of their citizenship status and integration prospects.[83]

CHP representatives in France did attend some diaspora meetings organised by the AKP. However, they also argued that conservative-nationalist and Sunni Islamic organisations receive more respect, attention and greater financial assistance and that the DİTİB has a 'mafia-like' structure in France, seeking to centralise and dominate every organisation. The CHP has formed positive relations with the ACORT and the FUAF, particularly since the Gezi uprisings, but they are not on good terms with Kurdish organisations: 'Kurds blame the CHP for the Turkish Republic's Kurdish massacres. It is hard for us to reconcile.'[84] In addition, the CHP in France maintains superficial communication with Alevis because they 'have a close-knit community and socialise through their *cemevis*, which are home to a considerable group of Kurdish Alevis. They are not very interested in French politics and remain entangled in Turkish affairs.'[85]

Officials from the secular TGD in Germany agreed that the Turkish diaspora's fragmentation had magnified in recent years[86] and further polarised the Turkish community.[87] Another TGD representative criticised Turkey's diaspora agenda for its religious and nationalistic focus:

> Things have changed in recent years. Before the 2000s, Turkish ministers would stop by our office when they visited Germany. Now Turkish bureaucrats ignore us. We are invited to official meetings in Ankara. However, we feel as if we are a minority in these meetings. Religious organisations outnumber us … Our relations with the [AKP] government have worsened since the Gezi Park protests. At a press conference, we condemned human rights violations committed by the AKP during the Gezi events. An AKP deputy cancelled a scheduled visit with us afterwards. The UID also suspended ties once it saw our political stance.[88]

Kenan Kolat, the former chairperson of the TGD who now serves as the leader of the CHP's Berlin branch, told journalists that the AKP government had let German Turks down: 'Before the Turkish elections, the AKP had promised that retirees would be allowed to work abroad, that paid military service would be €1,000, and that expatriates would receive 20 per cent discount on plane tickets. None of these promises were kept.'[89] The TGD's current chairperson, Gökay Sofuoğlu, has participated in several AKP-led diaspora meetings and official dinners. Yet he too suggested that the new Turkish diaspora policy should be approached with caution due to its divisive nature.[90]

By the same token, TBB representatives in Berlin drew attention to the lack of support from Turkish organisations: 'Even Joachim Gauck [German president between 2012 and 2017] visited our office. To the contrary, Turkish state organisations are implementing the "divide and rule" policy to assimilate us. They should just leave us alone.'[91] Yet another TBB leader found discrimination in Germany's stance towards Turks. Like many of my respondents, this official saw racism as one of the main reasons behind the Turkish diaspora's growing ties with the homeland. She argued that German politicians tend to place all Turks under the 'Muslim' category and constantly question diaspora Turks' attachment to Turkey. As she explained, this double standard again became evident when the Turkish-origin German football player Mesut Özil came under fire in 2018 after posing with Erdoğan.[92] Özil's warm relations with the Turkish president attracted ample criticism from the German football federation, the media and even some politicians. Consequently, Özil resigned from the German national football team, citing racism and disrespect in relation to the treatment of Turks in Germany.[93]

Kurdish organisations

The Kurdish diaspora resembles the other diaspora groups from Turkey in the sense that it comprises both pro- and anti-AKP camps. However, the major Kurdish diaspora organisations in Europe have made it clear that they do not endorse AKP policies. For example, in 2004, together with prominent Kurdish activists and intellectuals, the Kurdish Institute of Paris published the 'What Do the Kurds Want in Turkey?' declaration to urge Turkey to guarantee cultural diversity and political pluralism, and to become a true democracy.[94]

Other Kurdish associations in France have also become increasingly involved in anti-AKP protests since 2011. The 'Freedom to Öcalan, Peace to Kurdistan' march organised by the FEYKA in 2011 attracted 15,000 Kurds from all over Europe. Some members of the French Communist Party and the Party of the European Left also joined the demonstration, which contested the AKP government's unjust practices.[95] In 2014, at another FEYKA-organised rally in Paris, a large group of Kurds gathered with French Communist Party politicians to condemn the execution of three female PKK officials inside the Kurdish Information Centre in Paris.[96] Two years later, Kurds came together in Paris to oppose Turkish military operations aimed at the Kurdish population under the jurisdiction of the Kurdistan Regional Government in northern Iraq,[97] and the CDK-F administered a series of mass gatherings across France to decry the AKP's 'fascist' policies in south eastern Turkey.[98] In 2019, more than 20,000 Kurds gathered in Paris once again to counter the AKP's assault on Kurdish towns in north eastern Syria.[99]

Kurds in Germany also took to the streets after the 2010 Turkish ban on the Kurdish media channel *ROJ TV*. In the same year, the YEK-KOM championed Kurdish demands on Turkish policymakers, such as the lowering of the electoral threshold for political parties to enter the TBMM, the payment of reparations to Kurds who experienced forced displacement and the drafting of a new constitution in Turkey. Kurdish activists have also mobilised European policymakers and political parties by holding hunger strikes, vigils, acts of self-immolation[100] and other demonstrations.[101] For example, in 2016, over 30,000 protestors rallied against the AKP under the aegis of the NAV-DEM in Cologne.[102] Some 30,000 Kurds gathered in Berlin a year later to call for democracy in Turkey and to protest against the 2017 constitutional referendum.[103] In 2019, a new wave of Kurdish protests spread across Germany to denounce the AKP's military operations in north eastern Syria.[104]

Kurdish and Turkish diaspora groups often clash with each other, creating security challenges both for diaspora members and European host states. In 2015, PKK supporters in Germany vandalised a Grey Wolves-affiliated ATİB mosque in the district of Baden-Württemberg.[105] In 2016, an ultranationalist Turk stabbed a Kurdish protestor during a pro-Kurdish march in the same state.[106] A Kurdish leader in Germany claimed that the replacement of Gülen supporters with Grey Wolves cadres in the Turkish state apparatus negatively affects the co-existence of Turks and Kurds in Germany.[107] The ongoing tension between Turks and Kurds has alarmed the Federal Ministry of the Interior and the Federal Office for the Protection of the Constitution, culminating in a German-wide ban for the Grey Wolves in 2020, as noted in the previous chapter.[108]

Members of the Kurdish diaspora in both France and Germany pointed out that their stigmatisation has also been aggravated as a result of Turkey's new diaspora policy. In their opinion, Turkey's approach has done more harm than good, damaging Turkey's image in Europe and undercutting integration efforts. An official from the Kurdish Institute of Paris suggested that while Kurds were initially optimistic about the AKP's pre-2011 democratisation reforms, relations began to sour as soon as the peace process collapsed:

> Kurds do not trust the AKP government anymore. They expected a lot from Erdoğan. They thought that he was different ... When the AKP came to power, Kurds were still arrested but they were not tortured like they used to be in the 1980s. Diaspora Kurds could go back to Turkey freely and come back to France with no problems. Erdoğan even used the word 'Kurdistan' once. But he did not keep his promises later.[109]

Kurdish leaders in Germany expressed similar concerns. The chairperson of the YEK-KOM argued that Ankara's new diaspora policy seeks to control people and discredit Kurdish associations.[110] An official from the HDP's Berlin office, who is also active in various local Kurdish organisations, confirmed that the majority of the Kurdish diaspora in Germany are very critical of Erdoğan and his new diaspora strategy:

> These policies render our already negative image in Europe more negative and undermine our integration efforts. They also exacerbate the younger generation's identity crisis and leave them in limbo. AKP politicians use racism and the rise of far-right parties in Europe as a pretext to draw the diaspora closer to itself. And they are achieving their goal ... Political turbulence caused by the Gezi Park events and the coup attempt has atomised the Kurdish and Turkish diaspora here. I would have loved to get together and debate with AKP supporters, but they see us as 'monsters'.[111]

While prominent Kurdish organisations, such as the Ahmet Kaya Kurdish Cultural Centre and the YEK-KOM have organised many demonstrations against the wrongdoings of the AKP,[112] the KOMKAR have, at times, formed close relations with the AKP. For example, its leaders, including Kemal Burkay, praised the AKP's Kurdish Opening[113] and asked the Kurdish diaspora to support AKP policies and constitutional amendments.[114] These officials even expressed their willingness to attend formal diaspora meetings[115] and referred to the AKP as a better alternative to the Kemalist status quo. Turkish bureaucrats announced that they were indeed open to dialogue with the KOMKAR and praised the organisation's distancing from the PKK.[116] The 2010 'Kurdish Diaspora Meeting' that convened sixty Kurdish intellectuals in Cologne was one of the most crucial pro-AKP meetings organised by the KOMKAR.[117] The YEK-KOM boycotted the meeting, claiming that the KOMKAR had morphed into an AKP-controlled puppet and should be labelled a traitor. Other interviews conducted with various Kurdish-organisation members in Germany also revealed that Kurds shared conflicting views regarding the AKP's democratisation initiatives aimed at Kurds, such as the introduction of broadcasting in Kurdish and the disarmament of the PKK. Some diaspora Kurds found these reforms genuine and necessary while others viewed them as a political trap and part of a wider propaganda machine.[118]

Gülenist organisations

After the post-coup purge, the number of Turkish citizens seeking asylum in Europe skyrocketed, and Gülen affiliates have become the AKP's primary target in the diasporic arena. According to the Federal Office for Migration and Refugees, before 2016 Germany used to receive an average of 1,800 asylum applications from Turkish citizens per year.[119] In 2016, this number rose to 5,742, and to 11,423 in 2019. Roughly half of all applications for asylum in Germany in 2019 had been granted some form of protection compared to only 8.2 per cent of asylum applications in 2016.[120] Prior to 2016, approximately 80 per cent of asylum applications had been lodged by Turkish citizens of Kurdish-origin, but in 2019 more than half were submitted by non-Kurdish Turkish citizens.[121] The Federal Ministry of the Interior reported that between 2016 and 2018, 296 Turkey-originated asylum seekers carried a diplomatic passport, and 881 a service passport, granted to public sector employees, most of whom are believed to be Gülenists.[122]

Turkish officials have claimed that some 14,000 Gülenists fled Turkey for Germany in the aftermath of the thwarted coup attempt and have been receiving linguistic and monetary assistance from the Gülen Movement's non-governmental organisation, Aid Action for Refugees (Aktion für Flüchtlingshilfe).[123] In an effort to scrutinise fugitives, the AKP has asked Interpol and other European countries to help it clamp down on the Gülen Movement: German politicians from the Left Party reported that between 2016 and 2019 Ankara called Interpol 1,252 times to ask it to extradite or provide information about Gülenists and other dissidents in Germany. While spying allegations existed long before this, experts note that these operations are far larger and more extensive than previously.[124]

However, AKP officials have failed to find foreign allies. While Interpol did not object to arrest warrants targeting Islamic State fighters, it did not respond to Turkey's collaboration requests.[125] What is more, in 2017, German security investigated several DİTİB personnel on suspicion of spying on Gülen followers and raided the homes of four of them.[126] German newspapers wrote that thirteen imams in two different German states provided information to Turkish diplomats in Cologne about at least fourteen Gülen-affiliated institutions and forty-five Gülenists,[127] and that Turkish intelligence employed 6,000 spies in Germany.[128] Martin Schulz, an SPD politician, raised the espionage scandal in the 2017 German federal elections, proposing that Turkey's EU candidacy be terminated because of it.[129] Following the closure of the investigation without any charges, due to a lack of sufficient evidence, several Turkish imams escaped from Germany.[130]

As illustrated in a *Le Monde* article, France has also become a 'real fallback ground' for Gülenists.[131] In particular, the Strasbourg-Saint-Denis district of Paris has turned into a 'discreet ground of confrontation' between the AKP regime and oppositional forces. 'In France, the risk is real,' said Emre Demir, the editor-in-chief of the now-defunct *Zaman France*.[132] Even though the AKP had begun to monitor Gülenists well before the putsch, Demir noted that 'AKP threats are growing more and more. Insulting emails and hate speech, visible on social media, are plentiful, such as a Facebook post that threatened that "the turn will also come for the muzzled dogs of Fethullah Gülen who are in Europe".'[133]

Other Gülen supporters interviewed by the French media explained that they too are afraid of going back to Turkey, that their home country is no longer a 'safe place for them'. They reported that their life is highly uncertain and precarious.[134] Nihat Sarıer, the director of the Paris Platform, lamented vandalism targeting Gülen buildings in France and claimed that even some of his family members do not speak to him because he is viewed as a 'terrorist'.[135]

Many Gülenists in Germany also complained to reporters that they are being harassed and intimidated by Turkish political actors, such as the UID, as well as by members of the Turkish diaspora. Ercan Karakoyun, the chairperson of the Berlin-based Foundation for Dialogue and Education, explained:

> Many of us receive death threats. I have reported six death threats to the police and I know that many people have done the same. I am in constant touch with the police ... Parents have pulled their kids out of our schools. One reason is that, if they have a business in Turkey, they are afraid that something might happen to their business, and another reason is that they want to show loyalty to Erdoğan, and so they do not want to support the school anymore.[136]

Amid the AKP's crackdown that has led to the closure of Gülen institutions and forced the Gülen Movement to downsize its operations, Gülen representatives in Germany have called Ankara's diaspora engagement manipulative.[137] However, Gülenist groups have remained isolated from secular, Alevi and Kurdish diaspora groups that have voiced similar concerns. This is because these groups hold Gülen sympathisers responsible for Turkey's democratic backsliding.[138] Gülenists have also generally kept a low public profile and avoided public demonstrations against the AKP, unlike anti-Gülenists: immediately after the coup attempt, 35,000 Turks turned up in Cologne to show their support for Erdoğan in his fight against the Gülen Movement. Some AKP politicians, such as Akif Kılıç, the German-born Sport and Youth Minister, were present at the rally.[139]

Conclusion

The earlier years of the AKP were marked by progressive democratisation reforms. The party's inclusion of cultural pluralism into the state discourse, through the Alevi and Kurdish Openings in its second term, had one of the most profound impacts on Turkey's diaspora agenda. However, the AKP's political and legal reforms have significantly regressed since 2011. The party's third term is seen as a turning point, with the AKP's swift transition into an authoritarian ruler. The party's reframing of Alevism within a Turkish Islamic framework, encroachment on secularism and spiralling tension between the Turkish military and Kurdish groups have deepened the rupture between the AKP and the Alevi, secular and Kurdish community within and beyond Turkish borders.

At the same time, the tenuous alliance between the AKP and the Gülen Movement collapsed and Turkey's Europeanisation process entered an impasse. The AKP's authoritarianism targeting Alevi, secular, Kurdish and Gülenist groups has become even more palpable since the 2013 Gezi Park protests, the 2014 presidential elections, the 2016 aborted coup and the 2017 constitutional referendum. These events have led to a new wave of emigration from Turkey to Europe and unleashed additional turmoil within the diasporic field. Conflicts between the homeland and its dissident diasporas, as well as intra-diasporic difficulties, have prevented Turkey from reaching its full diaspora diplomacy potential, generated security problems on European soil and harmed Turkey–EU relations. The deterioration of Turkey's political conditions will continue to have significant implications for Turkey's relations with different segments of the diaspora in the years to come.

Notes

1 Interview, ACORT official, Paris, 22 January 2019.
2 H. Yılmaz, 'Euroscepticism in Turkey: Parties, elites, and public opinion', *South European Society and Politics* 16:1 (2011), 185–208.
3 F. Keyman and Z. Öniş, *Turkish Politics in a Changing World: Global Dynamics and Domestic Transformations* (Istanbul: Bilgi University Press, 2007).
4 M. Müftüler-Bac, 'Turkey's political reforms'.
5 G. Yılmaz, 'From Europeanisation to de-Europeanisation: The Europeanisation process of Turkey in 1999–2014', *Journal of Contemporary European Studies* 24:1 (2016), 86–100.
6 G. Noutcheva and S. Aydın-Düzgit, 'Lost in Europeanisation: The Western Balkans and Turkey', *West European Politics* 35:1 (2012), 59–78.
7 Y. Gürsoy, 'The impact of EU-driven reforms on the political autonomy of the Turkish military', *South European Society and Politics* 16:2 (2011), 293–308; G. Yılmaz, 'It is pull-and-push that matters for external Europeanisation! Explaining minority policy change in Turkey', *Mediterranean Politics* 19:2 (2014), 238–58.
8 M. Çınar, 'The electoral success of the AKP: Cause for hope and despair', *Insight Turkey* 13:4 (2011), 107–27; G. Yılmaz, 'From Europeanisation to de-Europeanisation'.
9 M. Heper, 'Civil–military relations in Turkey: Toward a liberal model?', *Turkish Studies* 12:2 (2011), 241–52.
10 E. Özbudun, 'Turkey's judiciary and the drift toward competitive authoritarianism', *International Spectator* 50:2 (2015), 42–55; B. Esen and S. Gumuscu, 'Why did Turkish democracy collapse? A political economy account of AKP's authoritarianism', *Party Politics* (2020), doi: 10.1177/1354068820923722
11 A. Kaya, *Europeanization and Toleration in Turkey: Myth of Toleration* (Basingstoke: Palgrave Macmillan, 2013); C. Lord, 'Rethinking the Justice and Development Party's Alevi "Openings"', *Turkish Studies* 18:2 (2016), 278–96; A. Karakaya-Stump, 'The AKP, sectarianism and the Alevis' struggle for equal rights in Turkey', *National Identities* 20:1 (2018), 53–67.

12 A. Çarkoğlu and E. Elçi, 'Alevis in Turkey', in *Routledge Handbook of Minorities in the Middle East*, ed. P. S. Lowe (London: Routledge, 2019), pp. 212–25; A. Arkilic and A. E. Gurcan, 'The political participation of Alevis'.

13 Ö. Kayhan-Pusane, 'Turkey's Kurdish Opening: Long awaited achievements and failed expectations', *Turkish Studies* 15:1 (2014), 81–99.

14 'Mavi Marmara: Why Did Israel Stop the Gaza Flotilla?', *BBC*, 27 June 2016, www.bbc.com/news/10203726

15 H. Taş, 'A history of Turkey's AKP–Gülen conflict', *Mediterranean Politics* 23:3 (2018), 395–402.

16 *Ibid.*

17 I. Yılmaz and G. Bashirov, 'The AKP after 15 years: Emergence of Erdoganism in Turkey', *Third World Quarterly* 39:9 (2017), 1812–30.

18 B. Balcı, 'Situating the Gülen Movement in France and in Europe'.

19 E. Özbudun, 'AKP at the crossroads: Erdoğan's majoritarian drift', *South European Society and Politics* 19:2 (2014), 155–67; C. B. Tansel, 'Authoritarian neoliberalism and democratic backsliding in Turkey: Beyond the narratives of progress', *South European Society and Politics,* 23:2 (2018), 197; S. Tepe, 'Populist party's challenge to democracy: Institutional capture, performance and religion', *Party Politics* (2021), doi: 10.1177/13540688211002478

20 G. Yılmaz, 'From Europeanisation to de-Europeanisation'.

21 N. Tocci, 'Turkey and the European Union: A journey in the unknown', *Brookings Institution Turkey Project Policy Paper Number 5* (November 2014), www.brookings.edu/wp-content/uploads/2016/06/turkey-and-the-european-union.pdf

22 T. Erdem, 'The end of Turkey's Europeanisation?', *Turkish Policy Quarterly* 12:1 (2013), 125–32.

23 S. Aydın-Düzgit and A. Kaliber, 'Encounters with Europe in an era of domestic and international turmoil: Is Turkey a de-Europeanising candidate country?', *South European Society and Politics* 21:1 (2016), 6.

24 C. Tuğal, *The Fall of the Turkish Model: How the Arab Uprisings Brought Down Islamic Liberalism* (London: Verso, 2016), p. 250.

25 T. Atay, 'The clash of "nations" in Turkey: Reflections on the Gezi Park incident', *Insight Turkey* 15:3 (2013), 39–44.

26 R. Imani-Giglou, L. d'Haenens and C. Ogan, 'Turkish diasporic responses to the Taksim Square protests: Legacy media and social media uses in Belgium, the Netherlands and Germany', *Telematics and Informatics* 34:2 (2017), 548–59.

27 H. Özen, 'An unfinished grassroots populism: The Gezi park protests in Turkey and their aftermath', *South European Society and Politics* 20:4 (2015), 534.

28 Interview, German Embassy official, Ankara, 28 June 2019.

29 Interview, Pir Sultan Abdal Cultural Association official, Ankara, 31 July 2013.

30 A. Karakaya-Stump, 'Alevizing Gezi', *Jadaliyya*, 26 March 2014, www.jadaliyya.com/pages/index/17087/alevizing-gezi; M. Bardakçı, A. Freyberg-Inan, C. Giesel and O. Leisse, *Religious Minorities in Turkey: Alevi, Armenians and Syriacs and the Struggle to Desecuritise Religious Freedom* (Basingstoke: Palgrave Macmillan, 2017).

31 B. Esen and S. Gumuscu, 'Rising competitive authoritarianism in Turkey', *Third World Quarterly* 37:9 (2015), 1581–1606; M. Somer, 'Understanding Turkey's democratic breakdown: Old vs new and indigenous vs global authoritarianism', *Southeast European and Black Sea Studies* 16:4 (2016), 481–503.

32 B. Kadercan, 'The year of the Grey Wolf: The rise of Turkey's new ultranationalism', *War on the Rocks* (2018), https://warontherocks.com/2018/07/the-year-of-the-gray-wolf-the-rise-of-turkeys-new-ultranationalism; D. Okcuoglu, 'Territorial Control and Minority Reforms: A Study of the Kurdish Borderlands in Turkey' (PhD dissertation, Queen's University, 2019); A. Arkilic, 'Turkish populist nationalism in transnational space'.

33 A. Kaya, 'Islamisation of Turkey under the AKP rule: Empowering family, faith and charity', *South European Society and Politics* 20:1 (2015), 47–69.

34 B. Esen and S. Gumuscu, 'Why did Turkish democracy collapse?'

35 H. Taş, 'The 15 July abortive coup and post-truth politics in Turkey', *Southeast European and Black Sea Studies* 18:1 (2018), 1–19.

36 E. Elçi, 'The rise of populism in Turkey: A content analysis', *Southeast European and Black Sea Studies* 19:3 (2019), 387–408.

37 I. Yilmaz and G. Bashirov, 'The AKP after 15 years'.

38 *Ibid.*

39 For more, see: A. Arkilic, 'The 2017 Turkish constitutional referendum'. To access the proposed amendments in Turkish, see: http://anayasadegisikligi.barobirlik.org.tr/Anayasa_Degisikligi.aspx

40 A presidential decree removed Melih Bulu from office on 14 July 2021. See: 'Boğaziçi University's appointed rector Melih Bulu removed from office', *Bianet*, 15 July 2021, https://m.bianet.org/english/education/247292-bogazici-university-s-appointed-rector-melih-bulu-removed-from-office

41 B. McKernan, 'Student Protests Grow as Turkey's Young People Turn against Erdoğan', *Guardian*, 4 February 2021, www.theguardian.com/world/2021/feb/04/turkey-student-protests-grow-young-people-vent-frustrations-with-erdogan

42 A. Arkilic and A. E. Gurcan, 'The political participation of Alevis'.

43 F. Ateş, 'Bochum'daki tepki yılların birikimidir', *Alevilerin Sesi* 158 (2012).

44 Interview, FUAF official, Paris, 16 January 2019.

45 'Avrupalı Aleviler Strasbourg'ta Eylem Yaptı', *Haberler*, 21 October 2012, www.haberler.com/avrupali-aleviler-strasbourg-ta-eylem-yapti-4032207-haberi/

46 A. Arkilic, 'The Alevi diaspora in France: Changing relations with the home and host states', in *The Alevis in Modern Turkey and the Diaspora: Recognition, Mobilisation and Transformation*, eds H. Markussen and D. Ozkul (Edinburgh: Edinburgh University Press, 2022), pp. 166–90.

47 'Fransa'da Erdoğan'a protesto', *CNN Türk*, 21 June 2014, www.cnnturk.com/haber/turkiye/fransada-erdogana-protesto

48 'Strasbourg'dan "RTE hoş gelmedin" mesajı', *ANF News*, 4 October 2015, https://anfturkce.com/guncel/strasbourg-dan-rte-hos-gelmedin-mesaji-55514

49 *Ibid.*

50 'Alevilerin Strasbourg'dan Gericiliğe Dur Mesajı', *FUAF*, 6 September 2016, http://alevi-fuaf.com/tr/2016/09/06/alevilerin-strasburgdan-gericilige-dur-mesaji-turan-eser/

51 'Basına ve Kamuoyuna', *FUAF*, 3 February 2017, https://alevi-fuaf.com/tr/2017/02/03/basina-ve-kamuoyuna/

52 Interview, FUAF official, Paris, 21 January 2019.

53 'Fransa'nin 7 Kentinde Adalet Nöbeti', *FUAF*, 15 June 2020, https://alevi-fuaf.com/tr/2020/06/15/fransanin-6-kentinde-adalet-nobeti/

54 'Almanya'da Erdoğan protestosu', *Hürriyet*, 28 October 2012, www.hurriyet.com.tr/gundem/almanya-da-erdogan-protestosu-21798464

55 'Köln'de Gezi eylemi', *Hürriyet*, 22 June 2013, www.hurriyet.com.tr/gundem/kolnde-gezi-eylemi-23565537

56 H. Topçu, 'Köln'de onbinlerce kişi Erdoğan'ı protesto etti', *BBC Türkçe*, 25 May 2014, www.bbc.com/turkce/haberler/2014/05/140524_koln_yuruyus

57 'Alevilerden Köln'de protesto mitingi,' *Deutsche Welle*, 12 October 2016, www.dw.com/tr/alevilerden-k%C3%B6lnde-protesto-mitingi/a-36366025

58 E. Yalaz, 'Berlin'de Boğaziçi'ne destek gösterisi', *Deutsche Welle*, 9 January 2021, www.dw.com/tr/berlinde-bo%C4%9Fazi%C3%A7ine-destek-g%C3%B6sterisi/a-56181758

59 *Ibid.*

60 Interview, Paris Alevi Cultural Centre official, Paris, 9 December 2013.

61 Interview, FUAF official, Paris, 16 January 2019.

62 Interview, AABF official, Berlin, 25 February 2019.

63 *Ibid.*

64 Y. Özdemir, 'Bir diaspora hayali'.

65 Interview, Paris Alevi Cultural Centre official, Paris, 9 December 2013.

66 'Diyanet Alevi Dedeleri Almanya'ya Gönderdi', *Hürriyet*, 4 February 2007, www.hurriyet.com.tr/diyanet-alevi-dedeleri-almanyaya-gonderdi-5890952

67 *Ibid.*

68 Interview, Ahlal Bayt Alevi Federation of Europe official, Cologne, 29 November 2013.

69 *Ibid.*

70 This official's speech is available at: https://ytbweb1.blob.core.windows.net/files/resimler/kitaplar_pdf/Almanya_ve_Goc_50_Yilinda_Almanya_da_Turkler_Sempozyumu.pdf

71 Interview, Paris Alevi Cultural Centre official, Paris, 9 December 2013; Interview, AABF official, Berlin, 25 February 2019.

72 Interview, ACORT official, Paris, 22 January 2019.

73 Interview, ACORT official, Paris, 12 December 2013.

74 Interview, ACORT official, Paris, 22 January 2019.

75 *Ibid.*

76 *Ibid.*

77 *Ibid.*

78 'Fransa'da Boğaziçi Üniversitesi'ne destek bildirisine STK, sendika ve partilerden destek', *Gazete Duvar*, 10 February 2021, www.gazeteduvar.com.tr/

fransada-bogazici-universitesine-destek-bildirisine-stk-sendika-ve-partilerden-destek-haber-1512983

79	Interview, ELELE official, Paris, 20 February 2013.
80	*Ibid.*
81	*Ibid.*
82	Interview, Paris Alevi Cultural Centre official, Paris, 21 January 2019.
83	*Ibid.*
84	Interview, CHP official, Paris, 18 January 2019.
85	*Ibid.*
86	Interview, TGD official, Berlin, 12 February 2019.
87	'Almanyalı Türklere itidal çağrısı', *Deutsche Welle*, 2 November 2015, https://t24.com.tr/haber/almanyali-turklere-itidal-cagrisi,315061
88	Interview, TGD official, Berlin, 29 October 2013.
89	S. Doğanay, 'Kenan Kolat: AKP Yurtdışındakilere verdiği sözleri tutmadı', *Haberler*, 25 July 2020, www.ha-ber.com/kenan-kolat-akp-yurtdisindakilere-verdigi-sozu-tutmadi/149932/
90	'Almanyalı Türklere itidal çağrısı'.
91	Interview, TBB official, Berlin, 25 February 2019.
92	Interview, TBB official, Berlin, 12 February 2019.
93	'Mesut Ozil Quits German National Team, Citing Racism', *New York Times*, 22 July 2018, www.nytimes.com/2018/07/22/sports/mesut-ozil-quits-germany.html#:~:text=BERLIN%20%E2%80%94%20Mesut%20Ozil%20is%20quitting,his%20retirement%20from%20international%20soccer
94	'What Do the Kurds Want?', *Kurdish Institute of Paris* (2004), www.institut-kurde.org/activites_culturelles/appels/what_do_the_kurds_want_in_turkey/
95	A. Kürdi, 'Paris'te en büyük Kürt yürüyüşü', *Rojbas Varto*, 8 October 2011, www.rojbasvarto.com/?p=3196
96	'Paris'teki en büyük Kürt yürüyüşü', *Avrupa Postası*, 13 January 2013, www.avrupa-postasi.com/avrupa/paristeki-en-buyuk-kurt-yuruyusu-h88005.html
97	'French Kurds Protest in Paris against Turkey's Attack on Kurdish Militants', *i24 News*, 26 July 2015, www.i24news.tv/en/news/international/europe/79707–150725-french-kurds-protest-in-paris-against-turkey-s-attack-on-kurdish-militants
98	'Fransa'daki Kürtler AKP'yi protesto gösterilerine hazırlanıyor', *ANF News*, 16 September 2016, https://anfturkce.com/guncel/fransa-daki-kurtler-akp-yi-protesto-gosterilerine-hazirlaniyor-77987
99	'Thousands Protest in Europe against Turkey's Syria Offensive', *France24*, 12 October 2019, www.france24.com/en/20191012-thousands-protest-in-europe-against-turkey-s-syria-offensive
100	B. Baser, 'The Kurdish diaspora in Europe'.
101	'Berlin'de Kürt konferansı yapıldı', *Evrensel*, 12 September 2009, www.evrensel.net/haber/199236/berlin-de-kurt-konferansi-yapildi
102	C. Winter, 'Thousands of Kurds in Germany Rally against Turkey', *Deutsche Welle*, 3 September 2016, www.dw.com/en/thousands-of-kurds-in-germany-rally-against-turkey/a-19525234

103 'Germany Turkey: 30,000 Kurds in Frankfurt Anti-Erdogan Protest', *BBC*, 18 March 2017, www.bbc.com/news/world-europe-39318461

104 'Türkiye'nin askeri harekatı Almanya'da protesto edildi', *Deutsche Welle*, 12 October 2019, www.dw.com/tr/t%C3%BCrkiyenin-askeri-harek%C3%A2t%C4%B1-almanyada-protesto-edildi/a-50808463

105 'PKK'lılar Almanya'da camiye saldırdı', *Anadolu Ajansı*, 7 August 2015, www.aa.com.tr/tr/dunya/pkklilar-almanyada-camiye-saldirdi/18764

106 'Almanya'da Türk-Kürt kavgası', *Deutsche Welle*, 7 February 2017, www.dw.com/tr/almanyada-t%C3%BCrk-k%C3%BCrt-kavgas%C4%B1/a-37440248

107 'The Grey Wolves Conquering Europe'.

108 C. Dalaman, 'Almanya'da Ülkücü Dernekler Yasaklanıyor'.

109 Interview, Kurdish Institute of Paris official, Paris, 2 June 2013.

110 Y. Aydın, 'The New Turkish Diaspora Policy'.

111 Interview, HDP official, Berlin, 15 February 2019.

112 A. lmanya'da Erdoğan protestosu'; 'Alevi örgütlerinden Erdoğan protestosu', *Sol*, 31 October 2012, https://editor.sol.org.tr/soldakiler/alevi-orgutlerinden-erdogan-protestosu-ortadogu-diktatorunu-almanyada-istemiyoruz-haberi; A. C. Morin, 'Paris'ten Taksim'e Destek', *ACORT*, 6 June 2013, http://acort.org/?p=355

113 S. Yıldız, 'Kemal Burkay Londra'da Kürt açılımını ve son süreci değerlendirdi', *KOMKAR* (2010), www.komkar.dk/side89.html

114 'Diyaspora Kürtlerinden Yetmez Ama Evet!', *Newroz* (2010), www.newroz.com/tr/forum-topic/diyaspora-kuerd-konferansi-mi

115 Y. Özdemir, 'Bir diaspora hayali'.

116 'Avrupa'daki Kürt Açılımı', *Haberler*, 27 June 2011, www.haberler.com/2-avrupa-daki-kurt-acilimi-2827224-haberi/

117 'Diyaspora Kürt konferansı sonuç bildirisi', *KOMKAR* (2010), www.komkar.dk/side173.html

118 B. Baser, 'The Kurdish diaspora in Europe'.

119 '47.4 Percent of Turkish Asylum Seekers Granted Protection in Germany in 2019', *Duvar English*, 11 January 2020, www.duvarenglish.com/human-rights/2020/01/11/47-4-percent-of-turkish-asylum-seekers-granted-protection-in-germany-in-2019/

120 *Ibid.*

121 *Ibid.*

122 'Thousands of FETO Members Sought Asylum in EU Countries in Two Years', *Daily Sabah*, 22 August 2018, www.dailysabah.com/investigations/2018/12/22/thousands-of-feto-members-sought-asylum-in-eu-countries-in-two-years

123 *Ibid.*

124 L. Rodeheffer, 'Turkey's Influence Network in Europe is Leading to Tension', *Global Risk Insights*, 3 June 2017, https://globalriskinsights.com/2017/06/turkey-influence-network-europe/; E. Topçu, 'Turkey Using Interpol to Track Down Dissidents', *Deutsche Welle*, 7 November 2019, www.dw.com/en/turkey-using-interpol-to-track-down-dissidents/a-51159723

125 E. Topçu, 'Turkey Using Interpol to Track Down Dissidents'.

126 C. Winter, 'Turkish Imam Spy Affair Extends across Europe', *Deutsche Welle*, 16 February 2017, www.dw.com/en/turkish-imam-spy-affair-in-germany-extends-across-europe/a-37590672

127 *Ibid.*

128 K. Hamberger, 'Grünen-Politiker beantragt Einberufung des Kontrollgremiums', *Deutschland Funk*, 22 August 2016, www.deutschlandfunk.de/bericht-ueber-tuerkische-spitzel-gruenen-politiker.1766.de.html?dram:article_id= 363736

129 B. Bruce, *Governing Islam Abroad.*

130 'Germany Drops Inquiry against Turkish Imams Suspected of Spying on Erdogan's Behalf', *Reuters*, 7 December 2017, www.reuters.com/article/uk-germany-turkey-spying/germany-drops-inquiry-against-turkish-imams-suspected-of-spying-on-erdogans-behalf-idUKKBN1E023C

131 S. Morinière, 'Turquie: l'angoisse des gulénistes de France', *Le Monde*, 27 July 2016, www.lemonde.fr/europe/article/2016/07/27/turquie-l-angoisse-des-gulenistes-de-france_4975507_3214.html

132 *Ibid.*

133 *Ibid.*

134 *Ibid.*

135 M. Fayolle and M. Chantreau, 'La répression du mouvement güleniste en France', *France Culture*, 12 August 2016, www.franceculture.fr/societe/la-repression-du-mouvement-guleniste-en-france

136 M. de la Baume and G. Paravicini, '"Sleepless" Nights for Gülen's Supporters in Europe'.

137 'Erdoğan'ın ziyareti ve Almanya'daki Türkler', *Deutsche Welle*, 1 August 2018, www.dw.com/tr/erdoğanın-ziyareti-ve- almanyadaki-türkler/a-44908071

138 Interview, TBB official, Berlin, 12 February 2019; Interview, AABF official, Berlin, 25 February 2019.

139 'Thousands March in Germany in Support of Turkey's President Erdogan', *BBC*, 31 July 2016, www.bbc.com/news/world-europe-36937891

6

'Let us learn from them': France's response to Turkey's changing relations with its diaspora

> The Turkish diaspora is secondary to the North African diaspora. Turks are sometimes discussed at the local level but they are never part of a national debate. They are few in number. They are not part of the colonial discussion. They are better integrated into France than Maghrebis ... I am aware of Turkey's ongoing diaspora diplomacy but we should not be afraid of Turks' transformation into active citizens. It is indeed a positive development.[1]

Compared to other major western European countries, France has historically permitted more Turkish influence within its borders. For example, French reaction to Turkey's diaspora rallies has been mild compared to other countries: when Austria and Germany furiously opposed pro-AKP diaspora rallies on their soil, French officials declared that such gatherings posed no threat to them.[2] In March 2017, French authorities in Metz gave the Turkish Minister of Foreign Affairs a warm welcome at the same time as the Netherlands had banned him from giving a scheduled speech.[3] As noted in Chapter 3, Turkey also plays a dominant role in the CFCM and even opened a religious high school in France in 2015.[4] The DİTİB's five-acre site in Strasbourg, which functions as 'the largest Muslim site in Europe',[5] and the *Millî Görüş*'s gargantuan Eyyûb Sultan Mosque project in the same city, which has received generous financial support from the Mayor of Strasbourg, are evidence of Turkey's growing presence in France. Turkey's important role in religious governance in France is in stark contrast to its limited involvement in the conduct of theology institutes and the DIK in Germany.

Another example of greater Turkish leeway in the country is France's reluctance to launch a Turkish language and civilisation CAPES (Certificate of Aptitude for Teaching in Secondary Education) programme that would train local certified teachers to be appointed to public schools.[6] France's historical dependency on teachers sent from Turkey through the ELCO programme is puzzling given that French universities have the capacity to train these teachers if the country wishes to (re)gain some control over Turkey's actions in this regard.[7] The increasing politicisation of Turkish Muslims has not attracted much attention in France either. As will be explained below, while the DİTİB and the *Millî Görüş* have been blacklisted or faced investigations and raids in most other European countries, they still maintain their political activities and representation in France. The UID and the COJEP have also lobbied at the national and EU level without any serious backlash.[8]

This does not mean, however, that Ankara's activities in France go unnoticed. For example, in 2018, *Le Point* published a piece alleging extensive corruption and spying activities within the DİTİB branches in France.[9] In a similar vein, French officials from the Ministry of the Interior warned that 'language teachers sent from Turkey convey nationalistic propaganda'[10] and that 'French policymakers should be sceptical of Ankara's tentacles because the AKP has developed not only a religious and educational transnational agenda but also a political one'.[11]

In 2018, Franco-Turkish interests clashed once again when President Macron met with members of the Kurdish-dominated Syrian Democratic Forces (SDF), led by the People's Protection Units (YPG), and offered mediation between them and Ankara. France sees the YPG as a key ally against the Islamic State, whereas for Turkey, the YPG remains a terrorist group. Consequently, Erdoğan rejected Macron's mediation offer and asked him to take a 'clear stance against all types of terrorism'.[12] One year later, Macron expressed discontent with Ankara's military operation against the YPG in northern Syria[13] and announced that 24 April would be 'a national day of commemoration of the Armenian genocide'.[14]

Further tension erupted in the second half of 2020 when Macron extended his support to Greece and Cyprus in the dispute over natural-gas reserves in the eastern Mediterranean and asked the EU to impose sanctions on Turkey because of Turkish drilling activities in the region.[15] A number of European heads of state and government have supported Macron by expressing similar views.[16] This call came two months after a French ship attempted to inspect a Turkish vessel as part of a UN arms embargo for Libya.[17] In addition to supporting rival sides in the Libyan civil war, Turkey and France vie for clout in predominantly Muslim West African countries.[18] President Macron has also accused Turkey of sending Syrian jihadists to defend Azerbaijan in the Nagorno-Karabakh conflict against Armenia.[19]

Perhaps more importantly, as described in Chapter 3, Macron's vow to limit foreign influence in the country drove a wedge between Ankara and Paris. Following a decision taken in February 2020, France now asks Turkish language teachers sent from Ankara to meet upper-intermediate French fluency requirements.[20] Macron even announced in October 2020 that France is determined to terminate the ELCO partnership with Turkey.[21] Erdoğan called the move 'an open provocation' and Macron 'impertinent'.[22] He went on to publicly question the state of Macron's mental health, which led France to recall its ambassador to Turkey. Turkey then urged its citizens to boycott French products.[23] However, damaged diplomatic relations softened a little when the French Delegation to NATO sent greetings to their 'ally' Turkey on Turkish Republic Day. The Turkish Delegation to NATO responded to the kind gesture with a thank-you note.[24] Since January 2021, Paris and Ankara have been following a roadmap to further improve ties.[25]

This chapter argues that France's traditionally less interventionist stance towards Turkey can be explained by several factors. Turks have a privileged status in the eyes of French policymakers vis-à-vis North Africans because of their smaller numbers. Turks also have a less contested historical relationship with France than that of North Africans who suffered under French colonialism and its inherent racial hierarchies.[26] But Turks' status stems not only from the lack of a colonial relationship between Turkey and France but from the popular French conception of Turkey as a country like France (both with strong state traditions and a secular regime) and of Turks as people with a liminal position between Europe and the Middle East. The chapter also examines France's *laïc* regime and relations with the Muslim community to account for the historically greater Turkish influence in the country. In order to elaborate on these points, the chapter will first outline France's broader immigration, citizenship and integration policies and then examine state policies towards religion, with a focus on the country's relations with the Turkish community.

Immigration, citizenship and integration policies in France

According to the French High Council for Integration, 'an immigrant is a non-French person born abroad and who lives in France'.[27] This definition includes the criterion of nationality at birth. An immigrant may decide to keep his or her citizenship or obtain French citizenship, yet immigrant status is permanent in both cases.[28] According to official statistics, in 2018 there were 6.5 million immigrants in France, 9.7 per cent of the total population of 67 million. Of these, 4.1 million were foreign nationals and 2.4 million had obtained French citizenship.[29] Around 13 per cent of immigrants in France were born in Algeria, 11.9 per cent in Morocco, 9.2 per cent in Portugal, 4.4 per cent in Tunisia, 4.3 per cent in Italy and 3.8 per cent in Turkey.[30] The French citizenship regime does not officially recognise the diversity of its citizens.[31] Since it is illegal to inquire about religious affiliation in the French census, there is no official statistical information on the Muslim population of France. However, estimations suggest France has around 5.7 million Muslims (8.8 per cent of the country's population),[32] and, as such, it hosts the largest Muslim population in Europe.[33]

During the early decades of immigration, especially at the height of the Industrial Revolution, France attracted emigrant workers mainly from other European countries, such as Poland, Belgium, Italy and Spain, to address demographic and economic concerns.[34] France's first significant encounter with Muslims occurred in the nineteenth century, with the colonisation of Algeria and Sub-Saharan Africa. French protectorates in Morocco and Tunisia, and mandates in Syria and Lebanon, magnified the French state's relationship with Muslims.[35] However, immigration has never defined France's national identity because of the 'myth of the ethnic homogeneity of its population'.[36] Until 1980, France's laissez-faire approach to immigration resulted in spontaneous and clandestine policies, and a failure to seriously address immigrant integration.[37]

France's current civic-territorial and assimilationist model – that aims to turn immigrants into citizens by cementing them into dominant culture and confines cultural difference to the private sphere – has made it difficult for immigrants and their children to blend into French society.[38] The fact that the French census does not gather data on ethnic origin or religious belief and refuses to consider French-born immigrant children part of the immigrant population, on the basis of the republican principles of unity and equality, has also rendered them statistically hidden.[39]

The 1889 Nationality Law forms the legal cornerstone of contemporary French nationality law. In the first half of the nineteenth century, most people born on French soil to foreign parents were not accepted as French citizens, and only a child born to a French father, either in France or abroad, was granted automatic French citizenship. This principle of *jus sanguinis* dominated French nationality legislation between 1803 and 1889.[40] Since 1889, French citizenship legislation has been a mixture of *jus soli* and *jus sanguinis*. Today citizenship is granted at birth if at least one of the child's parents is French or if the child was born in France and has one France-born parent. A person born in France whose parents are neither French nor were born in France automatically becomes French at the age of eighteen if they still reside in France and do not decline citizenship. Immigrants may also apply for naturalisation after five years of residence (although if an immigrant comes from a former colony or a Francophone country, there is no required period of residence). French citizenship can be acquired if a person remains married to a French citizen for five years and lives with their spouse.[41]

Models of citizenship create divergent opportunities and obstacles for immigrants. Rogers Brubaker argues that the persistently higher naturalisation rates in France compared to Germany can be explained by these countries' different historical traditions of citizenship.[42] Unlike France, *jus sanguinis* regimes, such as pre-2000 Germany, base citizenship on an ascriptive, ethno-cultural community of descent and common cultural traditions.[43]

Yet scholars suggest that France's unconditional dual citizenship, lower naturalisation requirements and strict colour-blind approach to race and ethnicity provide a more suitable context for immigrants than Germany's citizenship regime even after the 2000 German citizenship reform.[44]

The first significant emigration from Muslim colonies to France took place during World War I to supplement military personnel.[45] In the aftermath of the war, France once again sought to address its population decline through immigration, with most newcomers coming from Italy, Spain, Portugal, Eastern Europe and Russia.[46] The General Immigration Society, founded by employers, shaped immigration policy in this period: a 1927 law on naturalisation allowed foreigners that had been residing in the country for at least three years to become citizens.[47] France also welcomed North Africans living in French colonies to help meet labour shortages.[48] Yet economic recession in this decade halted the arrival of immigrants and spawned xenophobic sentiments.[49] The economic and political climate preceding World War II led France to embrace a hierarchical immigrant quota that placed Arab-origin immigrants at the bottom of the ladder and Europeans at the top.[50]

The period 1945–74 witnessed an expansion of the French economy and a series of attempts to create an inclusionary immigration policy. The Ordinance of 1945 (*Ordonnance*), the first legal immigration act, rejected the idea of selecting immigrants on the basis of ethnicity and natural origins, and prioritised economic and demographic needs instead.[51] While this immigration law still constitutes the backbone of French immigration policy, the idea of the better 'assimilability' of certain immigrant groups over others has not entirely faded and, in fact, returned in full force amid economic problems in the following decades.[52]

From the 1950s, the process of decolonisation in North and Sub-Saharan Africa led to the recruitment of non-white immigrants and the entry of people into the labour force without legal documents.[53] While internal and external restrictions were in place, immigration from former colonies also continued through family reunification.[54] These communities became the main non-white immigrant groups settling in metropolitan France in the post-World War II decades.[55] In particular, the 1954 Algerian War of Independence led to a major wave of emigrants from Algeria.[56] Yet the word 'integration' was rarely used by policymakers, journalists and scholars. Even though France lacked an integration policy, officials promoted specific treatments for emigrants coming from formerly colonised lands, who were seen as 'foreigners' and hard to assimilate.[57] These newcomers, particularly Algerians, struggled with racism.[58] The 1961 Massacre of Paris in the last years of the Algerian War of Independence caused the death of approximately fifty Algerians.[59]

The protests, marches and factory closures that resulted from such racism between May and June 1968 prompted a radical turn in French immigration policy. The government's reaction to the involvement of immigrants in the protests was harsh: France unilaterally restricted the number of Algerians who could enter the country, and this swift change was the first manifestation of the government's recognition of the potential danger of a large, disenfranchised and unassimilated North African population.[60] The oil crisis in 1973, a rise in unemployment and Valéry Giscard d'Estaing's presidency of 1974–81 marked the beginning of a restrictive immigration policy.[61]

With the election of the Socialist François Mitterrand to the presidency (1981–95), immigration policies moved towards a liberalising 'grand bargain'.[62] The Mitterrand government granted conditional amnesty to undocumented immigrants as well as residency and work permits to all immigrants.[63] After this decision, the wives and children of immigrants still living in their countries of origin moved to France – the largest number of newcomers in the following two decades. Yet most of these families settled in social housing in poor neighbourhoods and sent their children to failing schools.[64] The second generation of non-white immigrants, mostly of North African origin, realised that while they had been expected to become culturally French, they were socio-economically marginalised. Their grievances led to the first urban riots, in the *banlieues* of Lyon in the early 1980s.[65] In 1982, a new policy sought to upgrade the living conditions of socio-economically excluded immigrants. Although the policy did not highlight the ethnic composition of those living in the 'ghettos', North and Sub-Saharan African-origin individuals were the main target of this policy. The amendments improved housing, yet unemployment rates among these groups have remained high.[66]

Immigration became more politicised when the far-right National Front (FN), led by Jean-Marie Le Pen, won near 11 per cent of the vote in the 1984 European elections. This was the first time since 1945 that an extremist party on the right had gained national popularity.[67] Between the mid-1980s and the late 1990s, the FN garnered approximately 10 to 15 per cent of the popular vote in regional, national and European elections.[68] A one-time use of proportional representation in the 1986 legislative elections allowed the FN to send thirty-five deputies to the National Assembly.[69]

In 1990, the French government established the High Council for Integration, which questioned the assimilationist policies of the postcolonial era, emphasised the principle of equality and asserted that integration required the mutual efforts of immigrants and wider society.[70] Yet most administrative officials, local authorities and social workers resorted to a specific and pragmatic treatment of immigrants when they encountered suburban, socio-cultural and religious differences.[71] French immigration policy focused on public order and national security throughout the 1990s, and legislation, such as the 1993 Méhaignerie Law, set extensive residency requirements for North Africans claiming citizenship.[72] Official reports published in the 1990s perpetuated an exclusionary rhetoric and singled out Muslims as a group with deep-seated cultural and religious traits at odds with the core values of French society.[73] However, the left came back to power in 1997 and, once again, envisioned a liberalised immigration policy: an expert committee's recommendations served as the basis for a 1998 nationality law that facilitated the admission procedure for professionals, restored double *jus soli*, re-simplified the process for automatic *jus soli* at the age of eighteen and facilitated spousal naturalisation.[74]

The conservative government, in which Nicholas Sarkozy served as the new Minister of the Interior (2002–07), once again tightened immigration policy in the early 2000s.[75] The first Sarkozy Law, in 2003, sought to curb irregular immigration, facilitated expulsion and demanded harsher controls on marriage with foreign spouses.[76] Moreover, France introduced tighter controls on immigration in response to the 2005 *banlieue* riots by younger North and Sub-Saharan African immigrants.[77] By 2005, emigrants from the African continent outnumbered emigrants from Europe for the first time.[78] In 2006, the second Sarkozy Law introduced new rules on marriage and decreased the number of visas available.[79] This law also advocated for 'chosen immigration' to meet the needs of the French economy.[80] Under Sarkozy's presidency (2007–12), immigration policies remained restrictive.[81]

Even though Socialist François Hollande's presidency (2012–17) indicated a less draconian immigration policy, his term brought about no significant changes.[82] Hollande offered an entry visa for highly skilled immigrants, expanded the duration of residence authorisations from one to two years and liberalised naturalisation procedures. Yet he made it clear that every immigrant was required to learn French and complete civic training on republican values. He also failed to address discrimination in schools and the labour market, and immigrants' spatial segregation.[83] In addition, while Hollande had initially advocated for an open-door policy in the wake of the European refugee crisis and sworn an oath to accept 24,000 asylum seekers, he had admitted only 7,000 by 2016.[84] Yet even with these numbers, France became host to the second largest number of refugees in Europe.[85]

Following the *Charlie Hebdo* and Bataclan terrorist attacks in Paris in 2015, and the Nice truck attack in 2016, Hollande declared that there was a religious radicalisation problem with Islam.[86] This announcement reflected growing Islamophobia in the country.[87] An expert from the High Council for Integration similarly suggested that the French public was subject to overwhelming 'emotional aggression' from the Muslim community with the intensification of the public visibility of Islam over the last decade.[88]

Centrist Emmanuel Macron's election to presidency in 2017 – after a tight race with FN (National Rally, or RN, since 2018) candidate Marine Le Pen – initiated an increasingly tougher immigration policy. A bill passed in 2018 shortened asylum application deadlines, increased the detention period for new arrivals and mandated a one-year prison sentence for entering France illegally.[89] Under Macron's rule, asylum seekers are also required to wait three months to qualify for non-urgent health care and skilled migrants are subject to annual quotas.[90] In addition, Macron's policies led to the demolition of refugee camps across France.[91]

State policies towards religion

State policies towards religion in France have historically been shaped by an ideological battle between proponents of a combative secularism (*laïcité de combat*) and a pluralistic secularism (*laïcité plurielle*). Combative secularism aims to separate religion from the public sphere, whereas pluralistic secularism allows for the public visibility of religion. The principle of combative secularism is the dominant ideology in France and determines state policy on the accommodation of religious practices and groups.[92]

After the gradual loss of the Catholic Church's power in the aftermath of the 1789 French Revolution, the Third French Republic (1870–1940) institutionalised secularism.[93] The first two articles of the 1905 Law constitute the legal basis of French *laïcité*: Article 1 states that the Republic guarantees freedom of conscience, and free practise of religions is subject only to the restrictions set out in the interests of public policy. Article 2 stipulates that the state should not recognise nor subsidise any religion (*cultes*), although expenses related to chaplaincy services and designed to guarantee the free exercise of religions in public establishments (including schools, colleges, nursing homes, asylums and prisons) may be covered by specified state budgets.[94]

What makes the French system unique in Europe is that the 1905 Law ended state protection for Catholicism, Protestantism and Judaism, which had been previously acknowledged and funded by the state – that is, no religion is recognised by the French state, and all religions and beliefs stand on an equal legal footing.[95] The separation was specifically directed at the Catholic Church due to the 1801 Concordat signed between Napoleon I and Pope Pius XII, which granted the French state the right to nominate bishops and created a system of 'recognised religion' (*cultes reconnus*) in which three branches of Christianity (Roman Catholic, Lutheran and Calvinist) and Judaism were all equal, with Catholicism being the first among equals.[96] The Alsace-Moselle region is still subject to the Concordat, rather than the 1905 Law, because the region was under German authority in 1905; even when Alsace-Moselle was reintegrated into France, the 1905 Law did not abrogate the Concordat.[97] As a result, education in one of these religions is compulsory at primary and secondary school level, and the regional government pays the salaries of its religious ministers (pastors, priests and rabbis). Christian churches and Jewish subsidiaries also receive public grants, and the state finances the construction of places of worship that belong to the recognised religions.[98] The exclusion of Muslims from this arrangement – due to them being a post-1905 phenomenon – has encouraged the Muslim community 'to build their mosques in basements and to seek foreign support', as a French mayor from the region asserted.[99]

Religious groups are entitled to form religious associations in France. The definition and operation of these associations are subject to Sections 18 and 19 of the 1905 Law, according to which these associations can have no other purpose other than as religious organisations and are not allowed to receive subsidies from public funds.[100] They can benefit from tax exemptions when they receive donations if the state explicitly accepts their status as a religious association and grants them full legal capacity during the receipt of donations.[101]

While Muslim organisations are contingent on the 1905 Law, they rarely become religious associations under it and operate instead under the Law of 1 July 1901.[102] This law ensured that the right to form associations was a fundamental public right; any association that has legal status can be formed freely and should be disbanded only if it endangers public policy. Since 1981, foreigners have been allowed to establish associations in France.[103] In theory, these associations should only receive hand-delivered gifts with no tax benefits for the donor, but, under certain conditions, associations formed under the 1901 Law can be categorised as 'public utility associations' and receive major tax benefits, and even request subsidies from public authorities.[104] In other words, although the state provides no direct funding to religious organisations from the public budget, religious associations may receive indirect financial assistance.[105] This means that even though the constitution demands a strict separation of church and state in France, in reality the rules are at times relaxed in a way that provides financial benefits to Muslim organisations, and this is the opposite of what happens in Germany.[106] A bureaucrat from the French Ministry of the Interior explained further: 'Our law says: "You cannot intervene in religious organisations" ... This is the liberty of religions. This is why it's easier for foreign states to step in ... Umbrella organisations are formed easily in France. We don't evaluate the question of immigration from the perspective of Islam. Never. We don't want radicalists, we don't want political Islam, but we don't care about the rest. This is laïcité.'[107]

The Islamic-headscarf controversy is one of the most contentious issues with respect to the interplay between French *laïcité* and the accommodation of Muslim religious rights. In 1989, the director of a public high school in Creil, north of Paris, expelled three Muslim schoolgirls after they wore a headscarf (*hijab*).[108] When the school administrators and parents of the girls could not reach a mutually suitable solution, the then Minister of Education, Lionel Jospin, took the case to the Council of the State. The Council ruled that if teachers wore a headscarf, it would be a violation of the principle of *laïcité*; however, for students, it was permissible, in accordance with the 'freedom of conscience' principle.[109]

This ruling did not resolve the headscarf controversy: it came to the forefront again in 2003 when the then president, Jacques Chirac, set up a commission to reassess the implementation of the *laïcité* principle. The Stasi Commission's report[110] laid the grounds for a 2004 law on secularism and conspicuous religious symbols at public schools that prohibited the wearing of Islamic headscarves as well as Christian and Jewish religious symbols and dress.[111] This was a surprising decision given that only a marginal number of students were wearing headscarves at school before the law passed.[112] A new law, following a report by André Gerin, a member of the National Assembly, came into effect in 2011, prohibiting the wearing of full-face veils (*voile intégral*) in public.[113] According to the law, a woman wearing a full-face veil must pay €150 and take a compulsory French citizenship course, and individuals forcing women to wear a *burqa* or a *niqab* are subject to a €30,000 fine or one-year imprisonment.[114]

Education is another hallmark institution of France's *laïcité*. In keeping with the 1905 Law, the national curriculum does not teach religion as a formal subject in primary education, although primary schools are allowed to close one day a week, with the exception of Sunday, to permit parents to register their children in religious education organised by non-state entities.[115] In addition, chaplains are free to teach religion in secondary schools outside the school timetable. Yet this guideline does not benefit French Muslims because no Islamic chaplaincy operates in secondary schools (with the exception of the Alsace-Moselle region).[116] Although religion is not taught within the public school system, France provides significant funding for private religious schools that have been under contract with the state since the 1959 Debré Law, which deemed the state responsible for nearly 85 per cent of teachers' salaries and certain school expenditures. In return, these schools are required to follow the rules imposed on them and the curriculum devised by the Ministry of Education.[117]

Around one fifth of all secondary schools in France are private, most of which are owned by the Catholic Church, but there are also Jewish, Protestant and Muslim schools.[118] Muslims seeking public funding must prove that their school has been functioning for at least five years, their teachers are qualified to provide a good education, the size of the student body is relatively large and the school facilities are hygienic.[119] There are several prominent private Muslim schools in France.[120] In addition, there are private religious schools that do not have a contract with the French state and fund their operations themselves; these schools make up 3 per cent of all schools in France.[121] The establishment of private Gülenist and *Millî Görüş* schools was an important addition to the private Muslim school market and a watershed for the Turkish community in France (see Chapter 3).

With the growth of the Muslim population over time, various other religious issues – the construction of mosques, the allocation of Muslim cemetery spaces and the accreditation of imams – have challenged prevailing understandings of French secularism. As discussed previously, the French state established the CFCM in 2003 as a representative body that would serve as a bridge between French Muslims and state authorities, and ultimately create an Islam *of* France in lieu of an Islam *in* France. The very establishment of the institution ended up enhancing the continuing influence of foreign governments on the French Muslim community.[122] Macron's 2020 promise to reform Islam in the country seeks to amend this arrangement.

Situating Turks in France

Given the history of French state policies towards Muslims, how do Turks fit into the picture? As emphasised earlier, Turks arguably have a privileged status in the eyes of French policymakers vis-à-vis North Africans, who significantly outnumber the Turkish community. Turks' smaller numbers and minority status in France is the opposite of the situation in Germany, where Turks form the largest and, therefore, the most visible Muslim group.[123] My interviews with French bureaucrats confirmed this observation. According to an official from the Ministry of Europe and Foreign Affairs:

> In Germany, the size of the Turkish community is much bigger, and the way Germany has dealt with the immigration issue has ostracised Turks. Here, the Algerian, Tunisian and Moroccan population is much larger than the Turkish community and attracts more attention. Turkish integration has never been as problematic as North African integration. Turks have come to France more recently but have accomplished more than other migrant groups despite their smaller population. The majority of Islamic State terrorists here are home-grown Maghrebis ... We don't have in the French spirit, in the French mind, the idea that a Turk would be radicalised.[124]

Officials from the Ministry of Justice and the Ministry of the Interior made similar remarks: 'We view Turks as very integrated, peaceful and economically successful people … In confidential documents, I never see sentences discussing "the Turkish problem" … From a security perspective, Moroccan imams are more dangerous.'[125] A Ministry of Interior representative concluded: 'Turks in France are perceived as active, skilled workers. Their close-knit nature is not a problem for me because they are a small group and they have the right to stay closed … We have 100 radical Salafist mosques in France. Not a single one is Turkish.'[126]

Turks enjoy an advantageous position in France also because their historical relationship with the country is less contested than that of North Africans who endured French colonialism and its racial hierarchies, which marked those perceived as 'coloured' as inferior to white people.[127] In France, Frenchness and French identity were perceived as 'white', and North Africans, as a distinct group, were constructed and racialised as 'coloured'.[128] The presumed markers of race or 'non-whiteness' of North Africans are 'skin colour, hair, features, language varieties, and by extension family name, religion, in short, people's ways of being and knowing', which 'have long standing social meanings in France, underpinned and enlivened by ideologies and policies acting on them'.[129]

As Jennifer Fredette argues, despite their diversity and the fact that 'there is no one French Muslim identity', French elite discourse has commonly portrayed North Africans as a homogeneous group mainly concerned with religion, while simultaneously demarcating another identity, 'the good French citizen', that is superior to and threatened by the former identity.[130] In fact, even middle-class and educated descendants of North African immigrants face symbolic exclusion and are often viewed as foreigners.[131] David Theo Goldberg similarly notes that 'by the late Enlightenment racial hierarchization of national character, Immanuel Kant could wedge "the Arab", "possessed of an inflamed imagination", "between the basest of (Southern) Europeans and the Far East, but significantly above "the Negroes of Africa"'.[132] In his view, 'The idea of the European excludes those historically categorized as non-European, as being not white. You are here but don't (really or fully) belong. Your sojourn is temporary, so don't grow too comfortable. Hence the constant drumbeat about sending "them" back.'[133]

Turks in France have not been part of the racialised hierarchical structure. This is striking given that studies have found North Africans to be better integrated overall than Turks in socio-economic and political terms (as discussed in Chapter 3).[134] Turks are perceived as people with deep connections to Europe. As a diplomat from the Ministry of Europe and Foreign Affairs stated: 'I grew up with the idea that Turks and the French have been in connection for nearly 500 years, and Turkey is a very important and respectful partner.'[135] Another diplomat explained further:

> We have a very old history with Turkey. Don't forget that in 1536, almost five centuries ago, the French king Francis I and the Ottoman sultan Suleiman I signed a groundbreaking agreement to form an alliance. About eighty years after the conquest of Constantinople, in Christian Europe it was incredibly audacious for the French king to sign this accord with the Ottoman sultan. Turkey and France became equal partners with it. And since then we have formed very special relations in trade, military cooperation and culture. Whereas when you look at Turkey's historical relations with Germany, you will see that there was no equality. Germans always tried to dominate Turks ... There are many similarities between us. The Ottoman and Turkish constitutions were inspired by the French one. Turkish secularism took France as a model. Even our judicial systems are similar.[136]

A third diplomat added: 'As far as I can remember, we don't have [any account] in our history showing Turks as bad guys ... Atatürk was one of the greatest statesmen of the twentieth century. That's what we were told at school. He shared similarities with Charles de Gaulle. Like de Gaulle, Atatürk, as a military commander, experienced extreme wars and then founded a strong and centrist regime.' This diplomat also referred to how the Enlightenment, the French Revolution and French sovereignty and étatism had a profound influence on Atatürk and the leading Turkish republican elite, emphasising the smooth historical cooperation between the two countries: 'Turkey granted France a diplomatic representation on its soil in 1935 and even backed France at the UN General Assembly during the Algerian crisis.'[137]

His words are also telling in terms of Turks' liminal positionality in the eyes of French policymakers: 'Turks are probably the only Muslim community that is culturally similar to us. They are part of us.'[138] An official from the Ministry of the Interior added: 'France does not consider Turks as Muslims. Most people in France would say that they are part of Europe. They do not make a link between Islam and Turkishness.'[139] Another bureaucrat from the same institution said: 'I would argue that Turkish culture is very close to European culture. Istanbul is in Europe, so that's a natural connection ... Turkey is the only laïc country in the Muslim world ... Despite Erdoğan, we still see Turks this way, as secular, Western people ... Also, not every Turk here is an Erdoğan supporter. We have many Turks with French citizenship and secular identity.'[140]

Interestingly, Turks in France indeed 'think of themselves as being free from discrimination like the Europeans' even though they encounter the same obstacles as North Africans and experience discrimination at only slightly lower rates.[141] The majority of Turks are positive towards French society (with an average favourability score of 7.49 out of 10, with '1' being 'not at all' and '10' being 'very much') and feel accepted by their French colleagues and neighbours (average acceptance score of 8.96 out of 10).[142] Furthermore, only a limited number of Turks have reported a physical or verbal racist attack (average score of 1.69 out of 10) even though they experience many more attacks.[143]

France also sees Turkey as an experienced and reliable country, with valuable expertise to share regarding the governance of Islam, due to its *laïc* regime.[144] As a *Le Monde* reporter put it, 'France knows that Turkey has a lot of power over its diaspora and does not want to have a clash. France needs Turkey more than Germany, Austria, the Netherlands and the United Kingdom do. We need Turkey to administer Islam because, unlike these countries, we are a secular country.'[145] An expert from the Ministry of the Interior confirmed that French officials are more supportive of Turkey's diaspora outreach initiatives than their German counterparts because France does not have the necessary experience and tools to govern Islam in the country and, therefore, has to rely on Turkey for help: 'Very few people within French intelligence and diplomacy know Turkish. Our focus is on Arabic. That's why we are not even capable of detecting what kinds of messages are delivered by Turkish imams in Friday sermons.'[146] In other words, France is only able to *partly* govern Islam.[147]

In particular, the DİTİB is still seen as an important partner for the French state. In the words of an official from the Ministry of Europe and Foreign Affairs:

> Islam is new in France. It is not like Judaism or Protestantism, which are religions we are familiar with. We are grateful for the DİTİB's presence and support because it plays an important role in enhancing the co-existence of the Muslim and non-Muslim populations, and in helping French authorities form healthier relations with the Muslim population. Let us learn from them … We are less 'hands on' compared to Germany because we are a secular country and we do not have many young people that are eligible to become imams. Do you know that in the French Catholic church today, 20 per cent of the priests are foreigners, from Africa, Holland and Latin America? If we accept this for Catholics, we have to accept it for Muslims as well.[148]

Officials from the Ministry of the Interior agreed: 'The *Diyanet* is important. It fulfils some key roles for us … It keeps Turks away from radicalisation because it is state-controlled, it is moderate… Turkish influence is better than a void … This is convenient for us – that's why France has not demanded more say in religious affairs.'[149] Another bureaucrat from the Ministry of Justice informed me that *Diyanet* personnel should be respected if France wishes to empower its Muslim community: 'If we support strong, prestigious institutions like that, we will increase Muslims' profile in the country.'[150] French understanding of the *Diyanet* as a moderate religious authority and a key interlocutor is in line with the Turkish state's projection of the *Diyanet* since the early 2000s as an institution compatible with modernity, rationality and secularism, and as a model for 'European' or 'French Islam', unlike its extremist rivals in Shiite Iran or Wahhabi Saudi Arabia.[151]

Interviews also reveal that representatives of Turkish Muslim organisations in France believe that they enjoy a better status and less discrimination vis-à-vis other Muslim groups in the country. These leaders perceive France as a more accommodating country in terms of state policies towards Islam than Germany, and the CFCM as a more legitimate institution than the DIK.[152] According to them, French bureaucrats keep an equal distance from all religious groups, and view Turkish Muslims as reliable and legitimate dialogue partners. This stance prevents potential grudges and allows for better integration of Turkish Muslims into French society.[153]

For example, as noted in Chapter 3, the *Millî Görüş*, despite having a very negative image in Germany, has become a permanent member of the CFCM, and the DİTİB chaired the CFCM from 2017 to 2019: 'We feel free in the CFCM. Unlike Turks in Germany, we are a minority in France. Nobody meddles with our business.'[154] Turkish Muslim leaders also reported that they receive generous subsidies for their cultural and sporting activities from local authorities, contrary to the situation in Germany.[155] A French diplomat verified that 'Turks got inside the CFCM's structure and took over, which is a new and surprising development given that they have a shorter history in France … Turks have a strong potential to influence French and EU politics.'[156] While recent debates over the restructuring of Islam have strained relations between French authorities and Turkish Islamic organisations, these groups are still regarded more positively by French policymakers than by their German counterparts.

That said, while most French policymakers I spoke to are in favour of heightened Turkish influence in religious affairs in France, in siding with Macron some, including a bureaucrat from the Ministry of the Interior, follow these developments with suspicion: 'Ankara thinks "France is secular. We can do whatever we want to do. France will not interfere". And they are right … Islam is still not a French affair. It is seen as a foreign affairs issue. It is not localised yet, because of *laïcité*.'[157] He added that Turkey's engagement in France warrants attention because it is more assertive, institutionalised and expensive than that of Morocco, Algeria or Tunisia. Unlike these countries, according to this respondent, Turkey approaches its diaspora 'as part of the reimagination of Turkish identity'.[158] Another official from the same institution gave details about France's 'vexing negligence' and how his warnings had fallen on deaf ears: 'Turks want to dominate mosques in critical areas. This is a global project that will have important repercussions because Turks are the most important Muslim community in Europe and one of the most important in the world. Most French politicians think that Turkey is harmless, unable to see the connection between the AKP and the DİTİB.'[159]

While Macron is committed to curtailing foreign influence over the Muslim community in France, this master plan will be difficult to implement. As Olivier Roy put it, 'that's the paradox: to defend secularism with a plan based on the state's intervention in religion. That's why, for so many years, nothing has been done ... The state cannot force Muslims to exclusively attend sermons by "certified" imams. That would be anti-constitutional, and it'd be shut down immediately at the European Court of Human Rights.'[160] Furthermore, while Macron's strategy is aimed at Muslims, any eventual legislation would need to apply to other religions as well because the 1905 Law stipulates that all religions are on an equal footing before the law.[161] Other French experts on Islam, such as François Burgat and Alain Gabon, have called on France to put an end to this confrontational and marginalising atmosphere.[162] Left- and right-wing critics, including Jean-Luc Mélenchon, the head of the left-wing France Unbowed, and RN leader, Marine Le Pen, also argue that Macron risks undermining the very idea of *laïcité* by trying to influence Islamic institutions, by meddling in the training and financing of imams and by exercising 'disguised' hatred against Muslims.[163] Many Muslim groups in France have also fiercely objected to Macron's proposal.[164]

Conclusion

France is home to the largest Muslim population in Europe. The majority of Muslim emigrants came to France from North African countries, starting in the nineteenth century with the colonisation of North and Sub-Saharan Africa. As Muslim arrivals increased on the heels of the decolonisation of the African continent and the end of the Algerian War of Independence, new problems emerged between France and its Muslim population. France's colonial past provides a fertile ground for the modern racism aimed at the descendants of colonised peoples: the 'coloniality of power'[165] did not end with colonialism, and societal divisions and inequalities targeting the Maghrebi population are perpetuated on a daily basis in France. Turks, to some extent, are exempt from the hierarchical racial categorisation in France because of the lack of a colonial relationship between the two countries, and a shared understanding among many French public officials of Turks as people who are deeply embedded in Europe.

In order to understand why Turkey's engagement with its diaspora has traditionally been tolerated more in France than in Germany, this chapter has reviewed France's immigration, citizenship and integration policies, and its state policies towards religion. While the French state is not uniform and there are discrepancies between different ministries and different levels of government, Turks overall have a more positive image in France compared to other Muslim communities. Turks are less integrated into France than North Africans; however, they are viewed as a better assimilated and more harmonious immigrant group due to their smaller size and less turbulent historical relations. According to many French bureaucrats, the French and Turkish state traditions significantly resemble each other, and Turks, betwixt Europe and the Middle East, enjoy a liminal position. Paris also sees Ankara as an important ally in the governance of its Muslim community in the context of French *laïcité* and a perceived failure to 'localise' Islam.

Diplomatic relations between Ankara and Paris flared up in 2020 over disagreements in Libya, the eastern Mediterranean, the Nagorno-Karabakh conflict and, most significantly, Macron's declaration that foreign influence in the country should be curbed. Yet reformation of Islam is not an easy task in France. Given the domestic backlash from both political opposition and Muslims, such change will not take place overnight and it is likely that the French state will continue to work closely with Ankara in the management of Islam and Muslims, at least in the short-term. Moreover, tensions with Turkey could have strong ripple effects and negatively influence the status of French citizens in Turkey. In fact, Ankara announced, in a 2021 tit-for-tat speech, that if French policies do not change, French citizens working in French universities and schools in Turkey (such as Galatasaray University) will have to meet Turkish-language requirements or their work visas will not be renewed.[166]

Notes

1 Interview, French Ministry of Europe and Foreign Affairs official, Paris, 10 January 2019.
2 'Reality Check: Is Banning Turkish Rallies EU Policy?'
3 'Turkish Foreign Minister Expected in France as Dutch Rally Row Wages', *Local*, 12 March 2017, www.thelocal.fr/20170312/turkish-fm-expected-in-france-as-dutch-rally-row-rages
4 D. Aksel, *Home States*, p. 145.
5 J. Laurence, *Coping with Defeat*, p. 298.
6 S. Akgönül, 'Turkey's Next Crisis', *Institut Montaigne* (2020), www.institut-montaigne.org/en/blog/turkeys-next-crisis
7 *Ibid.*

8 A. Arkilic, 'Between the Homeland and Host States: Turkey's Diaspora Policies and Immigrant Political Participation in France and Germany' (PhD dissertation, University of Texas at Austin, 2016).

9 C. Pétreault, 'Exclusif: Les combines des religieux d'Erdogan', *Le Point*, 20 July 2018, www.lepoint.fr/societe/les-combines-des-religieux-d-erdogan-18–07–2018–2237379_23.php

10 Interview, French Ministry of the Interior official, Paris, 11 January 2019.

11 Interview, French Ministry of the Interior official, Paris, 11 March 2013.

12 'Syria War: Erdogan Rejects French Mediation Offer', *BBC*, 30 March 2018, www.bbc.com/news/world-europe-43595891?intlink_from_url=www.bbc.com/news/topics/c302m85qenyt/france&

13 'Macron Says "No Consensus" with Turkey over Definition of Terrorism', *France24*, 4 December 2019, www.france24.com/en/20191204-macron-says-no-consensus-turkey-definition-terrorism-syria-kurds-nato; A. Bonzon, 'L'escalade franco-turque', *Esprit*, December 2020, https://esprit.presse.fr/actualites/ariane-bonzon/l-escalade-franco-turque-43135

14 'France's Macron Announced National Day Marking Armenian Genocide', *France24*, 6 February 2019, www.france24.com/en/20190206-france-macron-announces-national-day-marking-armenian-genocide-turkey

15 J. Irish, 'Macron Seeks EU Sanctions over Turkish "Violations" in Greek Waters', *Reuters*, 23 July 2020, www.reuters.com/article/uk-france-cyprus-idUKKCN24O12M

16 S. Akgönül, 'Turkey's Next Crisis'.

17 M. Rose and E. Pineau, 'France's Macron Says He Set Red Lines with Turkey in Eastern Mediterranean', *Reuters*, 29 August 2020, www.reuters.com/article/us-france-macron-turkey-idUSKBN25O2OO

18 D. Jones, 'France–Turkey Dispute Grows over Cartoons and Influence in Africa', *Voice of America*, 29 October 2020, www.voanews.com/europe/france-turkey-dispute-grows-over-cartoons-and-influence-africa

19 M. Rose and J. Irish, 'France Accuses Turkey of Sending Syrian Jihadists to Nagorno-Karabakh', *Reuters*, 1 October 2020, www.reuters.com/article/us-armenia-azerbaijan-putin-macron/france-accuses-turkey-of-sending-syrian-mercenaries-to-nagorno-karabakh-idUSKBN26L3SB

20 F. Atalay, 'Fransa'nın imam ve Türkçe okutmanları sınırlamasına karşılık', *Cumhuriyet*, 13 February 2021, www.cumhuriyet.com.tr/haber/fransanin-imam-ve-turkce-okutmanlari-sinirlamasina-karsilik-fransiz-hocalara-turkce-sinavi-1813390

21 R. Kempin, 'France's foreign and security policy under Macron', *SWP Research Paper RP 04* (2021), www.swp-berlin.org/publikation/frances-foreign-and-security-policy-under-president-macron#fn-d25239e3599

22 'Erdogan Decries Macron's Plan against "Islamist Separatism"', *Al Jazeera*, 6 October 2020, www.aljazeera.com/news/2020/10/6/erdogan-decries-macrons-plan-against-islamist-separatism

23 'Turkey's Erdogan and French President Macron Butt Heads – Again', *Al Jazeera*, 26 October 2020, www.aljazeera.com/news/2020/10/26/islam-in-france-turkeys-erdogan-and-president-macron-butt-heads

24 'Republic Day Celebrated across Turkey, with Masks and Fervor', *NewsDay*, 30 October 2020, www.newsday24.com/turkey/republic-day-celebrated-across-tur-key-with-masks-and-fervor/

25 'Turkey Says Talks with France to Normalise Ties Going Well', *Reuters*, 7 January 2021, www.reuters.com/article/us-turkey-france/turkey-says-talks-with-france-to-normalise-ties-going-well-idUSKBN29C2PP

26 A. Lloyd, 'Writing Verdicts: French and Francophone Narratives of Race and Racism' (PhD dissertation, University of Pennsylvania, 2019).

27 'Understanding the measurement of foreign and immigrant populations', *INSEE* (2021), www.insee.fr/en/accueil

28 *Ibid.*

29 'How many immigrants are there in France?', *INED* (2020), www.ined.fr/en/everything_about_population/demographic-facts-sheets/faq/how-many-immi-grants-france/#:~:text=In%202018%2C%20there%20were%206.5,%25%2C%20had%20acquired%20French%20citizenship

30 *Ibid.*

31 R. Kılınç, *Alien Citizens*.

32 '5 facts about the Muslim population in Europe', *Pew Research Center* (2017), www.pewresearch.org/fact-tank/2017/11/29/5-facts-about-the-muslim-popu-lation-in-europe/

33 G. Bouvier, 'Les descendants d'immigrés plus nombreux que les immigrés', *INSEE* (2012), www.insee.fr/fr/statistiques/1374014?sommaire=1374025

34 J. Hollifield, 'French Republicanism and the limits of immigration control', in *Controlling Immigration: A Global Perspective*, eds W. Cornelius, P. Martin and J. Hollifield (Redwood City: Stanford University Press, 2004), p. 184.

35 R. Kılınç, *Alien Citizens*.

36 C. Wihtol de Wenden, 'France', in *European Immigration: A Sourcebook*, eds A. Triandafyllidou and R. Gropas (Aldershot: Ashgate, 2014), pp. 135–47.

37 G. Freeman, *Immigrant Labour and Racial Conflict in Industrial Societies: The French and British Experience, 1945–1975* (Princeton: Princeton University Press, 1979).

38 S. Castles, 'How nation-states respond to immigration and ethnic diversity', *Journal of Ethnic and Migration Studies* 21:3 (1995), 293–308.

39 J. Barou, 'Integration of immigrants in France: A historical perspective', *Identities* 21:6 (2014), 642–57.

40 P. Sahlins, *Unnaturally French: Foreign Citizens in the Old Regime and After* (Ithaca: Cornell University Press, 2004).

41 C. Bertossi, 'Country report: France', *European University Institute EUDO Citizenship Observatory Report* (2010), p. 1, http://cadmus.eui.eu/bitstream/handle/1814/19613/France.pdf?sequence=1

42 R. Brubaker, *Citizenship and Nationhood in France and Germany*.

43 *Ibid.*

44 C. Bertossi and J. W. Duyvendak, 'National models of immigrant integration: The costs of comparative research', *Comparative European Politics* 10:3 (2012), 237–47; K. Schönwalder and T. Triadafilopoulos, 'A bridge or barrier to incorporation? Germany's 1999 citizenship reform in critical perspective', *German Politics and Society* 30:1 (2012), 52–70.

45 J. Fetzer and C. Soper, *Muslims and the State in Britain, France and Germany*.

46 M. Schain, *The Politics of Immigration in France, Britain and the United States: A Comparative Study* (Basingstoke: Palgrave Macmillan, 2008).

47 *Ibid.*

48 R. Kılınç, *Alien Citizens*.

49 R. Schor, *L'opinion française et les étrangers en France, 1919–1939* (Paris: Sorbonne, 1985).

50 P. Weil, 'Races at the gate: Racial distinctions in immigration policy: A comparison between France and the United States', in *From Europe to North America: Migration Control in the Nineteenth Century*, eds A. Farhmeir, O. Faron and P. Weil (New York: Berghahn, 2003), pp. 368–402.

51 J. Hollifield, 'French Republicanism', p. 184; P. Weil, *La France et ses étrangers: L'aventure d'une politique de l'immigration de 1938 a nos jours* (Paris: Calmann-Lévy, 1995).

52 J. Barou, 'Integration of immigrants in France'.

53 G. Freeman, *Immigrant Labor*.

54 E. Kofman, M. Rogoz and F. Lévy, 'Family migration laws in France', *International Centre for Migration Development Report* (2010), https://pdfs.semantic-scholar.org/3122/4838fe1a44876182ab502e0ab5b262f779c3.pdf

55 D. Giubilaro, *Migration from the Maghreb and Migration Pressures: Current Situation and Future Prospects* (Geneva: International Labor Organization, 1997); R. Maxwell, *Ethnic Minority Migrants in Britain and France: Integration Trade-offs* (New York: Cambridge University Press, 2012).

56 'De 1945 à 1975', *Cité nationale de l'histoire de l'immigration* (2011), https://web.archive.org/web/20110902023107/www.histoire-immigration.fr/musee

57 J. Barou, 'Integration of immigrants in France'.

58 *Ibid.*

59 J. P. Brunet, *Police Contre FLN: Le drame d'octobre 1961* (Paris: Flammarion, 1999).

60 G. Freeman, *Immigrant Labour*, p. 86; J. Cesari, 'De l'immigré au minoritaire: les Maghrébins de France', *Revue européenne des migrations internationalies* 10:1 (1996), 109–26.

61 V. Giuraudon, 'Immigration policy in France', *Brookings Institution* (2001), www.brookings.edu/articles/immigration-policy-in-france/

62 P. Martin, *The Unfinished Story*.

63 P. Weil, *La France et ses étrangers*; P. Weil, *How to Be French? Nationality in the Making since 1789* (Durham: Duke University Press, 2008).

64 J. Barou, 'Integration of immigrants in France'.

65 F. Jobard, 'An overview of French riots: 1981–2004', in *Rioting in the UK and France: A Comparative Analysis*, eds D. Waddington, F. Jobard and M. King (London: Willan Publishing, 2009), pp. 27–38.

66 J. Barou, 'Integration of immigrants in France'.

67 J. Shields, 'Le Pen and the progression of the Far-right vote in France', *French Politics and Society* 13:2 (1995), 21–39.

68 *Ibid.*; E. Bleich, *Race Politics in Britain and France: Ideas and Policymaking since the 1960s* (Cambridge: Cambridge University Press, 2003), pp. 147–8.

69 *Ibid.*

70 J. Barou, 'Integration of immigrants in France'.

71 *Ibid.*

72 J. Beaman, *Citizen Outsider: Children of North African Immigrants in France* (Oakland: University of California Press, 2017), p. 19.

73 S. Duchesne, 'Identities, nationalism, citizenship and Republican ideology', in *Developments in French Ideology*, eds A. Cole, P. Le Galès and J. Lévy (Basingstoke: Palgrave Macmillan, 2005), pp. 230–44; C. Bertossi, 'The performativity of colour blindness: Race politics and immigrant integration in France, 1980–2012', *Patterns of Prejudice* 46:5 (2012), 427–44.

74 S. Duchesne, 'Identities, nationalism, citizenship and Republican ideology'; K. Hamilton, P. Simon and C. Veniard, 'The challenge of French diversity', *Migration Policy Institute* (2014), www.migrationpolicy.org/article/challenge-french-diversity

75 'Nationalité française et immigration: l'évolution du droit', *République Française Vie Publique* (2019), www.vie-publique.fr/eclairage/20181-nationalite-francaise-et-immigration-levolution-du-droit

76 E. R. Vickstrom, *Pathways and Consequences of Legal Irregularity: Senegalese Migrants in France, Italy and Spain* (Cham: Springer, 2019).

77 'En 2005 trois semaines d'émeutes urbaines', *Le Figaro*, 27 October 2015, www.lefigaro.fr/actualite-france/2015/10/25/01016–20151025ARTFIG00142-des-emeutes-urbaines-sans-precedent.php

78 M. Engler, 'France', *Focus Migration* (2007), http://focus-migration.hwwi.de/France.1231.0.html?&L=1

79 M. Schain, *The Politics of Immigration in France, Britain and the United States*, p. 41.

80 'French immigration policy', *French Ministry of Foreign Affairs* (2007), https://au.ambafrance.org/IMG/pdf/immigration_policy.pdf

81 C. Wihtol de Wenden, 'France', p. 137.

82 D. R. d'Allonnes, 'Immigration: la contre-offensive de Hollande', *Le Monde*, 15 December 2014, www.lemonde.fr/politique/article/2014/12/15/immigration-la-contre-offensive-de-hollande_4540644_823448.html

83 J. Carvalho, 'The Front National's influence on immigration during President François Hollande's term', in *Do They Make a Difference? The Policy Influence of Radical Right Populist Parties in Western Europe*, eds B. Biard, L. Bernhard and H. G. Betz (London: Rowman and Littlefield, 2019), pp. 37–57.

84 *Ibid.*

85 'World Migration Report 2020', *International Organization for Migration* (2020), www.un.org/sites/un2.un.org/files/wmr_2020.pdf

86 J. Carvalho, 'The Front National's influence on immigration'.

87 K. Najib and P. Hopkins, 'Islamophobia in London and Paris: How It Differs and Why?', *The Conversation*, 13 April 2018, https://theconversation.com/islamophobia-in-paris-and-london-how-it-differs-and-why-94793

88 Interview, French High Council for Integration official, Paris, 22 May 2013.

89 'France Approves Controversial Immigration Bill', *BBC*, 23 April 2018, www.bbc.com/news/world-europe-43860880

90 K. Piser, 'Migrants in France Are Paying the Price for Macron's Hard Line on Immigration', *World Politics Review*, 5 December 2019, www.worldpoliticsreview.com/articles/28390/in-macron-s-france-immigration-policy-is-getting-more-restrictive

91 *Ibid.*

92 A. T. Kuru, *Secularism and State Policies toward Religion: The United States, France and Turkey* (New York: Cambridge University Press, 2009), p. 106.

93 R. Kılınç, *Alien Citizens*, pp. 61–2.

94 'Loi du 9 décembre 1905 concernant la séparation des Eglises et de l'Etat', *République Française Légifrance* (2020), www.legifrance.gouv.fr/loda/id/JORFTEXT000000508749/2020-10-28/

95 J. Fetzer and C. Soper, *Muslims and the State in Britain, France and Germany*, p. 69.

96 J. Baubérot, *Laïcité 1905–2005, entre passion et raison* (Paris: Le Seuil, 2004); M. Fernando, *The Republic Unsettled: Muslim French and the Contradictions of Secularism* (Durham: Duke University Press, 2014).

97 *Ibid.*

98 *Ibid.*

99 S. Erlanger, 'A Pro-Church Law Helps a Mosque', *New York Times*, 6 October 2008, www.nytimes.com/2008/10/07/world/europe/07alsace.html

100 'Loi du 9 décembre 1905 concernant la séparation des Eglises et de l'Etat'.

101 *Ibid.*; B. Basdevant-Gaudemet, 'Islam in France', in *The Legal Treatment of Islamic Minorities in Europe*, eds R. Aluffi and G. Zincone (Leuven: Peeters, 2004), pp. 61–2.

102 J. Laurence and J. Vaïsse, *Integrating Islam: Political and Religious Challenges in Contemporary France* (Washington DC: Brookings Institution Press, 2006), pp. 85–6.

103 U. Schuerkens, 'Active civic participation of immigrants in France', *POLITIS Country Report* (2005), www.uni-oldenburg.de/politis-europe

104 B. Basdevant-Gaudemet, 'Islam in France', pp. 59–60.

105 *Ibid.*

106 A. Arkilic, 'The limits of European Islam'.

107 Interview, French Ministry of the Interior official, Paris, 11 March 2013.

108 Y. M. Ibrahim, 'Arab Girls' Veils at Issue in France', *New York Times*, 12 November 1989, www.nytimes.com/1989/11/12/world/arab-girls-veils-at-issue-in-france.html

109 C. Joppke, *Veil: Mirror of Identity* (Cambridge: Polity, 2009), p. 38.

110 Report (in French) is available here: www.vie-publique.fr/rapport/26626-commission-de-reflexion-sur-application-du-principe-de-laicite

111 J. R. Bowen, *Can Islam Be French? Pluralism and Pragmatism in a Secularist State* (Princeton: Princeton University Press, 2011).

112 J. Bowen, *Why the French Don't Like Headscarves: Islam, the State and Public Space* (Princeton: Princeton University Press, 2006).

113 J. R. Bowen and M. Rohe, 'Judicial framings of Muslims and Islam in France and Germany', in *European States and their Muslim Citizens: The Impact of Institutions on Perceptions and Boundaries*, eds J. R. Bowen, C. Bertossi, J. W. Duyvendak and M. L. Krook (Cambridge: Cambridge University Press, 2014), pp. 135–64.

114 J. Heider, 'Unveiling the truth behind the French burqa ban: The unwarranted restriction of the right to freedom of religion and the European Court of Human Rights', *Indiana International and Comparative Law Review* 22 (2012), 95–135; R. Kılınç, *Alien Citizens*, p. 73.

115 B. Basdevant-Gaudemet and F. Frégosi, 'L'Islam en France', in *Islam and the European Union*, eds R. Potz and W. Wieshaider (Leuven: Peeters, 2004), pp. 143–80.

116 *Ibid.*

117 R. Kılınç, *Alien Citizens*, pp. 13, 67–71.

118 T. Heneghan, 'French Muslim School Opens after Headscarf Ban', *Reuters*, 24 April 2007, www.reuters.com/article/us-religion-france-school-idUSSP28389 820070423

119 'France's First Private Muslim School Tops the Ranks', *France24*, 29 March 2013, www.france24.com/en/20130329-france-first-private-muslim-school-tops-ranks-averroes

120 C. Bourget, *Islamic Schools in France: Minority Integration and Separatism in Western Society* (Basingstoke: Palgrave Macmillan, 2019).

121 G. Tınmaz, 'Fransa'da İslami Anaokulları', *Perspektif*, 5 June 2020, https://perspektif.eu/2020/06/05/fransada-islami-anaokullari-kontrat-disi-ozel-okullar/

122 Z. Çıtak, 'Between "Turkish Islam" and "French Islam"'; B. Bruce, *Governing Islam Abroad*.

123 'German Population of Migrant Background Rises to 21 Million', *Deutsche Welle*, 28 July 2020, www.dw.com/en/german-population-of-migrant-background-rises-to-21-million/a-54356773

124 Interview, French Ministry of Europe and Foreign Affairs official, Paris, 15 January 2019.

125 Interview, French Ministry of Justice official, Paris, 24 January 2019.

126 Interview, French Ministry of the Interior official, Paris, 29 January 2019.

127 A. Lloyd, 'Writing Verdicts'.

128 J. Beaman, *Citizen Outsider*, p. 19.

129 T. D. Keaton, '"Black (American) Paris" and the French outer-cities: The race question and questioning solidarity', in *The Black Europe and the African Diaspora*, eds D. Clark Hine, T. D. Keaton and S. Small (Champaign: University of Illinois Press, 2009), p 108.

130 J. Fredette, *Constructing Muslims in France: Discourse, Public Identity and the Politics of Citizenship* (Philadelphia: Temple University Press, 2014), pp. 5–8.

131 J. Beaman, *Citizen Outsider*.

132 D. T. Goldberg, 'Racial Europeanisation', *Ethnic and Racial Studies* 29:2 (2006), 344.

133 *Ibid.*, 347.

134 A. Hargreaves, *Multi-ethnic France*; Z. Çıtak, 'Between "Turkish Islam" and "French Islam"'; F. Baskin, 'Turkish women in Alsace'; C. Beauchemin, C. Hamel and P. Simon (eds), *Trajectories and Origins: Survey on the Diversity of French Population*.

135 Interview, French Ministry of Europe and Foreign Affairs official, Paris, 15 January 2019.

136 Interview, French Ministry of Europe and Foreign Affairs official, Paris, 23 January 2019.

137 Interview, French Ministry of Europe and Foreign Affairs official, Paris, 15 January 2019.

138 *Ibid.*

139 Interview, French Ministry of the Interior official, Paris, 14 January 2019.

140 Interview, French Ministry of the Interior official, Paris, 29 January 2019.

141 Y. Brinbaum, M. Safi and P. Simon, 'Discrimination in France', p. 199; S. Brouard and V. Tiberj, *As French as Everyone?*

142 M. Hoffman, A. Makovsky and M. Werz, 'The Turkish diaspora in Europe: Integration, migration, and politics', *Center for American Progress* (2020), www.feps-europe.eu/attachments/publications/turkishdiaspora-report-final.pdf, pp. 16–7.

143 *Ibid*, p. 17.

144 Interview, French Ministry of the Interior official, Paris, 5 June 2013.

145 Interview, *Le Monde* reporter, Paris, 17 January 2019.

146 Interview, French Ministry of the Interior official, Paris, 11 March 2013.

147 B. Bruce, *Governing Islam Abroad*, p. 115.

148 Interview, French Ministry of Europe and Foreign Affairs official, Paris, 23 January 2019.

149 Interview, French Ministry of the Interior official, Paris, 14 January 2019.

150 Interview, French Ministry of Justice official, Paris, 24 January 2019.

151 Z. Çıtak, 'Between "Turkish Islam" and "French Islam"'.

152 A. Arkilic, 'The limits of European Islam'.

153 *Ibid.*

154 Interview, DİTİB official, Paris, 12 December 2013.

155 A. Arkilic, 'Between the Homeland and Host States'; A. Arkilic, 'The limits of European Islam'.

156 Interview, French Ministry of Europe and Foreign Affairs official, Paris, 23 January 2019.

157 Interview, French Ministry of the Interior official, Paris, 14 January 2019.

158 *Ibid.*

159 *Ibid.*

160 K. Piser, 'Macron Wants to Start an Islamic Revolution'.

161 *Ibid.*

162 'François Burgat: "Macron devrait mettre fin à cette atmosphère de confrontation"', *Anadolu Ajansı*, 11 September 2020, www.aa.com.tr/fr/journal-de-lislamophobie/francois-burgat-macron-devrait-mettre-fin-%C3%A0-cette-atmosph%C3%A8re-de-confrontation-entretien/1970183; A. Gabon,

'Macron's Islamic Charter Is an Unprecedented Attack on French Secularism', *Middle East Eye*, 3 February 2021, www.middleeasteye.net/opinion/macrons-islamic-charter-unprecedented-attack-french-secularism

163 J. Dettmer and L. Bryant, 'Macron's Ideas on Reform of Islam Draw Fire', *Voice of America*, 18 February 2018, www.voanews.com/europe/macrons-ideas-reform-islam-draw-fire; 'France's Jean-Luc Melenchon Condemns Political Islamophobia', *Morocco World News*, 14 November 2020, www.morocco-worldnews.com/2020/11/325931/frances-jean-luc-melenchon-condemns-countrys-islamophobic-secularism/

164 The 'Tribune de la dignité' petition initiated by the critics of this proposal is available at: https://docs.google.com/forms/d/e/1FAIpQLSdZiyHsEqtuyZNMs-D9LOzqLO0gXsY-NSbxjkSWm78u7DNkO5w/viewform

165 A. Quijano, 'Coloniality of power and Eurocentrism in Latin America', *International Sociology* 15:2 (2000), 215–32; W. Mignolo and E. Walsh, *On Decoloniality: Concepts, Analytics and Praxis* (Durham: Duke University Press, 2018).

166 F. Atalay, 'Fransa'nın imam ve Türkçe okutmanları sınırlamasına karşılık'.

7

'Islam does not belong to Germany': Germany's response to Turkey's changing relations with its diaspora

Freedom of speech and opinion needs to be protected, as long as it does not threaten the German Basic Law. However, we are not happy when mass pro-Turkish diaspora rallies are held on German soil and when homeland tensions are transplanted into Germany. We often witness street fights between pro- and anti-Erdoğan supporters. You need lots of police forces to keep these groups apart. Polarisation among the Turkish diaspora is growing and it is a problem for our peace and security … If you want Turks to integrate, you shouldn't address them as Turks. They are Germans with Turkish roots … Turks have two homes, not just one. And some of these Turks have only German citizenship. This makes the issue not a foreign but a domestic problem.[1]

German authorities have traded barbs with Turkey and reiterated on many occasions their desire to limit Ankara's influence on the Turkish diaspora. A pro-AKP referendum rally headlined by Turkey's then prime minister, Binali Yıldırım, saw 10,000 Turks gather in Oberhausen, a city in the Ruhr area, in February 2017 and stirred serious debate.[2] In the aftermath of the rally, German officials cancelled several events featuring AKP deputies and ministers that had been set to take place, citing the planned events' risks to public order. The cancellations were made permanent: when Chancellor Angela Merkel vocally supported local authorities' decision to call off pro-Turkish rallies, Yıldırım lashed out: 'You are not Turkey's boss. You are not a first-class country and we are not a second-class country … You should treat Turkey as an equal partner.'[3] Turkish officials went even further, likening the ban to Nazi practices and summoning the German Ambassador in Ankara.[4] In return, Heiko Maas, Germany's then Minister of Justice, argued that the comments were 'abstruse, malicious and absurd'.[5]

These rallies exacerbated the diplomatic row between Turkey and Germany that had broken out the year before. As discussed in Chapter 4, in 2016 the Bundestag passed a resolution that recognised as genocide the massacre and forced deportation of Armenians by Ottoman Turks in 1915.[6] In the same year, Erdoğan lodged a complaint against German satirist Jan

Böhmermann over a poem he shared on his television show that included crude language aimed at Erdoğan.[7] The post-coup imprisonment of human rights activists in Turkey, including German citizens, also led German officials to issue a travel warning against Turkey.[8] The capture of Deniz Yücel, a journalist holding both Turkish and German citizenship, for spreading PKK propaganda and for making contact with Fethullah Gülen further estranged Berlin and Ankara.[9]

The financing and training of *Diyanet* religious personnel is another source of outrage in Germany. Ninety per cent of imams serving in Germany come from foreign countries, and the DİTİB sends more than anyone else.[10] As explored in Chapter 4, the DİTİB came under fire in 2018 over the espionage scandal and the construction of a mega mosque in Cologne. In 2019, Germany proposed a new law that would require Turkish imams to learn German[11] and launched a pilot project at the University of Osnabrück to train local imams, with funding from the Federal Ministry of the Interior.[12] Furthermore, some states, including Hesse, terminated their Islamic religious teaching partnership with the DİTİB on the basis that the organisation is steered by Turkey.[13] Others, such as Lower Saxony, imposed a ban on DİTİB imams to prevent them from operating in prisons.[14]

The *Millî Görüş* has been accused of fraud and terrorist activities and has faced serious criminal investigations in Germany.[15] Even though these charges were later dropped, the organisation is still viewed with suspicion and was even barred from attending the DIK.[16] The ATİB and the UID have encountered comparable challenges in Germany, including the decision to forbid ATİB activities,[17] and the UID's representation in the German media as a promoter 'of Turkey's nationalist and Islamist parallel foreign policy in Europe'.[18] Since 2017, the UID has been placed on the Federal Office for the Protection of the Constitution list as a suspicious organisation due to its close links to the AKP, the DİTİB and the Grey Wolves.[19]

This chapter argues that Germany's traditionally more interventionist stance towards Turkey can be explained by several factors. First, Turks in Germany form the largest and, therefore, the most visible immigrant group. Second, Germany fulfilled its need for labour from bilateral worker agreements signed with Turkey rather than with former colonies. Therefore, migration and Islam debates have focused on Turks. Third, despite an official separation of church and state, religion still plays an important role in German politics. However, the German state has favoured other religions over Islam, and its relationship with Muslims has been intrusive and securitised. This chapter will delve into Germany's immigration, citizenship and integration policies, as well as state policies towards religion, focusing on its complex ties to the Turkish community.

Immigration, citizenship and integration policies in Germany

According to the Federal Statistical Office, as of 2019 there were 21.2 million immigrants in the country, around 26 per cent of the total German population of 83 million.[20] An individual is considered to have a 'migration background' if they, or at least one of their parents, were born without German citizenship.[21] Of all migrant-origin individuals, just over half were born as German citizens, with at least one parent obtaining or already holding German citizenship. Some 65 per cent of all individuals with a migration background came from another EU country, and 22 per cent from Asia.[22] But the largest single group of immigrants hails from Turkey, comprising 13 per cent of people with a migration background.[23] The proportion of Muslims in Germany is roughly 5 per cent of the total population, and Turks form the dominant Muslim group in the country, followed by individuals from Arab countries, the former Yugoslavia, Afghanistan and Iran. Of all Muslims, around 45 per cent are German citizens and the remainder are foreign nationals.[24]

Germany has attracted agricultural seasonal workers since the second half of the nineteenth century. However, in that period, the number of individuals who left Germany surpassed the number who poured in.[25] This pattern changed at the turn of the century when labourers from Poland were invited to work in the mining industry.[26] Towards the end of World War II, the term *Gastarbeiter* came to signify foreign civilian workers who laboured in the Nazi war economy on a voluntary basis in return for remuneration.[27] While these people were initially referred to as *Fremdarbeiter* (foreign workers), over time the term *Gastarbeiter* became more common, emphasising their temporary status.[28]

In 1944, there were 7.7 million foreign workers (2 million war prisoners and 5.7 million civilian workers), accounting for one third of the total German labour force.[29] Between 1945 and 1949, around 12 million German nationals returned home. These were people who had previously resided in areas intermittently under German jurisdiction prior to 1945, and ethnic German returnees from former German settlements in Eastern Europe and the former Soviet Union (*Aussiedler*).[30] Upon entry into Germany, they were granted various privileges, such as assistance with language training, employment and welfare, due to their ethnic origin.[31] In the 1960s, 1970s and 1980s, the immigrant population in Germany multiplied through the welcoming of foreign workers, asylum seekers and civil war refugees. Yet official rhetoric lagged behind these inflows of immigration, and the term *kein Einwanderungsland* (not a country of immigration) defined Germany's relationship with immigrants until the 2000s.[32]

Prior to the 1800s, the requirements for German citizenship contained a small territorial component, but, even back then, *jus sanguinis* was the dominant element defining citizenship in the regions that would later become Germany and informed the 1913 Nationality Law.[33] After defeat in World War II, Germany split into the Federal Republic of Germany (West Germany) and the German Democratic Republic (East Germany). Article 116, Paragraph 1 of the 1949 Federal Constitution (Basic Law, *Grundgesetz*) was initially based on the 1913 Law and described a German as 'a person who possesses German citizenship or who has been admitted to the territory of the German Reich within the boundaries of 31 December 1937 as a refugee or expellee of German ethnic origin or as the spouse or descendant of such person'.[34]

The acceptance of ethnic German immigrants contributed to the advancement of the war-torn German economy, although labour shortages endured.[35] The first guest-worker agreement was signed with Italy in 1955. Decisions regarding recruitment were made in the corporatist context of the Federal Ministry of Labour, and included employers and trade union representatives.[36] Germany signed other guest-worker agreements, with Spain (1960), Greece (1960) and Turkey (1961).[37] According to the rotation principle, guest workers were ostensibly required to return home at the end of their first year in Germany, yet tens of thousands of workers stayed upon expiration of their work visas. [38]

After the construction of the Berlin Wall in 1961, the end of movement from East to West Germany put a strain on economic growth. Consequently, guest-worker programmes in West Germany expanded.[39] Additional agreements were signed, with Portugal (1964), Tunisia (1965), Morocco (1963 and 1966) and Yugoslavia (1968).[40] The 1965 Act on Foreigners governed newcomers' entry into Germany without making a distinction between different immigrant groups' residence purposes or addressing questions of family reunification.[41] By 1973, some 2.6 million foreign workers had been recruited by Germany. Turks made up 23 per cent of all foreigners, followed by Yugoslavians (17 per cent), Italians (16 per cent), Greeks (10 per cent) and Spaniards (7 per cent).[42] Significantly, a number of these workers had already acquired residence permits, and Italians even enjoyed the right to free cross-border movement, a privilege bestowed on all European Community member-state citizens from 1968.[43]

The recruitment of guest workers was halted in 1973 due to economic recession caused by the oil crisis.[44] However, as Christian Joppke explains, three important legal changes mitigated this situation: (1) new legislation from 1973 limited the state's powers of deportation; (2) in 1978 the German government approved the automatic renewal of residence permits; and (3) in 1981, the government allowed family reunification, albeit with an eight-year residence qualification for the spouse and a one-year wait period outside Germany for the partner.[45] During this time, Germany came to acknowledge the permanent status of immigrants and the need to forge a formal integration policy.[46] Yet for German officials, integration meant 'acculturating Turks into German society without any attention paid to pluralism or multiculturalism'.[47]

These legal amendments expanded the Turkish population in Germany and saw the birth of second-generation Turks, who were denied German citizenship and were treated as outsiders.[48] According to unsealed confidential British documents, Helmut Kohl, who served as Chancellor of West Germany from 1982 to 1990 and of the reunited Germany from 1990 to 1998, proclaimed in 1982 that 'over the next four years, it would be necessary to reduce the number of Turks by 50 per cent' and that 'it was impossible for Germany to assimilate Turks in their present numbers', which stood at 1.5 million.[49] According to Kohl, 'Germany had no problems with the Portuguese, the Italians, even the South East Asians, because these communities integrated well ... But the Turks came from a very distinctive culture and did not integrate well ... Germany had integrated some 11 million Germans from East European countries. But they were European and therefore presented no problem.'[50] Kohl cited forced marriages, illegal employment and language incompetency as factors impeding Turkish integration and precipitating 'a clash of two different cultures',[51] an argument also voiced by some German scholars.[52] Kohl added that integration would only be possible if the Turkish population stopped surging.[53] Anti-Turkish sentiments were not restricted to Christian Democratic politicians like Kohl. His Social Democrat predecessor, Helmut Schmidt, also pledged that 'not one more Turk will come over the border', and Schmidt's chief of staff, Hans-Jürgen Wischnewski, looked down on Turks as 'Muslims who butcher their sheep in the bathtub'.[54]

Public opinion was equally hostile to Turks in this period, amid the eruption of the second oil crisis in the early 1980s and the deterioration of the German economy with the loss of 1.8 million jobs.[55] A 1982 survey found that 58 per cent of Germans wanted to reduce the number of foreigners in the country.[56] Anti-immigrant sentiments translated into strict policy decisions, such as the denial of the family reunion of immigrant children over the age of fifteen and the passing of a new law in 1983 to encourage Turks to return to their country of origin.[57] German officials hoped that a one-off lump-sum payment and the reimbursement of retirement-insurance payments would entice Turks to go back to Turkey. However, this measure did not prevent the growth of the Turkish immigrant population as only about 100,000 Turks exited Germany.[58]

From the beginning of the 1990s, political instability in Turkey swelled the number of people seeking asylum in Germany. Article 16a of the German constitution granted all persons prosecuted for political reasons the right to asylum in Germany.[59] The Turkish population also grew through a process of chain immigration.[60] In addition, the inflow of ethnic Germans as well as Yugoslavians, who had been granted temporary protection status (*Duldung*), accelerated dramatically following the collapse of the Iron Curtain and other political crises in continental Europe.[61] While in 1987 57,400 individuals applied for asylum, in 1992 applications had risen to 440,000.[62] These demographic changes led politicians from both the left and the right to promote tougher immigration policies. For example, a new law (*Ausländergesetz*) enacted in 1990 sought to prevent new immigrant arrivals and to encourage foreign nationals to return home.[63]

Germany experienced a spike in electoral support for anti-immigrant parties and xenophobic attacks. The ultranationalist anti-immigrant Republican Party (REP) gained an unexpected electoral victory in the 1989 national elections and took seats in the European Parliament between 1989 and 1994.[64] In 1991, anti-asylum-seeker protests shook multiple eastern and southern German cities.[65] To assuage increasing anti-immigrant sentiments, Article 16a was amended in 1993 to restrict the constitutional right to asylum.[66]

In the mid-1990s, job losses and the emergent multiculturalism debate once again sparked public backlash.[67] Most Germans blamed the centre-right coalition government – the CDU/Christian Social Union in Bavaria (CSU) and the Free Democratic Party (FDP) – for societal tensions. Against the backdrop of heated discussions on immigration and German identity, the SPD and the Green Party coalition's 1998 victory opened a window of opportunity for substantial immigration reform that transformed the old citizenship law in 2000. The most important change was the replacement of *jus sanguinis* with *jus soli*.[68]

As analysed in Chapter 4, although the 2000 citizenship reform overhauled Germany's naturalisation law, it did not lead to an immediate increase in immigrants' naturalisation rates. Germany does not allow dual citizenship, although exceptions are made for EU and Swiss citizens and individuals whose home countries (like Iran, Algeria, Syria and several Latin American countries) prohibit or make it very difficult to renounce citizenship. The preconditions for naturalisation remain gruelling compared to most European countries, and the 2000 citizenship reform made this process more onerous by increasing the application fee and by introducing a language and civic test, which resulted in declining naturalisation rates.[69] Moreover, unlike in France, the German version of *jus soli* does not include a provision for double *jus soli*, whereby the third-generation children of second-generation immigrants automatically receive citizenship regardless of their residency-permit condition. Due to this restriction, 60 per cent of the children born in Germany since the implementation of the 2000 Nationality Act have not obtained German citizenship.[70]

In 2004, Germany acknowledged for the first time its status as a country of immigration.[71] Following the 2005 federal elections and the appointment of Angela Merkel as chancellor, the Migration Act modified the structure of the legal immigration framework to adopt a more open policy, which included some integration measures (such as the introduction of privileged labour access and the provision of a residence permit of unlimited duration for high-skilled foreign graduates of German universities).[72] In contrast, family-reunification regulations remained the same, with the exception of the 2007 regulation that specified that spouses who wished to join their partners in Germany must attain basic German-language skills.[73] The 2007 National Integration Plan prioritised integration policy, and the 2012 National Action Plan on Integration put forward instruments to render the results of the integration policy measurable.[74] In addition to these federal-level measures, all German states embraced an integration concept and corresponding guidelines, and Berlin, North Rhine-Westphalia and Baden-Württemberg adopted laws seeking to increase the commitment to integration efforts.[75]

Despite these new laws, the implementation of immigration policy did not change drastically, and anti-immigrant attitudes, particularly against Turks, remained a part of mainstream German politics.[76] As a Green Party[77] and an SPD deputy[78] put it, since 9/11 the political environment has become increasingly negative for Turks, and Islamophobia has become normalised in the policy and public discourse.[79] Chancellor Merkel's statement in a 2010 meeting that Germany's attempts to create a multicultural society have 'utterly failed' stirred a nationwide anti-immigration debate.[80] The publication of a controversial book by Thilo Sarrazin, a former SPD politician, in the same year sparked further public discussion on the failure of Turkish/ Muslim integration and emboldened the far right.[81]

According to the 2014 Nationality Law, children of foreign parents living in Germany no longer had to choose between their current citizenship and German citizenship before they turned twenty-three, but, to obtain dual citizenship, they had to have been raised in Germany and, by the age of twenty-one, to have lived in Germany for at least eight years and attended a German school for at least six years.[82] These amendments are still viewed as discriminatory by immigration activists because not everyone meets the preconditions and the legislation does not apply retroactively.[83] In other words, the law applies only to young immigrants and does not cover those born abroad even if they have spent decades living in Germany.[84] Hence, dual citizenship for Turks is still not automatic: certain conditions must be fulfilled. This means that, despite improvements, the German citizenship model remains exclusionary for Turks.[85]

With the outbreak of the Arab uprisings and the Syrian civil war, Germany faced an acute humanitarian crisis, and in 2013 alone there were 1.2 million newcomers, a rate the country had not witnessed since 1993.[86] In 2015, Germany admitted more than 1 million refugees. The vast majority of them came from Syria, and the tension over the refugee crisis and Merkel's 'open-door policy' fortified PEGIDA and the AfD.[87]

The last monumental change to the German migration framework came in 2016 when the Integration Act and the Regulation on the Integration Act were adopted to facilitate the integration of refugees into German society.[88] Building on the 2005 Migration Act and the policy of 'support and challenge' (*Fördern und Fordern*), the Integration Act sought to provide willing refugees with integration classes on German language, history and culture, as well as education and employment opportunities.[89] As of 2018, 700,000 Syrians were living in Germany, forming the third largest group of foreigners, behind the Turkish and Polish communities.[90]

State policies towards religion

The German constitution guarantees the neutral treatment of religions and does not identify the state with any religious denomination.[91] However, this does not mean that the German state is indifferent to religions; there is political agreement that religions contribute to the cohesion of society.[92] In particular, Germany has developed a positive approach to the role of churches in public life, accepting them as a partner of the state that contributes to the public good (*Öffentlichkeitsauftrag der Kirchen*).[93] This means that, despite an official separation between religion and state, churches still play an important role in the country's politics, albeit less so in recent years.[94] For example, Christian leaders make public statements on key political and moral issues (such as abortion or the integration of foreigners), and German citizens can only officially cancel their church membership through a civil registry office or at a municipal court.[95] Moreover, the federal state collects a church tax (*Kirchensteuer*), first codified in 1803 in the Imperial Recess (*Reichsdeputationshauptschluss*),[96] to finance religious personnel, houses of worship and social welfare institutions, which are often administered by churches.[97]

This arrangement had its origins in the 1648 Peace of Westphalia, which confirmed the division of German territories between Catholic, Lutheran and Calvinist princes and the establishment of a strong connection between church and state.[98] In the aftermath of World War I, the first clauses of Articles 136 and 137 of the Weimar Constitution (1919–33) adopted the principle of church–state separation, declaring that 'civil and political rights and duties shall be neither dependent on nor restricted by the exercise of religious freedom' and that 'there shall be no state church'.[99] Yet the Weimar Constitution also introduced the status of corporation under public law, which extended certain subsidies and privileges to Catholic and Protestant churches.[100] In the post-World War II period, Article 140 of the new constitution maintained these religious clauses from the Weimar Constitution and, as such, the religious communities operating at the time of the enactment of the 1949 Basic Law – Catholic, Protestant and Jewish – automatically received the status of corporation under public law.[101]

A public-law corporation is entitled to levy church taxes that amount to 8 to 10 per cent of what is owed to the federal government in income taxes.[102] Public corporations can also administer businesses autonomously, decide upon the composition of their religious instruction, open religious places and send a representative to public institutions and broadcast councils, in addition to other rights.[103] This status provides not only material perks but also symbolic advantages, such as prestige and credibility.[104] Other religious communities that meet certain criteria can apply for this status in accordance with Article 140 of the 1949 Constitution, and jurisdiction for this lies within the authority of states.[105] However, some centralised requirements exist: in particular, the religious community must have been in existence for thirty years, possess a large number of members and show loyalty to the German state.[106] In 2013, the Ahmadiyya and the Baha'i communities gained this status in some German states.[107] Over the last decade, Alevi associations have also obtained public-corporation status in many states, such as Bremen, Hamburg and Lower Saxony.[108] However, Germany has yet to grant the status of corporation under public law to Sunni Muslim organisations.

Religious education, which falls under the jurisdiction of states, is another contentious issue for state policies on religion. According to Article 7 of the constitution, officially recognised religious societies (*Religionsgemeinschaft*) can develop curricula and offer religious courses.[109] Muslim organisations were forbidden from offering religious courses in public schools until the 1990s because they were unable to meet the state criteria.[110] After a legal battle stretching two decades, the IFB became the first Sunni Islamic organisation to obtain the right to provide Islamic education in public schools in Berlin.[111] However, the IFB has turbulent relations with German officials and continues to be viewed with suspicion. An IFB leader said: 'Until I was thirty-three years old, I would proudly declare that "I am German". Now I say "I am Turkish. You have made me Turkish".'[112] Since 2012, the DİTİB has also been providing Islamic religious education in some German states;

but the termination of the partnership between the state of Hesse and the DİTİB in Islamic religious education again attests to German authorities' growing suspicion.[113]

Similar to the French constitution, the German constitution permits the establishment of private faith-based schools, although the state is not required to provide financial assistance to them.[114] Only organisations that possess the status of corporation under public law can apply to open their own private schools with monetary aid. This rule has naturally restricted Islamic schools' activities in Germany (contrary to the situation in France, where multiple private Turkish schools freely operate).[115]

Moreover, while French headscarf law covers all religious symbols, the German law targets Islam specifically and makes explicit exemptions for Christian symbols.[116] In 1998, Fereshta Ludin, a German of Afghan background, was forced to quit her job as a teacher in Baden-Württemberg after a court ruled that her headscarf violated the religious freedom of her students.[117] In 2003, the Federal Constitutional Court called for each state parliament to pass laws on the status of the headscarf in public schools:[118] Several states, including Bavaria, Hesse, Lower Saxony, Saarland, Bremen, North Rhine-Westphalia and Berlin prohibited the wearing of headscarves in public schools. Yet some of these states made a distinction among religions and did not ban Christian symbols or clothing.[119]

In 2015, the Constitutional Court struck down its 2003 ban on Islamic headscarves for teachers when it ruled that the ban violated religious freedom, protected by Article 4 of the Basic Law.[120] However, this decision did not lead to major constitutional changes in Germany because it did not require the above-listed states to lift their ban. Among those states, only Lower Saxony voluntarily followed the court ruling and rescinded its ban.[121] In 2020, the Federal Labour Court ruled that a blanket ban on teachers wearing headscarves in Berlin was unconstitutional.[122] While a court in Hamburg ruled against a full-face-covering ban in public schools, Baden-Württemberg banned *burqas* and *niqabs* for all schoolchildren in primary and secondary schools.[123] Representatives of Turkish Muslim organisations in Germany explained that, similar to the public-law-corporation-status double standard, the fact that Christians are favoured over Muslims within the context of the headscarf ban attests to Germany's securitised approach towards them, as explored in detail in the following section.[124]

Situating Turks in Germany

How does the preceding background on state policies shape Turks' experiences and existence in Germany? Turks remain the least integrated immigrant group in Germany in terms of employment, language skills, school attendance, naturalisation and electoral participation and representation.[125] Studies indicate that Turks also experience and perceive discrimination at higher rates than other immigrant communities.[126] Turks are especially discriminated against in the labour market.[127] For example, students with a Turkish name looking for an internship have to send 14 per cent more applications than those with a German name in order to find one, even if the quality of their application is identical.[128] As a Federal Ministry for Economic Affairs and Energy bureaucrat and a CDU advisor elucidated, even highly skilled and integrated Turks face invisible discrimination because of their appearance or name.[129] This struggle resembles the challenges that middle-class and educated North African-origin citizens face in France.

A study conducted in 2016 revealed that only one in three Turks in Germany believed that every individual, regardless of their origin, enjoys the same opportunities in school or in the labour market.[130] Fifty-one per cent of Turks viewed themselves as second-class citizens in Germany, and 54 per cent believed that no matter how hard they tried, they would never be recognised as a member of German society. One in every two Turkish respondents argued that their own will and personal effort were insufficient to 'belong' because of the existence of grave structural barriers to their inclusion: 15 per cent of Turks cited their religion as the primary reason behind their discrimination, followed by their ethnic identity (9 per cent), language (7 per cent) and skin colour (3 per cent). Eighty-four per cent of Turks reported that they found it offensive when Muslims are the first to be suspected after a terrorist attack.[131] These responses demonstrate that feelings of rejection and discrimination characterise everyday Turkish life in Germany.

An expert from the European Council on Foreign Relations linked widespread prejudices against Turks in the country to the Turkish community's sheer size: 'Their large population is the main reason why Turks are at the heart of immigration debates in Germany. This raises a new question: who are you and what is your identity? We expected the third-generation Turks to integrate but that did not happen. Poles and Portuguese did but Turks did not and will not.'[132] Other respondents gave similar answers: according to an SPD deputy, 'because of the size of the Turkish community, any crisis that happens in Turkey naturally blows up in Germany and we don't want that. You cannot separate foreign affairs from domestic politics.'[133] Another German official noted: 'the *Diyanet* sends 151 imams to France and over 1,000 to us because the Turkish community is four times larger here. Turks here are naturally more influential than Turks in France. No wonder why our responses are different.'[134] A German bureaucrat from the Federal Foreign Office made a similar point: 'the size of the Turkish community, which can be compared to Maghrebis in France, creates serious security issues in Germany, particularly in small cities'.[135]

Germany does not have a colonial relationship or a shared history with Turkey.[136] Although Germany colonised some Pacific islands and parts of Africa with its participation in the Scramble for Africa in the nineteenth century, German colonies became British, French, Belgian, South African or New Zealand territories after World War I.[137] Germany sought to exert influence on the Ottoman Empire through its involvement in the modernisation of the Ottoman military and infrastructure, but this did not represent a direct colonisation of the Ottoman lands.[138] Germany thus covered its need for labour through bilateral worker agreements rather than through human capital from former colonies.[139] This is one of the reasons why postcolonial thought has not been an inherent part of German public debates on migration, integration and Islam,[140] and why Turks have become the scapegoats for the Islam debate in Germany. Some scholars and prominent members of the German Turkish community, such as Faruk Şen, the former director of the Centre for Turkish Studies in Essen, have even compared the ostracisation of Turks in contemporary Germany to that of Jews under the Third Reich – albeit in a different form and scale – and drawn parallels between anti-Turkish racism and anti-Semitism in the country.[141] Other scholars have questioned whether Turks can be positioned as 'the colonised of today' in Germany.[142] According to a Turkish diplomat serving in Germany:

> Recent developments, such as PEGIDA's and the AfD's growing popularity, are not very surprising when put in historical context. According to a recent poll conducted by the Körber Foundation, 95 per cent of Germans have a very negative perception of Turkey and an increasing number of Turkish-origin Germans no longer feel welcome in Germany. The Ottomans and the Prussians first interacted as late as 1701. Germany's stigmatisation of Turks dates back to Martin Luther, who wrote the infamous *On War against the Turk* in 1528, as well as to the Ottomans' Vienna siege in 1529 against the Holy Roman Empire.[143]

In a similar vein, another Turkish diplomat argued:

> Our military partnership reached its zenith during World War I when the Ottomans and the Germans fought side by side against the Allied Powers. However, this was not an equal partnership. Germans used Ottomans for their own interests. This asymmetrical relationship became all the way more obvious when Germany first requested *Gastarbeiter* to repair their war-torn economy and then asked them to leave once they got what they wanted.[144]

As analysed in Chapter 4, the 1990s saw dozens of large-scale violent attacks aimed at Turks in Germany. Anti-Turkish aggression started with the murder of Mete Ekşi, a nineteen-year-old Turkish student, by three Nazi sympathisers in the Kreuzberg district of Berlin in 1991.[145] In 1993, Neo-Nazis killed Mustafa Demiral, a fifty-six-year-old Turkish man, in Mülheim an der Ruhr.[146] Turks have also been the victims of savage arson attacks, including in Mölln and Solingen.[147] Xenophobic attacks against Turks continued into the early 2000s. Turkish shop owners were ambushed across the country between 2000 and 2007 in a series of murders derogatorily labelled 'Bosporus murders' or 'döner murders'.[148] Despite German authorities trying to convince the families of the victims that the Turkish mafia was responsible, in 2011 it was disclosed that the NSU was behind the killings.[149] In 2017, the victims' families sued the German government on the basis that both federal and state authorities made gross mistakes over the course of their investigations.[150] Turkish immigrant organisations also accused German intelligence of covering up the murders given that thirteen commissions established at federal and state parliament level were unable to unearth the facts due to restrictions imposed by intelligence officers.[151] Authorities in Hesse have recently decided to keep several key documents related to the murders confidential for 120 years, prompting further suspicion among the Turkish community regarding the NSU's possible ties to state officials.[152] Since the NSU homicides, Turkophobic attacks have been sporadically persistent in Germany.[153]

According to an SPD deputy, 'Germany's failure to seriously address the NSU murders sent shock waves to many Turks and compelled them to question their future here.'[154] An official from the Federal Foreign Office agreed that NSU violence continues to be a serious concern for the Turkish community in Germany. In her view, Germany's insufficient response to this pressing issue reflects the government's negative stance towards Turks. She concurred that while the 2000 citizenship reform was a big step, the majority of Turks still do not feel that they are part of German society: 'These policy changes did not spread to the masses. It is not in our DNA yet; we are still not an integration country. We have diversity but we are not fully aware of it … We should do more to enhance Turks' dual identity and belonging.'[155]

Other German policymakers similarly noted that Turks are still perceived as outsiders in the country as 'citizenship reforms and policy amendments have led to improvements on paper but not in hearts'[156] and that 'Turks' emotional and mental belonging is still missing'.[157] In the words of a Federal Foreign Office official, 'attacks targeting Turks are "a disgrace" for Germany, and even though the German government receives constant information from Turkish embassies regarding crimes targeting mosques, officials are still not committed enough to deterring these threats'.[158] In fact, despite promising policy changes, some German politicians continue to posit overtly that Turks do not belong to Germany because of their large population and cultural differences. For example, in 2018, AfD regional leader André Poggenburg called Germans of Turkish-origin 'camel drivers' and 'caraway traders that have the genocide of 1.5 million Armenians weighing them down'.[159] In the same year, Germany's new Minister of the Interior, Horst Seehofer, stated that 'Islam does not belong to Germany'.[160]

Germany's links with Turkish Muslim associations also remain hostile. As stated above, while Christian, Jewish, Baha'i, Ahmadiyya and Alevi groups have been granted the status of corporation under public law, Sunni Muslim organisations are yet to obtain it. Turkish representatives find this treatment discriminatory, suggesting that they have an adequate number of followers, and that most of their associations have a clear organisational structure and have been active for more than thirty years.[161] A DİTİB leader reported: 'Turkish Muslims face economic hardship in Germany because they do not receive state subsidies or tax revenues. Every year, tax revenue given to Christian churches equals €10 billion. Other Christian organisations … receive €50 billion. Under these circumstances, I find it unsurprising that we rely on Turkey's financial assistance.'[162]

To the contrary, German authorities from the Federal Ministry of the Interior claimed that Turkish Islamic organisations do not qualify for this status because they have either insufficient members or do not meet the permanency requirement.[163] Officials from the Federal Agency for Civic Education[164] and the Federal Ministry of Labour, Integration and Social Affairs[165] also argued that these groups would not obtain this status in the near future because Islam is different from other religions and difficult to integrate: 'It is not a hierarchical and unified religion. Communication with Muslims often stalls because of the decentralised nature of Islam.'[166]

German officials and parliamentarians also reprimanded the DİTİB for being politicised by the AKP as a 'patriarchic and ethnic-kin-based' actor that tightens Turkey's grip on the diaspora.[167] One official said:

Diaspora rallies are organised through DİTİB mosques. Friday sermons are used as a platform to recruit AKP supporters and to bring people to rallies. This is an unprecedented development. Catholic churches did something similar here in the past but never to this extent. Some Friday sermons even disseminate anti-integration messages. This is an issue for us … The DİTİB is slowly turning itself into an ethno-religious political institution. We are aware of this change; we are not stupid. The DİTİB does not share common values with us. It is no longer a reliable partner at the federal level.[168]

Local German officials voiced concerns as well: 'Immigrant organisations can ask for money but they need to justify why they need it. We cannot give any money to the DİTİB because we have certain rules and the DİTİB does not respect our rules. They need to be open. They need to show for what purposes they spend the money,' an official from the Berlin Senate for Immigration and Integration pointed out.[169] An immigration commissioner serving in Berlin's Turkish-populated Neukölln district also complained that 'the DİTİB sends us imams who cannot speak German. It is not easy for us to work with them if you cannot even communicate with them.'[170] While DİTİB officials acknowledged that they had made some mistakes in the past, they nonetheless argued that Germany's negative stance towards them perpetuates the 'us against them' binary and harms the Muslim community.[171]

As discussed previously, the creation of the DIK in 2006 was the first serious attempt at institutionalised dialogue between the state and Muslims in Germany. Like the CFCM in France, the DIK's recommendations are not binding, although there are major differences between them. For example, unlike in France, German officials have the authority to select participating organisations. The DIK also has a much more extensive focus on security and terrorism issues.[172] Due to its security-oriented rhetoric in its meetings and publications, and the German state's direct involvement in the process, Turkish Muslims view the DIK as a less inclusive platform than the CFCM.[173] This position is in line with some scholars' portrayal of the DIK as an institution that controls, defines and domesticates Islam; securitises immigration and integration debates; and divides Muslims into 'good' and 'bad'.[174]

For example, while the *Millî Görüş* and the Union of Islamic Cultural Centres were included in some DIK rounds, they were excluded from others.[175] During the first DIK round, German officials also revoked the DİTİB's participation due to the organisation's centralised administration and organic ties to Turkey. In order to join the DIK and to decentralise, the DİTİB reconstituted itself into fifteen regional associations.[176] Turkish Muslim leaders in Germany claimed that the DIK's intention is to pit Turkish organisations against each other so that they can 'divide and rule'. Unlike the situation in France, the DIK's exclusion of the *Millî Görüş* and the Union of Islamic Cultural Centres at the expense of the emancipation of Alevi and other 'provocative' figures, such as Seyran Ateş, a self-proclaimed liberal Muslim, is an indication of Germany's negative intentions, these leaders argued. They also denounced German officials' 'latent' racism and the rise of a new state discourse that focuses on 'core culture' (*leitkultur*).[177] An official from the Federal Ministry of the Interior responded to these allegations by suggesting that 'Germany is always happy to cooperate with Turkish Muslim organisations in the DIK but these organisations might not be capable of collaborating in the ways that Christians and Jews do'. For him, the DİTİB's close ties to Turkey, the *Millî Görüş*'s political and religious agenda and the Union of Islamic Cultural Centres' relatively limited role in the organisational landscape call into question these organisations' ability to serve as a dialogue partner of the federal state and in the DIK.[178] A bureaucrat from the Federal Ministry for Economic Affairs and Energy concluded that Turkish Muslim organisations' 'increasing politicisation is worrisome because they have never been this discernible in the public sphere before'.[179]

Conclusion

This chapter has critically explored why Turkey's engagement with its diasporas has traditionally created a more serious backlash in Germany than in France. Germany has attracted foreign workers since the second half of the nineteenth century, although it was not until the early 2000s that it officially recognised itself as a country of immigration and composed robust integration policies. Germany's *jus sanguinis* citizenship notion placed certain newcomers, such as ethnic Germans, above others. Although the acceptance of ethnic German immigrants in the aftermath of World War II contributed to the growth of the German economy, labour shortages continued. Consequently, in the 1950s and 1960s, Germany signed guest-worker agreements with many countries. However, German politicians singled out Turks as the most troublesome immigrant group due to their large numbers. This mentality persisted in the decades to come. German immigration policy also saw Turks as temporary workers, and this assumption led to policies that rendered Turkish integration harder. While the 2000 Nationality Act represented a significant change in German immigration and integration policies, the citizenship model is still exclusionary for Turks, and anti-Turkish sentiments remain ingrained in German politics, media and wider society. Today Turks continue to be the largest and the least integrated immigrant group in Germany. Turks' negative image in Germany is also linked to the contextualisation of Turks as 'the main other' due to the lack of a colonial history in the country. While in France North Africans have become the poster child of Islam, radicalisation and migration, in Germany Turks have been placed at the centre of public debates on these themes.

Moreover, despite an official separation between state and religion, the German state has extended certain privileges to Christian, Jewish, Baha'i, Ahmadiyya and Alevi communities through the status of corporation under public law. Sunni Muslim organisations, on the other hand, have yet to attain this status. Representatives of Turkish Islamic organisations find this treatment discriminatory given that their parties meet all the requirements. According to them, the German government does not rely on Turkish Muslim organisations to provide representation for its Muslim population in the way France does, and Islam remains an alien religion in Germany. Germany's increasingly intrusive and security-oriented approach since 9/11 has further stigmatised Turkish Muslims in the country. While Germany cannot afford a complete break with Ankara due to the sheer size of the German Turkish population, it is certain that Turkey's diaspora diplomacy efforts will continue to cause diplomatic tension in Germany.

Notes

1 Interview, Federal Foreign Office official, Berlin, 19 February 2019.
2 'German-Turkish leaders Alarmed by Yildirim Speech in Oberhausen', *Deutsche Welle*, 19 February 2017, www.dw.com/en/german-turkish-leaders-alarmed-by-yildirim-speech-in-oberhausen/a-37625555
3 'Dışişleri Bakanı Çavuşoğlu'ndan Almanya'ya Tepki', *Anadolu Ajansı*, 3 March 2017, www.aa.com.tr/tr/gunun-basliklari/disisleri-bakani-cavusoglundan-almanya ya-tepki-turkiyenin-patronu-degilsiniz/763011
4 E. Thomasson, 'Turkey Summons German Ambassador as Tensions Mount', *Reuters*, 19 September 2017, www.reuters.com/article/us-germany-turkey/turkey-summons-german-ambassador-as-tensions-mount-idUSKCN1BT1B4
5 'Turkey's Erdogan Makes Nazi Jibe over German Rally Ban', *BBC*, 5 March 2017, www.bbc.com/news/world-europe-39173296
6 D. Halm and S. Söylemez, 'Positionen von Migrantenorganisationen in grenzüberschreitenden politischen Debatten'.
7 'The Case of Satirist Jan Böhmermann', *Global Freedom of Expression* (2016), https://globalfreedomofexpression.columbia.edu/cases/the-case-of-satirist-jan-bohmermann/
8 'The Long Arm of the Sultan: How Recep Tayyip Erdogan Seduces Turkish Migrants in Europe', *The Economist*, 31 August 2017, www.economist.com/europe/2017/08/31/how-recep-tayyip-erdogan-seduces-turkish-migrants-in-europe
9 T. Jones, 'Journalist Deniz Yücel Sentenced to Almost 3 Years in Prison,' *Deutsche Welle*, 16 July 2020, www.dw.com/en/deniz-yucel-turkey-prison/a-54193689
10 S. Serdar and D. Akal, 'Almanya artık Türkiye'den imam istemiyor'; 'DİTİB Launches Education Program to Train Imams in Germany'.
11 'İmamlara Almanya şartı yürürlülüğe giriyor'.
12 S. Serdar, 'Germany Set to Take Charge of Imam Education Locally'.
13 'Hessen eyaleti DİTİB ile İslam dersi işbirliğini sonlandırdı', *Deutsche Welle*, 28 April 2020, www.dw.com/tr/hessen-eyaleti-ditib-ile-islam-dersi-i%C5%9F-birli%C4%9Fini-sonland%C4%B1rd%C4%B1/a-53272949
14 'Germany's Lower Saxony Imposes Ban on DİTİB's Imams, Refusing Their Service in Prisons', *Daily Sabah*, 8 February 2019, www.dailysabah.com/turkey/2019/01/30/germanys-lower-saxony-imposes-ban-on-ditibs-imams-refusing-their-service-in-prisons
15 C. Bolsover, 'Investigations into Muslim Organisation Milli Gorus Dropped'.
16 *Ibid.*
17 C. Dalaman, 'Almanya'da Ülkücü Dernekler Yasaklanıyor'.

18 N. Steudel, 'The Lobby behind Turkey's Prime Minister', *Deutsche Welle*, 21 May 2014, www.dw.com/en/the-lobby-behind-turkeys-prime-minister/a-17652516; 'Downplaying Erdogan's Influence inside Germany', *Deutsche Welle*, 8 June 2016, www.dw.com/en/downplaying-erdogans-influence-inside-germany/a-19 314758

19 E. Topçu, 'UID AKP'nin yurtdışına uzanan kolu mu?', *Deutsche Welle*, 10 February 2021, www.dw.com/tr/uid-akpnin-yurt-d%C4%B1%C5%9F%C4%B-1na-uzanan-kolu-mu/a-56518966

20 'German population of migrant background rises to 21 million'.

21 'Migration and integration', *Statistisches Bundesamt* (2021), www.destatis.de/EN/Themes/Society-Environment/Population/Migration-Integration/_node.html

22 'German Population of Migrant Background Rises to 21 Million'.

23 *Ibid.*

24 'Summary: "Muslim Life in Germany"', *Federal Ministry of the Interior* (2020), www.bamf.de/SharedDocs/Anlagen/EN/Forschung/Forschungsberichte/Kurz-berichte/muslimisches-leben-kurzfassung-englisch.pdf?__blob=publication-File&v=12

25 D. Vogel and V. Kovacheva, 'Germany', in *European Immigration: A Sourcebook*, eds A. Triandafyllidou and R. Gropas (Aldershot: Ashgate, 2014), p. 145.

26 V. Özcan, 'Germany: Immigration in transition', *Migration Policy Institute Country Profile* (2004), www.migrationpolicy.org/article/germany-immigration-transition

27 T. Schiller, *NS-Propaganda für den "Arbeitseinsatz" Lagerzeitungen für Fremdarbeiter im zweiten Weltkrieg: Entstehung, Funktion, Rezeption und Bibliographie* (Münster: LIT Verlag Münster, 1997).

28 C. Mueller, 'Integrating Turkish communities: A German dilemma'.

29 P. Martin, 'Germany: Reluctant land of immigration,' *German Issues* 21 (1998), www.aicgs.org/site/wp-content/uploads/2011/11/martin.pdf

30 V. Özcan, 'Germany: Immigration in transition'.

31 *Ibid.*

32 'The Impact of Immigration on Germany's Society', *Federal Office for Migration and Refugees* (2005), https://ec.europa.eu/home-affairs/sites/homeaffairs/files/what-we-do/networks/european_migration_network/reports/docs/emn-studies/illegally-resident/de-finalstudy-eng_en.pdf

33 R. Brubaker, *Citizenship and Nationhood in France and Germany*.

34 Basic Law for the Federal Republic of Germany in the revised version published in the Federal Law Gazette Part III, classification number 100–1, as last amended by Article 1 of the Act of 28 March 2019, www.gesetze-im-internet.de/englisch_gg/index.html

35 A. L. Messina, *The Logics and Politics of Post-WWII Migration to Western Europe* (New York: Cambridge University Press, 2007), p. 125.

36 A. Geddes, *The Politics of Migration and Immigration in Europe* (London: Sage, 2003), p. 81.

37 V. Özcan, 'Germany: Immigration in transition'.

38 S. Adar, 'Rethinking political attitudes of migrants from Turkey and their Germany-born children'.

39 V. Özcan, 'Germany: Immigration in transition'.

40 A. Geddes, *The Politics of Migration and Immigration in Europe*.

41 J. Gesley, 'Germany: The development of migration and citizenship law in post-war Germany', *The Law Library of Congress* (2017), www.loc.gov/law/help/migration-citizenship/germany.php#_ftnref12

42 V. Özcan, 'Germany: Immigration in transition'.

43 *Ibid*.

44 B. Klopp, *German Multiculturalism: Immigrant Integration and the Transformation of Citizenship* (Westport: Praeger, 2002).

45 C. Joppke, *Immigration and the Nation-state: The United States, Germany and Great Britain* (Oxford: Oxford University Press, 1999).

46 R. Chin, *The Guest Worker Question in Postwar Germany* (Cambridge: Cambridge University Press, 2009).

47 P. Martin, 'Germany: Reluctant land of immigration', 421.

48 V. Özcan, 'Germany: Immigration in transition'.

49 C. Hecking, 'Secret Thatcher Notes: Kohl Wanted Half of Turks Out of Germany', *Der Spiegel*, 1 August 2013, www.spiegel.de/international/germany/secret-minutes-chancellor-kohl-wanted-half-of-turks-out-of-germany-a-914376.html

50 *Ibid*.

51 *Ibid*.

52 W. Heitmeyer, J. Müller and H. Schröder, *Verlockender Fundamentalismus: Türkische Jugendliche in Deutschland* (Frankfurt/Main: Suhrkamp, 1997); H. Esser, *Sprache und Integration: Die sozialen Bedingungen und Folgen des Spracherwerbs von Migranten* (Frankfurt/Main: Campus Verlag, 2006).

53 C. Hecking, 'Secret Thatcher Notes'.

54 *Ibid*.

55 *Ibid*.

56 *Ibid*.

57 C. Wilpert, 'Identity issues in the history of the postwar migration from Turkey to Germany', *German Politics and Society* 31:2 (2013), 108–31.

58 C. Hecking, 'Secret Thatcher Notes'.

59 Basic Law for the Federal Republic of Germany.

60 D. Thränhardt, 'Germany's immigration policies and politics', in *Mechanisms of Immigration Control: A Comparative Analysis of European Regulation Policies*, eds G. Brochmann and T. Hammar (Oxford: Berg, 1999), pp. 29–57.

61 V. Özcan, 'Germany: Immigration in transition'. For more on *Duldung*, see: K. Koser and R. Black, 'Limits to harmonisation: The "temporary protection" of refugees in the European Union', *International Migration* 37:3 (1999), 521–43.

62 *Ibid*.

63 D. Vogel and V. Kovacheva, 'Germany', p. 148.

64 For more on the REP, see: T. Givens, *Voting Radical Right in Western Europe* (New York: Cambridge University Press, 2005).

65 S. Kinzer, 'A Wave of Attacks on Foreigners Stirs Shock in Germany', *New York Times*, 1 October 1991, www.nytimes.com/1991/10/01/world/a-wave-of-at-tacks-on-foreigners-stirs-shock-in-germany.html

66 A. L. Messina, *The Logics and Politics of Post-WWII Migration,* p. 128.

67 S. von Dirke, 'Multikulti: The German debate on Multiculturalism', *German Studies Review* 17:3 (1994), 513–36.

68 M. M. Howard, *The Politics of Citizenship in Europe.*

69 *Ibid.*; K. Schönwalder and T. Triadafilopoulos, 'A bridge or barrier to incorporation?'

70 M. M. Howard, 'The causes and consequences of Germany's new citizenship law', *German Politics* 17:1 (2008), 53.

71 P. L. Martin, 'Germany', in *Controlling Immigration: A Global Perspective*, eds W. A. Cornelius, P. L. Martin and J. F. Hollifield (Stanford: Stanford University Press, 2014), pp. 224–51.

72 A. L. Messina, *The Logics and Politics of Post-WWII Migration*, p. 132.

73 D. Vogel and V. Kovacheva, 'Germany', p. 149.

74 'National action plan on integration', *The Federal Government* (2012), https://polen.diplo.de/blob/485830/b3bada7b7614c18bb869326b0bef63aa/integration-nap-eng-data.pdf; 'Governance of migration integration in Germany', *European Commission* (2020), https://ec.europa.eu/migrant-integration/governance/germany

75 F. Gesemann and R. Roth, *Integration ist (auch) Ländersache! Schritte zur politischen Inklusion von Migrantinnen und Migranten in den Bundesländern* (Berlin: Friedrich-Ebert-Stiftung, 2014); V. Hanewinkel and J. Oltmer, 'Integration and integration policies in Germany', *Bundeszentrale für Politische Bildung* (2018), www.bpb.de/gesellschaft/migration/laenderprofile/262812/integration-and-integration-policies-in-germany

76 M. Kırıkçıoğlu, 'Anti-Turk Rhetoric in Germany Alienating Community, Jeopardizing Integration Efforts', *Daily Sabah*, 26 August 2017, www.dailysabah.com/eu-affairs/2017/08/26/anti-turk-rhetoric-in-germany-alienating-community-jeopardizing-integration-efforts-1503700806

77 Interview, Green Party deputy, Berlin, 27 February 2019.

78 Interview, SPD deputy, Berlin, 14 February 2019.

79 G. Pickel and C. Öztürk, 'Islamophobia without Muslims? The "contact hypothesis" as an explanation for anti-Muslim attitudes–Eastern European societies in a comparative perspective', *Journal of Nationalism, Memory and Language Politics* 12:2 (2018), 162–91.

80 'Chancellor Merkel says German Multiculturalism has "Utterly Failed"', *Deutsche Welle*, 17 October 2010, www.dw.com/en/chancellor-merkel-says-german-multiculturalism-has-utterly- failed/a-6118859

81 T. Sarrazin, *Deutschland schafft sich ab* (Munich: Deutsche Verlags-Anstalt, 2010); D. Crossland, 'German Author Thilo Sarrazin "Is Fuelling Fear of Muslims"', *The Times*, 31 August 2018, www.thetimes.co.uk/article/german-author-thilo-sarrazin-is-fuelling-fear-of-muslims-6w3rvpq5v

82 Conrad, 'Dual Citizenship Law Takes Place in Germany'.

83 *Ibid.*

84 'Germany to Grant Children of Immigrants Dual Citizenship', *Deutsche Welle*, 8 April 2014, www.dw.com/en/germany-to-grant-children-of-immigrants-dual-citizenship/a- 17551448

85 N. Conrad, 'Dual Citizenship Law Takes Place in Germany'.

86 'Merkel Freezes Germany's Debate over New Immigration Law', *Euractiv*, 4 March 2015, www.euractiv.com/section/social-europe-jobs/news/merkel-freezes-germany-s- debate-over-new-immigration-law/

87 'Anti-Islam Pegida March in German City of Dresden', *BBC*, 16 December 2014, www.bbc.com/news/world-europe-30478321

88 J. Gesley, 'Germany: The development of migration and citizenship law in post-war Germany'.

89 *Ibid.*

90 L. Hindy, 'Germany's Syrian refugee integration experiment', *The Century Foundation* (16 September 2018), https://tcf.org/content/report/germanys-syrian-refugee-integration-experiment/?agreed=1

91 Basic Law for the Federal Republic of Germany.

92 'Five facts about state and religion', *Deutschland* (2021), www.deutschland.de/en/topic/politics/state-and-religion-in-germany-the-five-most-important-facts#:~:text=In%20Germany%2C%20people%20can%20freely,percent%20belong%20to%20other%20religions

93 J. P. Willaime, 'Religion, state and society in Germany and France', *Hartford Institute for Religious Research* (15 August 2003), http://hirr.hartsem.edu/sociology/willaime.html

94 'Germany's Not-Quite-So-Secular Democracy', *Deutsche Welle*, 28 March 2006, www.dw.com/en/germanys-not-quite-so-secular-democracy/a-1942280

95 *Ibid.*

96 M. LeMieux, 'Religious Liberty in Germany and the United States: A Comparison' (PhD dissertation, University of Osnabrück, 2015).

97 'Germany's Not-Quite-So-Secular Democracy'.

98 J. Fetzer and C. Soper, *Muslims and the State in Britain, France and Germany*; T. Sealy, 'Country report: Germany', *Grease: Religion, Diversity and Radicalisation Project* (2019), https://cadmus.eui.eu/bitstream/handle/1814/69919/WP2%20Mapping_Germany%20report_Thomas%20Sealy.pdf?sequence=1&isAllowed=y

99 H. de Wall, 'Religious education in a religiously neutral state: The German model', in *Law, Religious Freedoms and Education in Europe*, ed. M. Hunter-Henin (London: Routledge, 2011), p. 182; T. Sealy, 'Country report: Germany'.

100 T. Sealy, 'Country report: Germany'.

101 J. Fetzer and C. Soper, *Muslims and the State in Britain, France and Germany*, pp. 105–7.

102 *Ibid.*, p. 107.

103 P. Loobuyck, J. Debeer and P. Meier, 'Church–state regimes and their impact on the institutionalisation of Islamic organisations in Western Europe: A comparative analysis', *Journal of Muslim Minority Affairs* 33:1 (2013), 61–76.

104 Interview, *Millî Görüş* official, Cologne, 22 November 2013.

105 M. Rohe, 'Islamic norms in Germany and Europe', in *Islam and Muslims in Germany*, eds A. Al-Hamarneh and J. Thielman (Leiden: Brill, 2008), pp. 49–81.
106 *Ibid.*
107 K. Krämer, '"Muslims in Germany Have Rights and Obligations"', *Deutsche Welle*, 18 June 2013, www.dw.com/en/muslims-in-germany-have-rights-and-obligations/a-16888992#:~:text=The%20Culture%20Ministry%20in%20the,the%20Jewish%20community%20in%20Germany; S. Demmrich, 'How to measure Baha'i religiosity', *Religions* 1:1 (2020), doi: 10.3390/rel11010029
108 'Alevis in Germany's Bremen Win Equal Status as Other Religious Communities', *Hürriyet Daily News*, 17 October 2014, www.hurriyetdailynews.com/alevis-in-germanys-bremen-win-equal-status-as-other-religious-communities-73141; 'Verordnung zur Verleihung der Rechte einer Körperschaft des öffentlichen Rechts an die Alevitische Gemeinde Deutschland mit Sitz in Köln', *Recht NRW* (2020), https://recht.nrw.de/lmi/owa/br_vbl_detail_text?anw_nr=6&vd_id=18981&ver=8&val=18981&sg=0&menu=1&vd_back=N
109 Basic Law for the Federal Republic of Germany.
110 K. Rosenow-Williams, *Organising Muslims and Integrating Islam.*
111 M. Peucker and S. Akbarzadeh, *Muslim Active Citizenship in the West.*
112 Interview, IFB official, Berlin, 27 February 2019.
113 'Hessen eyaleti DİTİB ile İslam dersi işbirliğini sonlandırdı'.
114 A. Yükleyen, *Localising Islam in Europe*, p. 161.
115 *Ibid.*
116 C. Joppke, *Veil: Mirror of Identity.*
117 V. Özcan, 'Germany's High Court allows teacher to wear Muslim headscarf', *Migration Policy Institute Analysis* (2013), www.migrationpolicy.org/article/germanys-high-court-allows-teacher-wear-muslim-headscarf
118 A. Boucher, 'The political participation of Berlin's Turkish migrants in the dual citizenship and headscarf debates'.
119 H. Chahrock, 'Discrimination in the name of neutrality: Headscarf bans for teachers and civil servants in Germany', *Human Rights Watch Report* (2009), www.hrw.org/report/2009/02/26/discrimination-name-neutrality/headscarf-bans-teachers-and-civil-servants-germany
120 T. Jones, 'Constitutional Court Strikes Down Absolute Headscarf Ban', *Deutsche Welle*, 13 March 2015, www.dw.com/en/constitutional-court-strikes-down-absolute-headscarf-ban/a-18313377
121 'German State Lifts Headscarf Ban for Public School Teachers', *Islamist Watch*, 7 September 2015, www.meforum.org/islamist-watch/47239/german-state-lifts-headscarf-ban-for-public
122 'Berlin Teacher Headscarf Ban Is Illegal, Rules Top Court', *Deutsche Welle*, 27 August 2018, www.dw.com/en/berlin-teacher-headscarf-ban-is-illegal-rules-top-court/a-54722770
123 'German State Bans Burqas, Niqabs in Schools', *Deutsche Welle*, 21 July 2020, www.dw.com/en/german-state-bans-burqas-niqabs-in-schools/a-54256541
124 Interview, *Millî Görüş* official, Berlin, 6 December 2013.
125 M. Anil, 'Explaining the naturalisation practices of Turks in Germany in the wake of the citizenship reform of 1999'; 'Study Shows Turkish Immigrants

Least Integrated in Germany'; E. Yalaz, 'Immigrant Political Incorporation'; S. W. McFadden, 'German citizenship law and the Turkish diaspora'.

126 E. Yalaz, 'Immigrant Political Incorporation'.

127 J. Wrench, 'Data on discrimination in EU countries: Statistics, research, and the drive for comparability', *Global Migration Policy Paper* (2010), www.globalmigrationpolicy.org/articles/integration/Data%20On%20Discrimination%20in%20EU-%20Statistics,%20Research,%20Comparability,%20WRENCH%202011.pdf

128 L. Kaas and C. Manger, 'Ethnic discrimination in Germany's labour market: A field experiment', *German Economic Review* 13:1 (2012), 1–20.

129 Interview, Federal Ministry for Economic Affairs and Energy official, Berlin, 5 February 2019; Interview, CDU advisor, Berlin, 26 February 2019.

130 D. Pelz, 'Angekommen, aber nicht anerkannt', *Deutsche Welle*, 16 June 2016, www.dw.com/de/angekommen-aber-nicht-anerkannt/a-19336147; O. Müller and D. Pollack, 'Angekommen und auch wertgeschätzt? Integration von Türkeistämmigen in Deutschland', *Bundeszentrale für politische Bildung* (2017), www.bpb.de/apuz/251227/angekommen-und-auch-wertgeschaetzt-integration-von-tuerkeistaemmigen-in-deutschland

131 *Ibid.*

132 Interview, European Council on Foreign Relations official, Berlin, 13 February 2019.

133 Interview, SPD deputy, Berlin, 14 February 2019.

134 Interview, Konrad Adenauer Foundation official, Berlin, 20 February 2019.

135 Interview, German Federal Foreign Office official, Berlin, 19 February 2019.

136 C. Mueller, 'Integrating Turkish communities: A German dilemma', *Population Research and Policy Review* 25:5/6 (2003), 419–41; A. Huyssen, 'Diaspora and nation: Migration into other pasts', *German Critique* 88, 147–64.

137 M. Albrecht, 'Postcolonialism, Islam and Germany', *Transit* 7:1 (2011), 16–25, https://escholarship.org/uc/item/04p001dj; 'New Zealand's Invasion of Samoa in 1914', *Radio New Zealand*, 17 August 2014, www.rnz.co.nz/national/programmes/new-zealand's-invasion-of-samoa/audio/20145902/nz's-invasion-of-samoa-in-1914

138 P. H. Christensen, *Germany and the Ottoman Railways: Art, Empire and Infrastructure* (New Haven: Yale University Press, 2017); G. Grüsshaber, *The 'German Spirit' in the Ottoman and Turkish Army, 1908–1938* (Berlin: De Gruyter Oldenbourg, 2018).

139 S. Albayrak, 'Being Muslim-Turks in Germany and Almancı (Turks living in Germany) in Turkey: Candidates for religious leaders (imams) in Germany training at Marmara University Faculty of Theology', *Marmara Üniversitesi İlâhiyat Fakültesi Dergisi* 52 (2017), 199–205.

140 S. Friedrichsmeyer, S. Lennox and S. Zantop (eds), *The Imperialist Imagination: German Colonialism and its Legacy* (Ann Arbor: University of Michigan Press, 1998); M. Albrecht, 'Postcolonialism, Islam and Germany'; E. Pape, 'Postcolonial debates in Germany – an overview', *African Sociological Review* 21:2 (2017), 2–14.

141 G. Yurdakul and M. Bodeman, 'We don't want to be the Jews of tomorrow', *German Politics and Society* 24:2 (2006), 44–67; 'Avrupa'nın Yeni Yahudileri Türkler dedi, işinden oluyor', *Hürriyet*, 27 June 2008, www.hurriyet.com.tr/gundem/avrupanin-yeni-yahudileri-turkler-dedi-isinden-oluyor-9288611; G. Yurdakul, 'Jews and Turks in Germany: Immigrant integration, political representation and minority rights', in *Rethinking the Public Sphere through Transnationalising Processes*, eds A. Salvatore, O. Schmidtke and H. J. Trenz (London: Palgrave McMillan, 2013), pp. 251–68.

142 M. Albrecht, 'Postcolonialism, Islam and Germany'.

143 Interview, Turkish Embassy official, Berlin, 13 February 2019.

144 Interview, Turkish Consulate official, Berlin, 26 February 2019.

145 'Discrimination against Turks Lingers 25 Years after Solingen Tragedy', *Daily Sabah*, 30 May 2018, www.dailysabah.com/politics/2018/05/30/discrimination-against-turks-in-germany-lingers-25-years-after-solingen-tragedy

146 *Ibid.*

147 *Ibid.*

148 T. Meaney and S. Schäfer, 'The Neo-Nazi Murder Trial Revealing Germany's Darkest Secrets', *Guardian*, 15 December 2016, www.theguardian.com/world/2016/dec/15/neo-nazi-murders-revealing-germanys-darkest-secrets

149 *Ibid.*

150 R. Staudenmaier, 'NSU Victims' Families Sue German Government over Investigation Errors', *Deutsche Welle*, 18 June 2017, www.dw.com/en/nsu-victims-families-sue-german-government-over-investigation-errors/a-39298486; S. Aust, Helmar Büchel and D. Laabs, 'Spuren, die keine sein dürfen', *Die Welt*, 24 April 2017, www.welt.de/politik/deutschland/article163970309/Spuren-die-keine-sein-duerfen.html

151 A. Şimşek, 'Germany: Turks Demand New Probe on Neo-Nazi Murders', *Anadolu Ajansı*, 18 July 2018, www.aa.com.tr/en/europe/germany-turks-demand-new-probe-on-neo-nazi-murders/1207890

152 *Ibid.*

153 'Discrimination against Turks Lingers 25 Years after Solingen Tragedy'.

154 Interview, SPD deputy, Berlin, 14 February 2019.

155 Interview, German Federal Foreign Office official, Berlin, 19 February 2019.

156 Interview, Expert Council of German Foundations on Integration and Migration official, Berlin, 22 February 2019.

157 Interview, Federal Ministry of Labour, Integration and Social Affairs official, Düsseldorf, 20 November 2013.

158 Interview, German Federal Foreign Office official, Berlin, 19 February 2019.

159 'AfD Regional Leader Andre Poggenburg Resigns Following Anti-Turkish Speech', *Deutsche Welle*, 8 March 2018, www.dw.com/en/afd-regional-leader-andre-poggenburg-resigns-following-anti-turkish-speech/a-42882995; K. Knipp, 'Turkey's Economic Woes Reveal Complicated German Ties', *Deutsche Welle*, 16 August 2018, www.dw.com/en/turkeys-economic-woes-reveal-complicated-germany-ties/a-45112271

160 'Seehofer: Der Islam gehört nicht zu Deutschland', *Süddeutsche Zeitung*, 15 March 2018, www.sueddeutsche.de/politik/integration-seehofer-der-islam-gehoert-nicht-zu-deutschland-1.3908644

161 K. Rosenow-Williams, *Organising Muslims and Integrating Islam*; A. Arkilic, 'The limits of European Islam'; A. Arkilic, 'Between the Homeland and Host States'.

162 Interview, DİTİB official, Cologne, 27 November 2013.

163 Interview, Federal Ministry of the Interior official, Berlin, 7 November 2013.

164 Interview, German Federal Agency for Civic Education official, Berlin, 19 February 2019.

165 Interview, Federal Ministry of Labour, Integration and Social Affairs official, Düsseldorf, 20 November 2013.

166 Interview, German Federal Agency for Civic Education official, Berlin, 19 February 2019.

167 Interview, European Council on Foreign Relations official, Berlin, 13 February 2019; Interview, German Federal Foreign Office official, Berlin, 19 February 2019; Interview, Konrad Adenauer Foundation official, Berlin, 20 February 2019; Interview, Left Party official, Berlin, 25 February 2019.

168 Interview, Konrad Adenauer Foundation official, Berlin, 20 February 2019.

169 Interview, Berlin Senate for Immigration and Integration official, Berlin, 12 September 2013.

170 Interview, Neukölln immigration commissioner, Berlin, 19 September 2013.

171 'DİTİB'den Almanya'ya "yeni başlangıç" çağrısı', *Deutsche Welle*, 7 January 2019, www.dw.com/tr/ditibden-almanyaya-yeni-ba%C5%9Flang%C4%B1%C3%A7-%C3%A7a%C4%9Fr%C4%B1s%C4%B1/a-46989705

172 A. Arkilic, 'The limits of European Islam'.

173 *Ibid.*

174 L. Hernández Aguilar, *Governing Islam and Muslims in Contemporary Germany: Race, Time and the German Islam Conference* (Leiden: Brill, 2018).

175 Interview, *Millî Görüş* official, Cologne, 19 November 2013.

176 Interview, DİTİB official, Cologne, 27 November 2013.

177 Interview, *Millî Görüş* official, Berlin, 6 December 2013; Interview, *Millî Görüş* official, Berlin, 27 February 2019; Interview, TGB official, Berlin, 27 February 2019.

178 Interview, Federal Ministry of the Interior official, Berlin, 7 November 2013.

179 Interview, Federal Ministry for Economic Affairs and Energy official, Berlin, 5 February 2019.

8

Conclusion

This book has explored Turkey's diaspora diplomacy. Diaspora diplomacy is a relatively new phenomenon. Scholars have defined it as 'engaging a country's overseas community to contribute to building relationships with foreign countries'.[1] In this book, I have defined the term as the home state's desire to advance foreign policy interests, relations and negotiations via diasporic communities at local, national and supranational levels. Yet the outcome of these efforts may or may not be mutually beneficial for the home state, the host state(s) and the diasporas. This conceptualisation of diaspora diplomacy takes into consideration the fact that not all segments of a diaspora community might be loyal or willing to promote the foreign policy goals of their home states. The book's central goal is thus to identify some general mechanisms that help explain when the outcome of diaspora diplomacy efforts is positive or negative, and to generate a definition that emphasises the agency of the diaspora group itself in explaining such outcomes.

In unpacking Turkey's diaspora diplomacy, the book first examined the continuities and changes in Turkey's diaspora engagement policies from the 1960s to the present day, and offered a conceptual framework to understand this transformation. It then provided the first in-depth examination of the Turkish diaspora's post-2003 role as an agent of diplomatic goals and examined the plethora of transnational and international tensions that have arisen from this change. It illustrated that Turkey's conservative-nationalist and Sunni Islamic diaspora groups have become a tool of political leverage and have sought to enhance Turkey's official diplomatic endeavours. Yet Turkish diaspora diplomacy has worsened Ankara's relations with the non-conformist segments of the diaspora. It has also complicated relations with Europe as the majority of European countries have interpreted Turkey's diaspora diplomacy as an intervention in their domestic affairs and as a security threat. While diaspora diplomacy is not the only element harming Turkey's relationship with Europe, it has made a significant and overlooked contribution to the deterioration of relations.

Diasporas may communicate to multiple stakeholders and audiences, including non-state actors, and thus affect governance and society in both the sending and the receiving countries. Yet the literature on diasporas and diplomacy has paid scant attention to the question of how diasporas blur the strict division between the domestic and the foreign. Diaspora scholars have either investigated diasporas as an issue of domestic politics – they have been primarily concerned with the impact of the diaspora on the politics of the homeland or the host country rather than with international relations – or have only referred to diasporas in passing, mostly as a vehicle for public diplomacy or a mode of soft power. This study contributes to the blossoming literature on diaspora diplomacy, particularly contested diaspora diplomacy, made more significant by Turks forming the largest Muslim immigrant community in Europe.

As Chapter 2 revealed, the Turkish state's diaspora policies were mainly driven by economic incentives but, since the 2000s, its agenda has been shaped by political goals. Turkish officials have actively sought to mobilise select, ideologically proximate diaspora groups in favour of Turkey's five foremost foreign policy goals: (1) the denial of the Armenian genocide; (2) the establishment of closer relations with the EU; (3) the promotion of Turkey as an independent and strong regional power, and the preservation of a distinct Turkish identity in Europe; (4) the disempowerment of Kurdish and Gülenist groups abroad; and (5) combating Islamophobia and racism in Europe. Turkey's diaspora outreach policies have also aimed to consolidate the political power of the incumbent AKP and its leader, Erdoğan, by drumming up expatriate votes. Chapter 2 argued that Turkey's shift from a passive to a proactive diaspora engagement policy is a result of events unfolding at three levels: domestically, the AKP's rise to power in 2002; transnationally, the Turkish émigré community's shift from temporary to permanent settlement; and internationally, Turkey's changing relations with Europe since the 1999 Helsinki Summit, 9/11 and the European refugee crisis. The chapter emphasised that domestic factors have played the most significant role in shaping Turkey's diaspora agenda. The AKP's emergence as a new political elite has changed the ways in which Turkey interacts with its overseas population and perceives its international position vis-à-vis European countries.

The book then transferred the analysis to the impact of Turkey's diaspora policy change on the conservative elements of the Turkish diaspora in France and Germany, two key EU member states, which also host the highest number of Turks in Europe. Chapters 3 and 4 detailed Turkey's engagement with conservative-nationalist and Sunni Islamic organisations in France and Germany. They did so through a focus on the outreach activities of various state institutions and these diaspora organisations' perceptions of and responses to Turkey's increasing sway over them. The chapters demonstrated that Turkey's engagement with its loyal supporters in Europe advances deliberate policy goals, such as increasing the lobbying potential of the Turkish diaspora in favour of the AKP government, canvassing diaspora votes and strengthening national legitimacy by evoking a sense of loyalty among diaspora Turks. The German case is particularly important given the position of the German Turkish population as a large constituency for Turkish, German and EU elections. These two chapters also documented the ways in which the AKP has encouraged conservative diaspora organisations' political mobilisation by presenting them as Turkey's ambassadors and by bolstering their organisational capabilities against the backdrop of the rise of Islamophobia in Europe.

In order to shed light on the limitations of diaspora diplomacy, Chapter 5 looked at intra-diasporic politics as well as at the ongoing clashes the AKP government has been experiencing with the seemingly 'disloyal' segments of the diaspora. The AKP's democratisation reforms have significantly slowed since 2011 with the increasing violation of political rights and civil liberties. The party's third term is seen as a turning point as Erdoğan has swiftly transitioned into an authoritarian ruler. The party's reframing of Alevism within a Turkish Islamic framework, its encroachment on secularism and spiralling tension between the Turkish military and Kurds have deepened the rupture between the AKP and Alevi, secular and Kurdish communities within and beyond Turkish borders. At the same time, the fraying alliance between the AKP and the Gülen Movement started to collapse and Turkey's Europeanisation process entered a period of stalemate. The AKP's targeting of Alevi, secular, Kurdish and Gülenist groups has become even more conspicuous since the 2013 Gezi Park protests, the 2014 presidential elections, the 2016 aborted coup and the 2017 constitutional referendum. These events have led to a new wave of Turkish emigration to Europe, spearheaded by secularists, highly skilled emigrants, students, sacked public employees and academics. The chapters demonstrated that new tensions between Gülenists and AKP supporters, and Kurds and ultranationalists have unleashed additional turmoil within the diasporic field. Although it was not the focus of this book, there is also an emerging clash between Turks who came to Europe as 'guest workers' and the white-collar, brain-drainer 'new wave Turks' who made Europe their new home in the post-2000 era. The latter's attitude towards the former is often characterised by prejudice, aversion and ignorance.[2] The growing polarisation within the émigré community has weakened the effectiveness of Turkey's diaspora diplomacy, generated unrest within European host states and negatively affected Turkey–EU relations.

The final part of the book examined how Turkey's expanding sphere of influence over its diaspora shapes Ankara's diplomatic relations with

European host states. More specifically, Chapters 6 and 7 delved into the French and German governments' responses to Turkish diaspora engagement policy and diaspora diplomacy. The AKP's new diaspora agenda complicated Ankara's and Turkey-originated expatriates' relations with policymakers in both countries, but more so in Germany than in France. To explain this variation between France and Germany, these chapters charted France and Germany's different citizenship and immigrant integration models, as well as policies towards Islam and Muslims. In particular, in comparing Turkish and other immigrant experiences in France, Chapter 6 affirmed that Turks have historically been exempt from the hierarchical racial categorisation in France that placed North and Sub-Saharan citizens originating from former colonies below white French citizens. Turks' exemption from this placement stems not only from the lack of a colonial relationship between Turkey and France but also from the popular French conception of Turkey as a country like France (both with strong state traditions and a secular regime) and of Turks as people with a liminal position between Europe and the Middle East. Paris has also tended to view Ankara as an important ally in the governance of its Muslim community within the context of French *laïcité* and a perceived failure to 'localise' Islam. However, Turks' privileged status started to change in 2020, particularly after French President Macron's vow to curb foreign influence in the country. Conversely, Germany covered most of its need for labour from a bilateral worker agreement signed with Turkey (and other countries) rather than from former colonies. Ever since the first wave of Turkish emigration to Germany, German politicians saw Turks as the most troublesome immigrant group due to their large numbers and unique historical relations with the country. This mentality persisted in the decades to come. Moreover, unlike French *laïcité*, which places all religions and beliefs on an equal legal footing, the German state has periodically favoured other religions over Islam, as evidenced by the extension of the status of corporation under public law to all major religions except Islam; and Germany's intrusive and security-oriented approach towards Turkish Muslims worsened after 9/11. Chapters 6 and 7 concluded that any diplomatic row France and Germany have with Turkey has negative consequences for Turkey–EU relations given that these are the most influential EU member states.

Broader tensions across Europe

Other EU member states have bristled at Turkey's diaspora diplomacy in similar ways. For example, the Netherlands followed Germany's decision and cancelled a series of planned Turkish rallies in March 2017. The Dutch prime minister, Mark Rutte, announced that Turkish election campaigns would no longer be allowed within the Dutch territory.[3] This Turkish–Dutch spat escalated when Dutch officials barred the Turkish Minister of Foreign Affairs, Mevlüt Çavuşoğlu, from entering the country and expelled the then Minister of Family and Social Policies, Fatma Betül Sayan Kaya, prior to her scheduled rally in Rotterdam.[4] At the outset of the intensifying diplomatic crisis, Turkey's Minister of the Interior, Süleyman Soylu, threatened to 'blow the mind' of Europe by breaking the 2016 EU–Turkey refugee deal, which would send 15,000 refugees a month to the EU.[5]

In a similar vein, Erdoğan antagonistically referred to the Netherlands as 'fascist', a 'Nazi remnant' and a 'banana republic'.[6] In February 2018, the Netherlands announced that its ambassador to Turkey would be withdrawn for an undetermined period and that no new Turkish ambassador would be appointed to the Hague. Furthermore, the Dutch Foreign Affairs Ministry officially declared that diplomatic talks with Turkey had been suspended. The acrimony continued to magnify when Ankara summoned the Dutch chargé d'affaires to condemn the Dutch House of Representatives' decision to recognise the mass killings of Armenians in 1915 as genocide.[7] An impasse with the Netherlands does not bode well for Turkey's economic interests given that 85 per cent of Turkey's foreign investments come from the West, with the Netherlands being the top investor in Turkey.[8]

Other western European countries have voiced discontent too. Austria advocated the prevention of AKP officials launching rallies, ruling that the events might increase friction and hinder Turkish integration into Austria. Austrian policymakers even called for a collective European policy banning Turkish rallies in EU territory.[9] Belgian authorities also announced that local councils could decide whether or not to cancel rallies based on security considerations.[10]

The DİTİB's espionage scandal in Germany has leaked into the rest of Europe as well. German Green Party politician Volker Beck filed a criminal complaint and warned other European countries that 'the *Diyanet*, religious attachés at consulates and the local DİTİB associations are ... capable of acting as a secret service ... The Turkish state's collection of information on Gülen activities has likely occurred all over the world.'[11] German newspapers similarly reported that Turkish religious attachés serving in the Netherlands, Austria, Switzerland and Belgium sent espionage reports to Ankara.[12] In 2017, Austrian Green Party deputy Peter Pilz expressed his concerns regarding a clandestine 'global spying network' at Turkish diplomatic missions.[13] Austrian Chancellor Sebastian Kurz announced in 2018 that his country would extradite sixty *Diyanet*-funded imams and their families and close down one ATİB-affiliated mosque.[14] AKP officials condemned this 'ideologically charged' decision, arguing that it validated the Islamophobic and far-right populist movements in the country.[15] In 2020, the Austrian Minister of the Interior, Karl Nehammer, reported that Austrian intelligence had caught another Turkish spy: 'This is about an exertion of influence by a foreign power … Turkish espionage has no place in Austria. There is no place for Turkish influence on liberty and fundamental rights. We will fight against it vehemently,' he added, and gave an official account of the incident to Europol and the European Council.[16] Belgium also responded to the espionage allegations by rejecting visa applications from Turkish imams who had applied for long-term visas to work in the country,[17] and by suspending subsidies to mosques.[18] Similarly, Dutch officials said that they were wary of Ankara's 'long arm' in the country and summoned the Turkish Ambassador to the Hague after a DİTİB official admitted that he was compiling information about Gülenists.[19]

Political parties formed by Turks in Europe have also inflamed tensions across the continent, most recently in the Netherlands and Sweden. For example, the DENK in the Netherlands has been accused of 'fanning flames of immigrant discontent' and being 'Netherlands haters' by some Dutch media channels.[20] In 2018, Mikail Yüksel, a Turkish-origin politician, claimed to have been expelled from Sweden's left-wing Centre Party ahead of local and general elections because of his close connections to the AKP.[21] Mehmet Kaplan, another Swedish politician with Turkish roots, who had previously served as the Minister of Housing, Urban Development and Information Technology was also forced to resign after photos were revealed showing him attending a dinner with the ultranationalist Grey Wolves.[22]

These disagreements are likely to have long-lasting consequences in Europe, jeopardising Turkey's EU membership and broader partnerships with EU countries, and damaging Turkey's international image. In fact, in 2017, European Commission President Jean-Claude Juncker suggested that Turkey was fully to blame for the breakdown of its EU membership talks and that Ankara was withdrawing from Europe with 'giant steps'.[23] Erdoğan's response was surprising, as he declared that Turkey has no intention to leave Europe: 'We see ourselves nowhere else but in Europe. We contemplate to build our future together with Europe … We believe that we do not have any problem with any country or institution that cannot be solved through politics, diplomacy and dialogue.' He also invited the EU to keep its promises not to discriminate against Turkey nor disseminate 'explicit hostility'.[24]

A representative from the Delegation of the EU to Turkey confirmed that while the EU does not want to cut off ties with Turkey, 'the process is stuck and it is not going anywhere' and that 'tensions over the Turkish diaspora do not help'. This bureaucrat also shared concerns regarding Turkey's threats to abort the refugee deal.[25] Two diplomats from the German and

French embassies in Ankara also suggested that Turkey's reliability as a partner for the EU has significantly declined due to the diaspora rally rows, the detainment of both Turkish and European citizens by the Turkish government and the overall curtailment of freedom of speech within and beyond Turkey'.[26]

Implications beyond the diaspora diplomacy scholarship

The breadth of the implications of this research goes beyond the diaspora diplomacy scholarship and speaks to other enduring debates in anthropology, international relations, political science, sociology and public policy. These include, but are not limited to, the continuing supremacy of the nation-state in the globalised age, populist nationalism, authoritarianism and non-democratic politics and immigrant integration.

Emigration is a phenomenon that simultaneously fortifies and subverts territorial understandings of state sovereignty and borders.[27] Its impact is felt in terms of both de-territorialising and re-territorialising.[28] Some scholars have explained the global rise of diaspora institutions by paying closer attention to the 'regional and global standards of migration management'[29] and 'international forces shaping state behaviour from the outside', such as the UN.[30] Others have contended that globalisation has led to the loss of control of borders and states in a way that renders sovereignty and even citizenship redundant, creating a 'post-national citizenship'.[31] This approach has alleged that state sovereignty has declined in an era characterised by the growth of international ties and networks that traverse national borders and cultures. While this book does not disregard the significance of international or transnational forces, it provides evidence for the relevance of the nation-state in an age of globalisation.[32]

As many studies have already demonstrated, host states play a key role in the governance of Muslim communities in Europe. For example, Jonathan Laurence has noted that between 1990 and 2010, European governments sought to shape European Islam by 'a dual movement of expanding religious liberty and increasing control exerted over religion'.[33] In order to achieve this, they have converged and cooperated on a broad range of issues concerning their Muslim communities. They have also introduced restrictive immigration policies to rebuild the connection between territory and sovereignty and reimpose their authority.[34] This book reveals that the policies of sending states matter at least as much as the policies of receiving states for the governance of immigrants. As seen in the case of Turkish long-distance politics,[35] sending states may establish 'new institutions and rights to incorporate their extraterritorial citizens into a global nation defined less by territory and more by national belonging'.[36] In doing so, they 'bind together immigrants, their descendants, and those who have remained in their home-land into a single transborder citizenry ... and view emigrants and their descendants as part of the nation, whatever legal citizenship the émigrés may have'.[37] Engagements between the home state and its nationals abroad significantly influence the ways in which host states interact with their Muslim communities.

The findings presented in this book are also relevant for populist nation-alism scholarship. Populism can appear in a myriad of forms, such as revo-lutionary intellectual populism, peasant populism and populist dictatorship.[38] The minimal definition of populism refers to an 'anti-elite discourse in the name of the sovereign People'.[39] Populist nationalism, which has been on the rise especially since the latter half of 2010, juxtaposes populism and nation-alism.[40] Populist nationalist leaders mobilise 'the people' around common heritage, myths, stories and symbols,[41] and address a certain ethnic or racial group that are said to be the 'pure' people.[42] They revitalise a sense of peo-plehood that is central to the ethnic nation rooted in an historical context and emphasise their attachment to a glorious historical past.[43] President Erdoğan is the poster child of populist nationalism, as evidenced by his anti-establishment and neo-Ottoman appeals at diaspora rallies, direct link-ages between himself and his followers, and his positioning of Turkey as the protector of overseas Turks and ethno-nationalist and religious values against the threat of European states. As discussed thoroughly in this book, Ankara's reconfiguration of its diaspora as an inseparable component of the 'great' Turkish nation has evoked unrest in Europe. However, populist nationalism is not a phenomenon specific to Turkey. In fact, it is gaining ground in Europe, too, which contributes to the further marginalisation of the Turkish diaspora and pushes them closer to the homeland. Indeed, my recent research has shown that diaspora Turks who face more discrimina-tion in their respective European host states are more likely to be wooed by Ankara's populist-nationalist discourse and to vote for the AKP and Presi-dent Erdoğan in Turkish parliamentary and presidential elections.[44]

Turkey's deepening authoritarianism and its ramifications for the trans-national arena constitute another source of anxiety for Europe. A state's regime type influences patterns of state–diaspora engagement as well as the nature of the diaspora's role in international relations.[45] Diaspora groups are central in the forging of cooperative foreign policy ties between their home and host countries when both these countries have democratic regimes. However, in democratic–authoritarian, authoritarian–democratic and authoritarian–authoritarian dyads, diasporas are more likely to have a limited political impact on the formalisation and strengthening of coopera-tive foreign policy ties.[46] Other scholars have theorised authoritarian emi-gration states' 'peculiar' practices of transnational repression, legitimation and co-optation, which form part of these states' survival strategies.[47] Unlike democracies, which tend to encourage external voting in order to boost democratic participation, authoritarian states may introduce external voting to monitor and repress their nationals abroad.[48] In fact, as Fiona B. Adamson has suggested:

> the location of diasporic spaces outside the physical boundaries of the state does not necessarily remove them from the pressures and effects of state authoritarianism. Rather, state repressive power can extend into the spaces of other states and take the form of 'transnational' or 'extraterritorial' repression, acting as a 'long-distance' deterrent to political organising and posing a threat to populations living abroad.[49]

As illustrated in this study, some Turkish state institutions' and diaspora organisations' involvement in 'illiberal, anti-democratic or authoritarian' activities[50] has become a serious concern for European host states.

Finally, this research has broader implications for the relationship between migrants' involvement in homeland politics and their integration into host states.[51] While migrant integration was initially viewed as a 'one-way' process – that is, the responsibility of migrants – scholars came to consider it as a 'two-way' process, where migrants and host states interconnect and transform each other. And since the 1990s, integration has been understood as a 'three-way' process in which migrants, countries of origin and countries of settlement take part. This body of work delineates the role home states play in migrant integration and is useful in explaining why some migrants fare better than others in terms of integration even if they live in the same host state and share similar characteristics.[52] Although allegiance to the sending state raises questions concerning the integration of migrants and their descendants in the receiving country, the assumed negative relationship is yet to be explored.[53] Initial data suggests that Turkey's paternalistic approach towards its nationals abroad has hampered the Turkish diaspora's integration prospects and relations with European host states. Yet given the complexity of the nature of migrants' multiple identities and belongings, we need a longitudinal analysis to properly examine the effects of this relationship. The long-term implications of Turkish Muslims' politicisation in host states are also important for the governance of the broader Muslim population in the EU against the backdrop of a record influx of refugees and the growing popularity of anti-migrant parties and movements.

Concluding remarks

Can the book's arguments be generalised to other cases? This research has revealed that sending states do not reach out equally to all groups within their diasporas. Instead, they launch sophisticated and effective diaspora engagement policies that work to achieve concrete political ambitions aimed at certain diasporic communities. Turkey's bifurcated diaspora engagement policy arguably resembles those of India and the People's Republic of China. These countries distinguish between Sikh, Tamil, Muslim and Hindu groups, and Tibetan, Uyghur and Han Chinese diaspora groups respectively.[54] In a similar vein, the Egyptian and Israeli governments have developed a multi-tiered diaspora policy taking into consideration diaspora groups' intergenerational differences or diverging economic and foreign policy potentials.[55]

North African countries have empowered specific pro-regime diaspora groups for security and political purposes as well.[56] Morocco, in particular, is akin to Turkey in terms of diaspora engagement objectives and strategies. In recent years, the Moroccan government has strived to preserve the moral and material interests of its diaspora, to empower Moroccan expatriate organisations, to deepen Moroccan immigrants' allegiance to their homeland and to consolidate the political regime at home. It has sought to re-establish forms of belonging and commitment among the diaspora based not only on nationality but also on Islamic identity.[57]

Parallels can also be drawn between Turkey and other authoritarian countries in terms of the home state's favouring of certain diaspora groups and stigmatising others. As Katrina Burgess has pointed out, the Dominican Republic and the Philippines are two interesting cases in point. The incumbent Dominican government has seen potential in its diasporas and sought to include them in its transnational patronage networks. The transnationalisation of political parties has created incentives for political leaders to court migrants as potential voters and to cultivate partisan loyalties, and expatriates that have responded to the state's expectations have received selective benefits.[58] However, the Dominican diaspora is not a homogeneous entity. Mirroring the 2013 Gezi Park protests in Turkey, Dominicans inside and outside the country organised the Green March (*Marcha Verde*) protests in 2017, which cast doubt on the regime's grip on the diaspora.[59]

Filipino President Rodrigo Duterte has also presented himself as the advocate of his country's interests at home and abroad and has been committed to establishing a strong connection between the Filipino state and expatriates. However, he has prioritised the formation of clientelistic relationships with 'loyal' diaspora. Amid the country's democratic backsliding, certain diaspora communities have shown a strong resistance to his engagement efforts and coordinated counter-mobilisations outside the electoral arena. In return, echoing Erdoğan, Duterte has engaged in repressive policies to counter overseas challenges to his political rule. He has called his opponents 'terrorists', collaborated with loyal diaspora members to subdue them and sponsored pro-regime Filipino groups abroad. His authoritarian actions have even prompted new overseas resistance movements, such as the Malaya Movement, launched in the United States.[60] This development resembles the creation of new Turkish resistance groups across Europe in early 2021 in response to Erdoğan's appointment of Melih Bulu, a businessman known for his close ties to the AKP, to Turkey's prestigious Boğaziçi University as rector. These protests marked the largest display of civil uprising within and beyond Turkey's borders since the 2013 Gezi events.[61]

While this study has raised novel questions, it has certain limitations that future studies should address. It has focused on how loyal immigrant organisations' officials have become politically mobilised at the homeland's behest. As the de facto representatives of immigrant-origin individuals in Europe, immigrant organisations constitute the main claims-making actors and co-constructors of political debates pertinent to immigration and integration. They also serve as a bridge between their home states and local communities, and advocate for migrant interests in various areas.[62] Moreover, since 9/11, Turkish immigrant organisations have become increasingly influential actors in Europe.[63] However, Nina Glick-Schiller has warned scholars about the 'ethnic association fetish'.[64] In her view, an excessive focus on immigrant organisations presents a limited portrayal of transnational immigrant behaviour because these organisations make up a small portion of the diaspora community. She has also noted that by concentrating on specific ethno-religious immigrant associations, scholars and policymakers wrongfully portray migrants as people who are culturally 'different' to others and live in ghettos separated from local, national and transnational forms of civil society. Keeping this in mind, future studies should analyse the impact of diaspora engagement activities on individuals who are not part of any organisation. After all, not every member of the diaspora community joins an organisation. Research is thus needed on the extent to which – and how – empowerment at the leadership and organisational level filters down, as well as on the ways in which diaspora diplomacy is exercised by ordinary members of the expatriate community.

In fact, the extant literature still tends to deal with how and why home states engage their diasporas, rather than with what results. Many researchers in this field have developed a state-centred perspective, which has discouraged them from collecting much needed empirical data from individuals in the diaspora. Beyond the fetishisation of the state in the field, there are also logistical and financial difficulties with engaging in multi-site fieldwork, particularly in non-democratic settings. This book acknowledges these challenges but emphasises that there is a need for extensive multi-site ethnographic fieldwork that focuses not only on home and host states but also on members of the diaspora. This methodological approach would help scholars to further unpack the diaspora. How does preferential treatment of diaspora communities affect intra-diasporic relations in other countries? Does it lead to fragmentation in the diaspora as in the Turkish case or does it not matter as much? What effect does it have on diaspora mobilisation? These are questions that require further research.

Other interesting avenues for future research would be to investigate whether declining homeland support leads to an environment where less favoured diaspora organisations would be more prone to de-transnationalise, as Jonathan Laurence put it.[65] In fact, my research on the Alevi diaspora in France has found that, as Alevi leaders feel increasingly excluded by Turkey, they have formed closer relations with French officials.[66] It would be interesting to explore whether this observation holds for other non-conformist diaspora groups from Turkey, particularly those operating in Germany, where racist attacks targeting Turks in various cities have shattered the Turkish community's trust in German society and their politicians. Furthermore, scholars could investigate in more detail how, when and why disregarded diaspora groups form solidarity networks and engage in diplomatic activities.

The impact of the COVID-19 pandemic on state–diaspora relations provides another fruitful research platform. Kemal Kirişçi has argued that the pandemic has led to increasing authoritarianism in Turkey.[67] Since the identification of the first COVID-19 case in the country, in March 2020, President Erdoğan has reinforced his one-man rule by debilitating state institutions, by eroding opposition parties' attempts to fight the pandemic and by detaining scores of journalists and social media users due to their alleged spread of 'provocative news'.[68] Yet this is a global phenomenon. From the People's Republic of China to Hungary, states around the world have used the pandemic as an excuse to repress domestic opposition and violate civil liberties through heightened surveillance and tracing.[69] Scholars should thus pay closer attention to how the pandemic and other global crises exacerbate authoritarian states' repressive extraterritorial practices and how they then impact diaspora diplomacy. The ever changing nature of politics begets novel and intriguing questions that require the attention of scholars and policymakers, as this book has demonstrated.

In conclusion, this study contributes to the growing literature on diasporas and diplomacy. Diasporas have become identified as influential actors that transform relations at the state-to-state level and blur the strict division between the domestic and the foreign. A case study of Turkey's diasporas is thus a significant addition to the scholarly literature at a time when emigrants from Turkey in Europe have reached 5.5 million, and when issues of diplomacy, migration, citizenship and authoritarianism have become more salient than ever.

Notes

1 K. S. Rana, 'Diaspora diplomacy and public diplomacy', p. 70.
2 C. Nurtsch, 'Turkish Brain Drainers versus Guest Workers', *Qantara*, 6 March 2019, https://en.qantara.de/content/new-istanbul-in-berlin-turkish-brain-drain-ers-versus-guest-workers
3 'Erdogan: Austria Will "Pay a Price" for Banning Turkish Campaigning', *Euractiv*, 23 April 2018, www.euractiv.com/section/global-europe/news/erdogan-austria-will-pay-a-price-for-banning-turkish-campaigning/
4 'Turkey Referendum: Clashes as Dutch Expel Minister', *BBC*, 12 March 2017, www.bbc.com/news/world-europe-39246392
5 'Turkey Threatens to Send Europe "15,000 Refugees a Month"', *Euractiv*, 18 March 2017, www.euractiv.com/section/global-europe/news/turkey-threatens-to-send-europe-15000-refugees-a-month
6 *Ibid.*
7 'Turkey's Erdogan Calls Dutch Authorities "Nazi Remnants"', *BBC*, 11 March 2017, www.bbc.com/news/world-europe-39242707; A. Arkilic, 'How Turkey's Outreach to Its Diaspora is Inflaming Tensions with Europe'.
8 M. Sönmez, '85% of Turkey's Foreign Investors Still from the West', *Hürriyet Daily News*, 4 January 2016, www.hurriyetdailynews.com/85-percent-of-tur-keys-foreign-investors-still-from-west-93356; A. Arkilic, 'How Turkey's Outreach to Its Diaspora is Inflaming Tensions with Europe'.
9 'Turkey's Erdogan Accuses Germany of "Nazi Practices" over Rally Cancellations', *Deutsche Welle*, 5 March 2017, www.dw.com/en/turkeys-erdogan-accuses-germany-of-nazi-practices-over-rally-cancellations/a-37816320
10 'Reality Check: Is Banning Turkish Rallies EU Policy?'
11 C. Winter, 'Turkish Imam Spy Affair Extends across Europe'.
12 *Ibid.*
13 *Ibid.*
14 'Austria to Shut Down Mosques and Expel Foreign-funded Imams', *Reuters*, 8 June 2020, www.reuters.com/article/us-austria-politics-islam-idUSKCN1 J40X1
15 'Avusturya Türkiye'nin finanse ettiği 60'a yakın imamı ve ailelerini sınırdışı edi-yor', *BBC*, 8 June 2018, www.bbc.com/turkce/haberler-dunya-44410584
16 K. Knolle, 'Austria to File Charges against Turkish Spy, Interior Minister Says', *Reuters*, 1 September 2020, www.reuters.com/article/us-austria-turkey-espio-nage/austria-to-file-charges-against-turkish-spy-interior-minister-says-idUSKBN-25S4R1
17 'Belgium Rejects Visa Applications of Turkish Imams', *Hürriyet Daily News*, 16 March 2017, www.hurriyetdailynews.com/belgium-rejects-visa-applications-of-turk-ish-imams--110875
18 T. Heneghan, 'Turkish-financed Mosques in Europe Allegedly Spying for Erdo-gan', *Religious News*, 19 April 2017, https://religionnews.com/2017/04/19/turk-ish-financed-mosques-in-europe-allegedly-spying-for-erdogan/

19 T. Sterling, 'Netherlands Says It Wary of "Long Arm" of Turkish State', *Reuters*, 15 December 2016, www.reuters.com/article/us-turkey-security-netherlands-idUSKBN1431BS

20 N. Siegal, 'A Pro-Immigrant Party Rises in the Netherlands', *New York Times*, 29 July 2016, www.nytimes.com/2016/07/30/world/europe/dutch-denk-party.html

21 'Turkish-origin Swedish Expelled from Centre Party', *Daily Sabah*, 23 August 2018, www.dailysabah.com/europe/2018/08/23/turkish-origin-swedish-politi-cian-expelled-from-centre-party

22 M. Norell, 'Erdogan's Influence in Europe: A Swedish Case Study', *Washington Institute* (2020), www.washingtoninstitute.org/policy-analysis/erdogans-influ-ence-europe-swedish-case-study

23 'EU's Juncker Said Turkey Leaving Europe by "Giant Steps"', *France24*, 29 August 2017, www.france24.com/en/20170829-eus-juncker-says-turkey-leaving-europe-giant-steps

24 'We Contemplate to Build a Future with Europe, says Erdoğan', *Hürriyet Daily News*, 21 November 2020, www.hurriyetdailynews.com/we-contemplate-to-build-our-future-with-europe-erdogan-says-160229

25 Interview, EU Delegation to Turkey representative, Ankara, 28 June 2019.

26 Interview, German Embassy official, Ankara, 24 June 2019; Interview, French Embassy official, Ankara, 28 June 2019.

27 L. Brand, *Citizens Abroad*; H. Mylonas, *The Politics of Nation-building: Making Co-Nationals, Refugees and Minorities* (New York: Cambridge University Press, 2012); M. Collyer (ed.), *Emigration Nations: Policies and Ideologies of Emigrant Engagement* (Basingstoke: Palgrave Macmillan, 2013).

28 L. Basch, N. Glick-Schiller and C. Szanton-Blanc, *Nations Unbound: Transna-tional Projects and the Deterritorialised Nation-state* (New York: Gordon and Breach, 1994); N. Glick-Schiller, L. Basch and C. Szanton-Blanc, 'From immi-grant to transmigrant: Theorizing transnational migration', *Anthropology Quar-terly* 68:1 (1995), 48–63.

29 A. Gamlen, *Human Geopolitics*, p. 49.

30 *Ibid.*, p. 12.

31 Y. Soysal, *Limits of Citizenship: Migrants and Postnational Memberships in Europe* (Chicago: University of Chicago Press, 1994); S. Sassen, *Losing Control: Sovereignty in an Age of Globalisation* (New York: Columbia University Press, 1996).

32 J. F. Hollifield, 'Migration, trade and the nation-state: The myth of globalisation', *Journal of International Law and Foreign Affairs* 3:2 (1998), 595–636; J. F. Hol-lifield, 'The politics of international migration'.

33 J. Laurence, *The Emancipation of Europe's Muslims*, p. 6.

34 K. Burgess, *Courting Migrants*.

35 A. Arkilic, 'Long-distance politics and diaspora youth'.

36 K. Burgess, *Courting Migrants*, p. 21.

37 N. Glick-Schiller and G. Fouron, *Georges Woke Up Laughing: Long Distance Nationalism and the Search for Home* (Durham: Duke University Press, 2001), p. 20.

38 M. Canovan, *Populism* (New York: Harcourt, 1981).

39 P. Aslanidis, 'Is populism an ideology? A refutation and a new perspective', *Political Studies* 64:1 (2016), 96.

40 For more information, see: A. Arkilic, 'Turkish populist nationalism in transnational space'.

41 D. Johnson and E. Frombgen, 'Racial contestation and the emergence of populist nationalism in the United States', *Social Identities* 15:5 (2009), 635.

42 F. Lopes-Alves and D. Johnson, 'The rise of populist nationalism in comparative perspective: Europe and the Americas', in *Populist Nationalism in Europe and the Americas*, eds F. Lopes-Alves and D. Johnson (London: Routledge, 2019), pp. 3–19.

43 J. De Matas, 'Making the nation great again: Trump, Euro-skepticism, and the surge of populist nationalism', *Journal of Comparative Politics* 10:2 (2017), 19–36; D. Johnson and E. Frombgen, 'Racial contestation'.

44 A. Arkilic, 'Turkish populist nationalism in transnational space'.

45 F. B. Adamson, 'Non-state authoritarianism and diaspora politics', *Global Networks* 20:1 (2020), doi: 10.1111/glob.12246

46 N. Mirilovic, 'Regime type and diaspora politics: A dyadic approach', *Foreign Policy Analysis* 14 (2018), 346–66.

47 G. Tsourapas, 'The Peculiar Practices of "Authoritarian Emigration States"', *British Academy* (2018), www.thebritishacademy.ac.uk/publishing/review/32/peculiar-practices-authoritarian-emigration-states/; G. Tsourapas, *The Politics of Migration in Modern Egypt*; G. Tsourapas, 'Global autocracies'.

48 L. Brand, 'Authoritarian states and voting from abroad: North African experiences', *Comparative Politics*, 43:1 (2010), 81–99.

49 F. B. Adamson, 'Non-state authoritarianism and diaspora politics', 153.

50 *Ibid.*

51 R. Waldinger, 'Between "here" and "there": Immigrant cross-border activities and loyalties', *International Migration Review* 42:1 (2008), 3–29; A. Chaudhury, 'Transnational politics and immigrant political participation in Europe', *Oxford International Migration Institute Working Paper 127* (2016).

52 A. Weinar, A. Unterreiner and P. Fargues, 'Introduction: Integration as a three-way process', in *Migrant Integration Between Homeland and Host Society Volume 1: Where Does the Country of Origin Fit?*, eds A. Weinar, A. Unterreiner, and P. Fargues (Berlin: Springer, 2017), pp. 1–19; T. Givens, A. Arkilic and E. Davis, 'Immigrant integration', in *Introduction to International Migration: Population Movements in the 21st Century*, eds J. Money and S. Lockhart (London: Routledge, 2021), pp. 175–95.

53 L. Mügge, 'Transnationalism as a research paradigm and its relevance for integration', in *Integration Processes and Policies in Europe: Contexts, Levels and Actors*, eds B. Garcés-Mascareñas and R. Penninx (Dordrecht: Springer, 2016), pp. 109–26.

54 J. To, *Qiaowu: Extra-Territorial Policies for the Overseas Chinese* (Leiden: Brill, 2014); F. B. Adamson, 'Sending states'.

55 G. Tsourapas, 'Why do states develop multi-tiered emigration policies?'; Y. Abramson, 'Making a homeland, constructing a diaspora: The case of Taglit-birthright Israel', *Political Geography* 58 (2017), 14–23.

56 L. Brand, *Citizens Abroad*; L. Brand, 'Expatriates and home state development', *Mashriq & Mahjar* 5:1 (2018), 11–35.

57 A. Contreras and M. Martinez, 'Religion and migration in Morocco: Governability and diaspora', *New Diversities* 17:1 (2015), 111–27; Ö. Bilgili and S. Weyel, 'Diaspora engagement policies of countries with similar emigration histories: Morocco and Turkey', in *Adjusting to a World in Motion: Trends in Global Migration and Migration Policy*, eds D. Beshavor and M. Lopez (Oxford: Oxford University Press, 2016), pp. 390–413.

58 K. Burgess, *Courting Migrants*, pp. 11, 191. Also see: M. A. Paarlberg, 'Transnational militancy: Diaspora influence over electoral activity in Latin America', *Comparative Politics* 49:4 (2017), 541–59.

59 K. Burgess, *Courting Migrants*, pp. 192–3.

60 *Ibid.*, pp. 11, 195–200.

61 B. McKernan, 'Student Protests Grow as Turkey's Young People Turn against Erdoğan'.

62 M. Schrover and F. Vermeulen, 'Immigrant organisations'; S. Carol and R. Koopmans, 'Dynamics of contestation over Islamic religious rights in Western Europe'.

63 R. Kastoryano, *Negotiating Identities*; K. Rosenow-Williams, *Organising Muslims and Integrating Islam*; A. Arkilic, 'The limits of European Islam'.

64 N. Glick-Schiller, 'The transnational migration paradigm', in *Migration and Organised Civil Society: Rethinking National Policy*, eds D. Halm and Z. Sezgin (London: Routledge, 2015), pp. 25–43.

65 J. Laurence, 'From the Élysée salon to the table of the Republic: State–Islam relations and the integration of Muslims in France', *French Politics, Culture and Society* 23:1 (2005), 37–64; J. Laurence, *The Emancipation of Europe's Muslims*.

66 A. Arkilic, 'The Alevi diaspora in France'.

67 K. Kirişçi, 'The coronavirus has led to more authoritarianism in Turkey', *Brookings Institution* (2020), www.brookings.edu/blog/order-from-chaos/2020/05/08/the-coronavirus-has-led-to-more-authoritarianism-for-turkey/

68 *Ibid.*

69 'Autocrats See Opportunity in Disaster', *The Economist*, 25 April 2020, www.economist.com/leaders/2020/04/23/autocrats-see-opportunity-in-disaster; S. Hamid, 'Reopening the world: How the pandemic is reinforcing authoritarianism', *Brookings Institution*, 16 June 2020, www.brookings.edu/blog/order-from-chaos/2020/06/16/reopening-the-world-how-the-pandemic-is-reinforcing-authoritarianism/

Select bibliography

The following sources are the most important references consulted in this book. For references of all sources, please refer to the endnotes provided at the end of each chapter.

Abadan-Unat, N. *Bitmeyen Göç: Konuk İşçilikten Ulus-Ötesi Yurttaşlığa* (Istanbul: Bilgi University, 2002).

Abramson, Y. 'Making a homeland, constructing a diaspora: The case of Taglit-birthright Israel', *Political Geography* 58 (2017), 14–23.

Adamson, F. B. 'Non-state authoritarianism and diaspora politics', *Global Networks* 20:1 (2020), doi: 10.1111/glob.12246

Adamson, F. B. 'Sending states and the making of intra-diasporic politics: Turkey and its diaspora(s)', *International Migration Review* 53:1 (2019), 210–36.

Adamson, F. B., and Demetriou, M. 'Remapping the boundaries of "state" and "national identity": Incorporating diasporas into IR theorising', *European Journal of International Relations* 13:4 (2007), 489–526.

Adamson, F. B., and Tsourapas, G. 'Migration diplomacy in world politics', *International Studies Perspectives* 20:2 (2019), 113–28.

Akgönül, S. *La Turquie 'nouvelle' et les Franco-Turcs: Une interdépendence complexe* (Paris: L'Harmattan, 2020).

Akgönül, S. 'Turkish Islam in Europe: Political Activism and Internal Conflicts', *Oasis*, 18 July 2019, www.oasiscenter.eu/en/turkish-islam-in-europe-akp-vs-gulen

Akgündüz, A. *Labour Migration from Turkey to Western Europe, 1960–1974: A Multidisciplinary Analysis* (Aldershot: Ashgate, 2008).

Akıncı, M. A. 'Fransa'daki Türk toplumun Türkçe ile ilişkisi', *HAL Archives-Ouvertes* (2018), https://hal.archives-ouvertes.fr/hal-02367261/

Aksel, D. *Home States and Homeland Politics: Interactions between the Turkish State and Its Emigrants in France and the United States* (London: Routledge, 2019).

Al-Hamarneh, A., and Thielman, J. eds. *Islam and Muslims in Germany* (Leiden: Brill, 2008).

Alonso Délano, A., and Mylonas, H. 'The microfoundations of diaspora politics: Unpacking the state and disaggregating the diaspora', *Journal of Ethnic and Migration Studies* 45:4 (2019), 473–91.

Aluffi, R., and Zincone, G. eds. *The Legal Treatment of Islamic Minorities in Europe* (Leuven: Peeters, 2004).

Amelina, A., and Faist, T. 'Turkish immigrant associations in Germany: Between integration pressure and transnational linkages', *Revue Européenne des Migrations Internationales* 24:2 (2008), 91–120.

Amiraux, V. *Acteurs de l'Islam entre Allemagne et Turquie: Parcours militants et expériences religieuses* (Paris: L'Harmattan, 2001).

Arkilic, A. 'The Alevi diaspora in France: Changing relations with the home and host states', in *The Alevis in Modern Turkey and the Diaspora: Recognition, Mobilisation and Transformation*, eds H. Markussen and D. Ozkul (Edinburgh: Edinburgh University Press, 2022), pp. 166–90.

Arkilic, A. 'Long-distance politics and diaspora youth: Analyzing Turkey's diaspora engagement policies aimed at post-migrant generations', in *Routledge International Handbook of Diaspora Diplomacy*, ed. L. Kennedy (London: Routledge, 2022), pp. 214–29.

Arkilic, A. 'Explaining the evolution of Turkey's diaspora engagement policy: A holistic approach', *Diaspora Studies* 14:1 (2021), 1–21.

Arkilic, A. 'Turkish populist nationalism in transnational space: Explaining diaspora voting behaviour in homeland elections', *Journal of Balkan and Near Eastern Studies* 23:4 (2021), 585–605.

Arkilic, A. 'Empowering a fragmented diaspora: Turkish immigrant organisations' perceptions of and responses to Turkey's diaspora engagement policy', *Mediterranean Politics* (2020), doi: 10.1080/13629395.2020.1822058

Arkilic, A. 'How Turkey's Outreach to Its Diaspora Is Inflaming Tensions with Europe', *Washington Post*, 26 March 2018, www.washingtonpost.com/news/monkey-cage/wp/2018/03/26/how-turkeys-outreach-to-its-diaspora-is-inflaming-tensions-with-europe/

Arkilic, A. 'Between the Homeland and Host States: Turkey's Diaspora Policies and Immigrant Political Participation in France and Germany' (PhD dissertation, University of Texas at Austin, 2016).

Arkilic, A. 'The limits of European Islam: Turkish Islamic umbrella organisations and their relations with host countries – France and Germany', *Journal of Muslim Minority Affairs* 35:1 (2015), 17–43.

Arkilic, A., and Gurcan, A. E. 'The political participation of Alevis: A comparative analysis of the Turkish Alevi Opening and the German Islam Conference', *Nationalities Papers: The Journal of Nationalism and Ethnicity* 49:5 (2021), 949–66.

Arkilic, A., and Macdonald, L. 'The European Union's disintegration over refugee responsibility-sharing', *Women Talking Politics* (November 2019), 26–9.

Avcı, G. 'Religion, transnationalism and Turks in Europe', *Turkish Studies* 6:2 (2005), 201–13.

Aydın, Y. 'The New Turkish Diaspora Policy', *Stiftung Wissenschaft und Politik* (2014), www.swp-berlin.org/fileadmin/contents/products/research_papers/2014_RP10_adn.pdf

Balcı, B. 'Situating the Gülen Movement in France and in Europe', *Politics, Religion and Society* 19:1 (2018), 69–80.

Barou, J. 'Integration of immigrants in France: A historical perspective', *Identities* 21:6 (2014), 642–57.

Basch, L., Glick-Schiller, N., and Szanton-Blanc, C. *Nations Unbound: Transnational Projects and the Deterritorialised Nation-state* (New York: Gordon and Breach, 1994).

Baser, B. 'Governing Turkey's diaspora(s) and the limits of diaspora diplomacy', in *The Routledge Handbook of Turkish Politics*, eds A. Özerdem and M. Whiting (London: Routledge, 2019), pp. 202–13.

Beaman, J. *Citizen Outsider: Children of North African Immigrants in France* (Oakland: University of California Press, 2017).

Beauchemin, C., Hamel, C., and Simon, P. eds. *Trajectories and Origins: Survey on the Diversity of French Population* (Berlin: Springer, 2018).

Berridge, G. R., and Lloyd, L. *The Palgrave Macmillan Dictionary of Diplomacy* (Basingstoke: Palgrave Macmillan, 2012).

Bertossi, C. 'The performativity of colour blindness: Race politics and immigrant integration in France, 1980–2012', *Patterns of Prejudice* 46:5 (2012), 427–44.

Birka, I., and Klavins, D. 'Diaspora diplomacy: Nordic and Baltic perspective', *Diaspora Studies* 13:2 (2020), 115–32.

Bjola, C., and Holmes, M. eds. *Digital Diplomacy: Theory and Practice* (London: Routledge, 2015).

Bleich, E. *Race Politics in Britain and France: Ideas and Policymaking since the 1960s* (Cambridge: Cambridge University Press, 2003).

Bonnafous, S. 'La presse française et les "événements immigrés" de 1974 à 1984', *L'Homme et la société* 87:1 (1988), 53–62.

Bowen, J. R. *Can Islam Be French? Pluralism and Pragmatism in a Secularist State* (Princeton: Princeton University Press, 2011).

Bozdoğan, S., and Kasaba, R. eds. *Rethinking Modernity and National Identity in Turkey* (Seattle: University of Washington Press, 1997).

Brand, L. 'Expatriates and home state development', *Mashriq & Mahjar* 5:1 (2018), 11–35.

Brand, L. 'Authoritarian states and voting from abroad: North African experiences', *Comparative Politics* 43:1 (2010), 81–99.

Brand, L. *Citizens Abroad: State and Emigration in the Middle East and North Africa* (New York: Cambridge University Press, 2006).

Brettell, C. B., and Hollifield, J. F. eds. *Migration Theory: Talking across Disciplines* (London: Routledge, 2000).

Brouard, S., and Tiberj, V. *As French as Everyone? A Survey of French Citizens of Maghrebin, African and Turkish Origin* (Philadelphia: Temple University Press, 2011).

Brubaker, R. 'The diaspora "diaspora"', *Ethnic and Racial Studies* 28:1 (2005), 1–19.

Brubaker, R. *Citizenship and Nationhood in France and Germany* (Cambridge, MA: Harvard University Press, 1992).

Bruce, B. *Governing Islam Abroad: Turkish and Moroccan Muslims in Western Europe* (Basingstoke: Palgrave McMillan, 2018).

Burgess, K. *Courting Migrants: How States Make Diasporas and Diasporas Make States* (Oxford: Oxford University Press, 2020).

Castles, S. 'How nation-states respond to immigration and ethnic diversity', *Journal of Ethnic and Migration Studies* 21:3 (1995), 293–308.

Caymaz, B. *Les mouvements islamiques turcs à Paris* (Paris: L'Harmattan, 2002).

Cesari, J. 'De l'immigré au minoritaire: les Maghrébins de France', *Revue européenne des migrations internationales* 10:1 (1996), 109–26.

Chin, R. *The Guest Worker Question in Postwar Germany* (Cambridge: Cambridge University Press, 2009).

Christou, A., and Mavroudi, E. eds. *Dismantling Diasporas: Rethinking the Geographies of Diasporic Identity, Connection and Development* (Farnham: Ashgate, 2015).

Collyer, M. 'A geography of extra-territorial citizenship: Explanations of external voting', *Migration Studies* 2:1 (2014), 55–72.

Collyer, M. ed. *Emigration Nations: Policies and Ideologies of Emigrant Engagement* (Basingstoke: Palgrave Macmillan, 2013).

Cooper, A. F., English, J., and Thakur, R. C. *Enhancing Global Governance: Towards a New Diplomacy* (New York: United Nations University Press, 2002).

Çıtak, Z. 'Between "Turkish Islam" and "French Islam"': The role of the Diyanet in the Conseil Français du Culte Musulman', *Journal of Ethnic and Migration Studies* 36:4 (2010), 619–34.

Davutoğlu, A. 'Turkish foreign policy and the EU in 2010', *Turkish Policy Quarterly* 8:3 (2009), 11–7.

De Haas, H. 'Between courting and controlling: The Moroccan state and "its" emigrants', *COMPAS Working Paper 54*, Oxford Centre on Migration, Policy and Society (2007).

Délano, A. *Mexico and Its Diaspora in the United States: Policies of Emigration since 1848* (Cambridge: Cambridge University Press, 2011).

Délano, A., and Gamlen, A. 'Comparing and theorizing state–diaspora relations', *Political Geography* 41 (2014), 43–53.

Diyanet İşleri Başkanlığı. 'Kurumsal' (2021), www.diyanet.gov.tr/tr-TR/Kurumsal/Indeks/

Ekşi, M. *Kamu Diplomasisi ve AK Parti Dönemi Türk Dış Politikası* (Ankara: Siyasal Kitabevi, 2018).

Ercan-Argun, B. *Turkey in Germany. The Transnational Sphere of Deutschkei* (London: Routledge, 2003).

Erdoğan, M. *Euro-Turks Barometer 2013*, Ankara Hacettepe University Migration and Politics Research Centre (2013), http://fs.hacettepe.edu.tr/hugo/dosyalar/ETB_rapor.pdf

Erzan, R., and Kirişçi, K. *Turkish Immigrants in the European Union: Determinants of Immigration and Integration* (London: Routledge, 2008).

Esen, B., and Gumuscu, S. 'Rising competitive authoritarianism in Turkey', *Third World Quarterly* 37:9 (2015), 1581–606.

Esser, H. *Sprache und Integration: Die sozialen Bedingungen und Folgen des Spracherwerbs von Migranten* (Frankfurt/Main: Campus Verlag, 2006).

Faist, T. ed. *Dual Citizenship in Europe: From Nationhood to Social Integration* (Aldershot: Ashgate, 2007).

Fargues, P. 'International migration and the nation state in Arab countries', *Middle East Law and Governance 5* (2013), 5–35.

Fernando, M. *The Republic Unsettled: Muslim French and the Contradictions of Secularism* (Durham: Duke University Press, 2014).

Fetzer, J. S., and Soper, C. J. *Muslims and the State in Britain, France and Germany* (Cambridge: Cambridge University Press, 2005).

Fredette, J. *Constructing Muslims in France: Discourse, Public Identity and the Politics of Citizenship* (Philadelphia: Temple University Press, 2014).

Freeman, G. *Immigrant Labour and Racial Conflict in Industrial Societies: The French and British Experience, 1945–1975* (Princeton: Princeton University Press, 1979).

Freeman, G. P., and Ögelman, N. 'Homeland citizenship policies and the status of third country nationals in the European Union', *Journal of Ethnic and Migration Studies* 24:4 (1998), 769–88.

Gamlen, A. *Human Geopolitics: States, Emigrants and the Rise of Diaspora Institutions* (Oxford: Oxford University Press, 2019).

Gamlen, A. 'The emigration state and the modern geopolitical imagination', *Political Geography* 27:8 (2008), 840–56.

Gamlen, A. 'Diaspora engagement policies: What are they and what kind of states use them?', *COMPAS Working Paper 32*, Oxford Centre on Migration, Policy and Society (2006).

Gesemann, F., and Roth, R. *Integration ist (auch) Ländersache! Schritte zur politischen Inklusion von Migrantinnen und Migranten in den Bundesländern* (Berlin: Friedrich-Ebert-Stiftung, 2014).

Givens, T. *Voting Radical Right in Western Europe* (New York: Cambridge University Press, 2005).

Givens, T., Arkilic, A., and Davis, E. 'Immigrant integration', in *Introduction to International Migration: Population Movements in the 21st Century*, eds J. Money and S. Lockhart (London: Routledge, 2021), pp. 175–95.

Glick-Schiller, N., Basch, L., and Szanton-Blanc, C. 'From immigrant to transmigrant: Theorizing transnational migration', *Anthropology Quarterly* 68:1 (1995), 48–63.

Goldberg, D. T. 'Racial Europeanisation', *Ethnic and Racial Studies* 29:2 (2006), 331–64.

Gonzalez, J. J. *Diaspora Diplomacy: Philippine Migration and Its Soft Power Influences* (Maitland: Mill City Press, 2012).

Gözaydın, İ. *Diyanet: Türkiye Cumhuriyeti'nde Dinin Tanzimi* (İstanbul: İletişim, 2009).

Green, S. *The Politics of Exclusion: Institutions and Immigration Policy in Contemporary Germany* (Manchester: Manchester University Press, 2004).

Halm, D., and Sezgin, Z. eds. *Migration and Organised Civil Society: Rethinking National Policy* (London: Routledge, 2015).

Hargreaves, A. *Multi-ethnic France: Immigration, Politics, Culture and Society* (London: Routledge, 2007).

Haug, S., Müssig, S., and Stichs, A. *Muslimisches Leben in Deutschland* (Nürnberg: Bundesamt für Integration und Flüchtlinge, 2009).

Hernández Aguilar, L. *Governing Islam and Muslims in Contemporary Germany: Race, Time and the German Islam Conference* (Leiden: Brill, 2018).

Hintz, L. *Identity Politics Inside Out: National Identity Contestation and Foreign Policy in Turkey* (Oxford: Oxford University Press, 2018).

Ho, E. L. '"Claiming" the diaspora: Elite mobility, sending state strategies and the spatialities of citizenship', *Progress in Human Geography* 35:6 (2011), 757–72.

Ho, E. L., and McConnell, F. 'Conceptualizing "diaspora diplomacy": Territory and populations betwixt the domestic and foreign', *Progress in Human Geography* 43:2 (2019), 235–55.

Hollifield, J. F. 'The politics of international migration: How can we "bring the state back in?"', in *Migration Theory: Talking across Disciplines*, eds C. Brettell and J. F. Hollifield (London: Routledge, 2000), pp. 137–85.

Hollifield, J. F. 'Migration, trade and the nation-state: The myth of globalisation', *Journal of International Law and Foreign Affairs* 3:2 (1998), 595–636.

Howard, M. M. *The Politics of Citizenship in Europe* (Cambridge: Cambridge University Press, 2009).

Huyssen, A. 'Diaspora and nation: Migration into other pasts', *German Critique* 88 (2003), 147–64.

Hüküm, U., Petek, G., and Gürsoy, D. *Turcs en France* (Paris: Saint-Pourçain-sur-Sioule, 2007).

Ireland, P. *The Policy Challenge of Ethnic Diversity* (Cambridge, MA: Harvard University Press, 1994).

Iskander, N. *Creative State: Forty Years of Migration and Development Policy in Morocco and Mexico* (Ithaca: Cornell University Press, 2010).

İçduygu, A. 'International migration and human development in Turkey', *Human Development Research Paper No. 2009/52*, United Nations Development Program Human Development Reports (2009).

İçduygu, A., and Aksel, D. 'Turkish migration policies: A critical historical retrospective', *Perceptions* 18:3 (2013), 167–90.

Jonker, G. *Eine Wellenlange zu Gott: der 'Verband der Islamischen Kulturzentren' in Europa* (Bielefeld: Transcript, 2000).

Joppke, C. *Immigration and the Nation-state: The United States, Germany and Great Britain* (Oxford: Oxford University Press, 1999).

Jönsson, C., and Langhorne, R. *Diplomacy: Problems and Issues in Contemporary Diplomacy* (Thousand Oaks: Sage, 2004).

Kadirbeyoğlu, Z., and Okyay, A. 'Turkey: Voting from abroad in 2015 general elections', *Global Governance Program Report* (2015), https://globalcit.eu/voting-from-abroad-in-turkey-s-general-elections-2015/

Kalın, İ. 'Soft power and public diplomacy in Turkey', *Perceptions* 16:3 (2011), 5–23.

Karakaya-Stump, A. 'The AKP, sectarianism and the Alevis' struggle for equal rights in Turkey', *National Identities* 20:1 (2018), 53–67.

Kastoryano, R. *Negotiating Identities: States and Immigrants in France and Germany* (Princeton: Princeton University Press, 2002).

Kaya, A. 'Migration as a leverage tool in international relations: Turkey as a case study', *Uluslararası İlişkiler* (January 2021), 1–19.

Kaya, A. *Turkish-origin Migrants and Their Descendants: Hyphenated Identities in Transnational Space* (Basingstoke: Palgrave Macmillan, 2019).

Kaya, A., and Kentel, F. *Euro-Türkler: Türkiye ile Avrupa Birliği Arasında Köprü mü, Engel mi?* (Istanbul: Bilgi University Press, 2005).

Kennedy, L. ed. *Routledge International Handbook of Diaspora Diplomacy* (London: Routledge, 2022).

Kepel, G. *Les banlieues de l'Islam: Naissance d'une religion en France* (Paris: Le Seuil, 1987).

Kerr, P., and Wiseman, G. *Diplomacy in a Globalising World* (Oxford: Oxford University Press, 2013).

Kılınç, R. *Alien Citizens: The State and Minorities in Turkey and France* (Cambridge: Cambridge University Press, 2019).

Kirişci, K. 'Disaggregating Turkish citizenship and immigration practices', *Middle Eastern Studies* 36:3 (2000), 1–22.

Klopp, B. *German Multiculturalism: Immigrant Integration and the Transformation of Citizenship* (Westport: Praeger, 2002).

Koinova, M. 'Diaspora mobilisation for conflict and post-conflict reconstruction: Contextual and comparative dimensions', *Journal of Ethnic and Migration Studies* 44:8 (2017), 1–19.

Koinova, M., and Tsourapas, G. 'How do countries of origin engage migrants and diasporas? Multiple actors and comparative perspectives', *International Political Science Review* 39:3 (2018), 311–21.

Koopmans, R., and Statham, P. eds. *Challenging Immigration and Ethnic Relations Politics* (Oxford: Oxford University Press, 2001).

Kösebalaban, H. *Turkish Foreign Policy: Islam, Nationalization, and Globalization* (Basingstoke: Palgrave Macmillan, 2011).

Kuru, A. T. *Secularism and State Policies toward Religion: The United States, France and Turkey* (New York: Cambridge University Press, 2009).

Küçükcan, T., and Güngör, V. eds. *Turks in Europe: Culture, Identity, Integration* (Amsterdam: Türkevi Research Center, 2009).

Lafleur, J. M. 'Why do states enfranchise citizens abroad? Comparative insights from Mexico, Italy and Belgium', *Global Networks* 11:4 (2011), 481–501.

Laurence, J. *Coping with Defeat: Sunni Islam, Roman Catholicism, and the Modern State* (Princeton: Princeton University Press, 2021).

Laurence, J. *The Emancipation of Europe's Muslims: The State's Role in Minority Integration* (Princeton: Princeton University Press, 2012).

Laurence, J., and Vaïsse, J. *Integrating Islam: Political and Religious Challenges in Contemporary France* (Washington DC: Brookings Institution Press, 2006).

Lemmen, T. *Islamische Organisationen in Deutschland* (Bonn: Friedrich Ebert Stiftung, 2000).

Levitt, P., and De la Dehesa, R. 'Transnational migration and the redefinition of the state: Variations and explanations', *Ethnic and Racial Studies* 26:4 (2005), 587–611.

Lord, C. 'Rethinking the Justice and Development Party's Alevi "Openings"', *Turkish Studies* 18:2 (2016), 278–96.

Mandel, R. *Cosmopolitan Anxieties: Turkish Challenges to Citizenship and Belonging in Germany* (Durham: Duke University Press, 2008).

Maritato, C. 'Addressing the blurred edges of Turkey's diaspora and religious policy: Diyanet women preachers sent to Europe', *European Journal of Turkish Studies* 27 (2018), doi: 10.4000/ejts.6020

Martin, P. L. *The Unfinished Story: Turkish Labour Migration to Western Europe* (Geneva: International Labour Office, 1991).

Maxwell, R. *Ethnic Minority Migrants in Britain and France: Integration Trade-offs* (New York: Cambridge University Press, 2012).

McFadden, S. W. 'German citizenship law and the Turkish diaspora', *German Law Journal* 20:1 (2019), 72–88.

Melissen, J. *The New Public Diplomacy: Soft Power in International Relations* (Basingstoke: Palgrave Macmillan, 2005).

Menjívar, C., Ruiz M., and Ness, I. eds. *The Oxford Handbook of Migration Crises* (Oxford: Oxford University Press, 2019).

Messina, A. L. *The Logics and Politics of Post-WWII Migration to Western Europe* (New York: Cambridge University Press, 2007).

Mirilovic, N. 'Regime type and diaspora politics: A dyadic approach', *Foreign Policy Analysis* 14 (2018), 346–66.

Money, J., and Lockhart, S. eds. *Introduction to International Migration: Population Movements in the 21st Century* (London: Routledge, 2021).

Müftüler-Bac, M. 'Turkey's political reforms: The impact of the European Union', *Southeast European Politics and Societies* 10:1 (2005), 16–30.

Mügge, L. 'Managing transnationalism: Continuity and change in Turkish state policy', *International Migration* 50:1 (2012), 20–38.

Mylonas, H. *The Politics of Nation-building: Making Co-Nationals, Refugees and Minorities* (New York: Cambridge University Press, 2012).

Naujoks, D. *Migration, Citizenship and Development: Diasporic Membership Policies and Overseas Indians in the United States* (Oxford: Oxford University Press, 2013).

Nye, J. S. *Soft Power: The Means to Success in World Politics* (New York: Public Affair, 2004).

Okyay, A. 'Diaspora Making as a State-led Project: Turkey's Expansive Diaspora Strategy and Its Implications for Emigrant and Kin Populations' (PhD dissertation, EUI, 2015).

Ögelman, N. 'Directing Discontent: Turkish-origin Associations in Germany' (PhD dissertation, University of Texas at Austin, 2003).

Öktem, K. *Turkey's New Diaspora Policy: The Challenge of Inclusivity, Outreach and Capacity* (Istanbul: Istanbul Policy Centre, 2014).

Özbudun, E. 'Turkey's judiciary and the drift toward competitive authoritarianism', *International Spectator* 50:2 (2015), 42–55.

Østergaard-Nielsen, E. *Transnational Politics: Turks and Kurds in Germany* (London: Routledge, 2003).

Østergaard-Nielsen, E. ed. *International Migration and Sending Countries: Perceptions, Policies and Transnational Relations* (Basingstoke: Palgrave Macmillan, 2003).

Paçacı Elitok, S., and Straubhaar, T. eds. *Turkey, Migration and the EU: Potentials, Challenges, and Opportunities* (Hamburg: Hamburg University Press, 2012).

Parolin, G. *Citizenship in the Arab World: Kin, Religion and Nation State* (Amsterdam: Amsterdam University Press, 2009).

Petek-Şalom, G. 'Les ressortissants turcs en France et l'évolution de leur projet migratoire', *Revue hommes et migrations* 1212 (1998), 14–24.

Peucker, M., and Akbarzadeh, S. *Muslim Active Citizenship in the West* (London: Routledge, 2014).

Pojmann, W. ed. *Migration and Activism in Europe since 1945* (Basingstoke: Palgrave Macmillan, 2008).

Potz, R., and Wieshaider, W. eds. *Islam and the European Union* (Leuven: Peeters, 2004).

Ragazzi, F. 'A comparative analysis of diaspora policies', *Political Geography* 41 (2014), 74–89.

Riordan, S. *The New Diplomacy* (Cambridge: Polity Press, 2003).

Rosenow-Williams, K. *Organising Muslims and Integrating Islam: New Developments in the 21st Century* (Leiden: Brill, 2012).

Sahin-Mencutek, Z., and Baser, B. 'Mobilizing diasporas: Insights from Turkey's attempts to reach Turkish citizens abroad', *Journal of Balkan and Near Eastern Studies* 20:1 (2018), 86–105.

Sahlins, P. *Unnaturally French: Foreign Citizens in the Old Regime and after* (Ithaca: Cornell University Press, 2004).

Sassen, S. *Losing Control: Sovereignty in an Age of Globalisation* (New York: Columbia University Press, 1996).

Sayarı, S. 'Migration policies of sending countries: Perspectives on the Turkish experience', *Annals of the American Academy of Political and Social Science* 485 (1986), 87–97.

Schain, M. *The Politics of Immigration in France, Britain and the United States: A Comparative Study* (Basingstoke: Palgrave Macmillan, 2008).

Schor, R. *L'opinion française et les étrangers en France, 1919–1939* (Paris: Sorbonne, 1985).

Schönwalder, K., and Triadafilopoulos, T. 'A bridge or barrier to incorporation? Germany's 1999 citizenship reform in critical perspective', *German Politics and Society* 30:1 (2012), 52–70.

Schrover, M., and Vermeulen, F. 'Immigrant organisations', *Journal of Ethnic and Migration Studies* 31:5 (2005), 823–32.

Shain, Y., and Barth, A. 'Diasporas and international relations theory', *International Organisation* 57:3 (2003), 449–79.

Shankland, D. *The Alevis in Turkey: The Emergence of a Secular Islamic Tradition* (London: Routledge, 2003).

Sirkeci, İ., and Pusch, B. eds. *Turkish Migration Policy* (London: Transnational Press, 2016).

Sirkeci, İ., Şeker, B. D., and Çağlar, A. eds. *Turkish Migration, Identity and Integration* (London: Transnational Press London, 2015).

Smith, R. C. 'Migrant membership as an instituted process: Transnationalisation, the state and the extra-territorial conduct of Mexican politics', *International Migration Review* 37:3 (2003), 297–343.

Soysal, Y. *Limits of Citizenship: Migrants and Postnational Memberships in Europe* (Chicago: University of Chicago Press, 1994).

Sökefeld, M. *Struggling for Recognition: The Alevi Movement in Germany and in Transnational Space* (Oxford: Berghahn, 2008).

Stone, D., and Douglas, E. 'Advance diaspora diplomacy in a networked world', *International Journal of Cultural Policy* 24:6 (2018), 710–23.

Şenay, B. *Beyond Turkey's Borders: Long-distance Kemalism, State Politics and the Turkish Diaspora* (London: I. B. Tauris, 2013).

Tepe, S. 'Populist party's challenge to democracy: Institutional capture, performance and religion', *Party Politics* (2021), doi: 10.1177/13540688211002478

Thibos, C. 'Imputing diaspora: An examination of Turkish political rhetoric in Germany', *Diaspora* 19:2–3 (2017), 170–94.

Torrealba, A. A. 'Three main approaches of diaspora diplomacy in foreign policy', *Actual Problems of Economics and Law* 11:2 (2017), 154–69.

Triandafyllidou, A., and Gropas, R. eds. *European Immigration: A Sourcebook* (Aldershot: Ashgate, 2014).

Tribalat, M. *Faire France: Une enquête sur les immigrés et leurs enfants* (Paris: La Découverte, 1995).

Tsourapas, G. 'Global autocracies: Strategies of transnational repression, legitimation and co-optation in world politics', *International Studies Review* (2020), doi: 10.1093/isr/viaa061

Tsourapas, G. *The Politics of Migration in Modern Egypt: Strategies for Regime Survival in Autocracies* (Cambridge: Cambridge University Press, 2018).

Tsourapas, G. 'Why states develop multi-tier emigrant policies? Evidence from Egypt', *Journal of Ethnic and Migration Studies* 41:13 (2015), 212–14.

Tuğal, C. *The Fall of the Turkish Model: How the Arab Uprisings Brought Down Islamic Liberalism* (London: Verso, 2016).

Türkiye Büyük Millet Meclisi. *Constitution of the Republic of Turkey* (1982), https://global.tbmm.gov.tr/docs/constitution_en.pdf

Ünver, C. 'Changing diaspora politics of Turkey and public diplomacy', *Turkish Policy Quarterly* 12:1 (2013), 181–9.

Varadarajan, L. *The Domestic Abroad: Diasporas in International Relations* (Oxford: Oxford University Press, 2010).

Waldinger, R. 'Between "here" and "there": Immigrant cross-border activities and loyalties', *International Migration Review* 42:1 (2008), 3–29.

Weil, P. *How to Be French? Nationality in the Making since 1789* (Durham: Duke University Press, 2008).

Weinar, A., Unterreiner, A., and Fargues, P. eds. *Migrant Integration between Homeland and Host Society Volume 1: Where Does the Country of Origin Fit?* (Berlin: Springer, 2017).

White, J. *Muslim Nationalism and the New Turks* (Princeton: Princeton University Press, 2013).

Wihtol de Wenden, C. 'Generational change and political participation in French suburbs', *Journal of Ethnic and Migration Studies* 21:1 (1995), 69–78.

Wilpert, C. 'Identity issues in the history of the post-war migration from Turkey to Germany', *German Politics and Society* 31:2 (2013), 108–31.

Yalaz, E. 'Immigrant Political Incorporation: Institutions, Groups and Inter-Ethnic Context' (PhD dissertation, Rutgers University, 2014).

Yanaşmayan, Z., and Kaşlı, Z. 'Reading diasporic engagements through the lens of citizenship: Turkey as a test case', *Political Geography* 70 (2019), 24–33.

Yavuz, H. ed. *The Emergence of a New Turkey* (Salt Lake City: University of Utah Press, 2006).

Yener-Roderburg, İ. Ö. 'Party organisations across borders: Top-down satellites and bottom-up alliances: The case of AKP and HDP in Germany', in *Political Parties Abroad: A New Arena for Party Politics*, eds T. Kernalegenn and E. van Haute (London: Routledge, 2020), pp. 218–37.

Yılmaz, G. 'From Europeanisation to de-Europeanisation: The Europeanisation process of Turkey in 1999–2014', *Journal of Contemporary European Studies* 24:1 (2016), 86–100.

Yılmaz, I., and Bashirov, G. 'The AKP after 15 years: Emergence of Erdoganism in Turkey', *Third World Quarterly* 39:9 (2017), 1812–30.

Yurdakul, G. *From Guest Workers into Muslims: The Transformation of Turkish Immigrant Associations in Germany* (Newcastle upon Tyne: Cambridge Scholars, 2009).

Yurtdışı Türkler ve Akraba Topluluklar Başkanlığı. *About Us* (2021), www.ytb.gov. tr/en/corporate

Yükleyen, A. *Localising Islam in Europe: Turkish Islamic Communities in Germany and the Netherlands* (New York: Syracuse University Press, 2012).

Yükleyen, A., and Yurdakul, G. 'Islamic activism and immigrant integration: Turkish organisations in Germany', *Immigrants and Minorities* 29:1 (2011), 64–85.

Zanfrini, L. *The Challenge of Migration in a Janus-faced Europe* (Basingstoke: Palgrave Macmillan, 2018).

Index

Page numbers followed by *t* refer to tables. References to notes are indicated by a note-number suffix after the page number, e.g. 22n18.

EU authorised representative for GPSR:
Easy Access System Europe, Mustamäe tee 50,
10621 Tallinn, Estonia
gpsr.requests@easproject.com